BAD MOON RISING:
AMERICAN OUTLAWS
OF THE ROARING 1920'S & 1930'S
(A LOOK AT THE GOOD,
THE BAD AND THE UGLY
WHO DEFIED AUTHORITY)

By
J. Wayne Frye

This book is written in Canadian English.

BAD MOON RISING: AMERICAN OUTLAWS OF THE ROARING 1920'S AND 1930'S

TO: VADA CRANFORD FRYE

I have known many outlaws in my life, foremost among them the grand ones who refused to bow to the authority of the ministers of the perverted word of God, others who never accepted the unjustness of an economic system based on greed and nepotism, many who never wavered before governments that promoted patriotic babble, the intrepid few who refused to accept the sanctimonious arrogance of intuitions that promoted ignorance rather than enlightenment and finally those who never allowed convention to keep them in the abyss of intellectual prison. My beloved grandmother, Vada Cranford Frye was a bulwark against ignorance. Though uneducated, she never ceased in the eternal search for truth and justice. My revolutionary zeal, my refusal to accept the unacceptable, my devotion to fairness and justice in a world where it is too often trampled under the jack-booted feet of repression in the name of expediency was developed, honed and refined sitting at her feet and absorbing the wisdom that flowed from her like a mighty river roaring through a gorge. Each day, the treasures of wisdom she imparted are the guiding principles of my life.

AND AS ALWAYS, TO MY MUSE
Lynton Viñas

Catalogue Number: 2017-3453599

ISBN: 978-1-928183-29-7

Fireside Books – Victoria, British Columbia
Part of the Peninsula Publishing Consortium

J. Wayne Frye

BAD MOON RISING: AMERICAN OUTLAWS OF THE ROARING 1920'S AND 1930'S

TABLE OF CONTENTS

BAD MOON RISING: AMERICAN OUTLAWS OF THE ROARING 1920'S AND 1930'S

ABOUT THE AUTHOR

Wayne Frye's *Aaron Adams* mysteries, Chablis Louise Chavez adventures, *Girl* series books and *Lynton* adventures have titillated the brains of those who enjoy tantalizing tales that challenge the mind. His life, like those of the heroes he writes about, has been filled with adventure and excitement. He has been a college hockey coach, university professor, and at one time, the youngest university president in the USA. Called a marketing genius by the LOS ANGELES TIMES, he has been a promotional consultant to hockey teams and motion picture companies. He has been cited for his work with inner-city gang children in the Los Angeles area and been active in the anti-globalization movement. He became a Canadian citizen in 2003 and lives in Ladysmith, British Columbia and Laguna, Philippines. He provides satirical political commentary to many Canadian newspapers, and his books on politics have created a great deal of controversy.

Some Other Books by J. Wayne Frye

Hockey Mania and the Mystery of Nancy Running Elk
Something Evil in the Darkness at Hopkins House
How Hockey Saved a Jew From the Holocaust
Fighting for Justice in the Land of Hypocrisy
The Girl Who Stirred up the Whirlwind
The Girl Who Motivated Murder Most Foul
The Girl Who Said Goodbye for the Last Time
Fall From Apocalypse
Armageddon Now
Worth
When Jesus Came to Jersey as the Son of Thunder
When Jesus Came to Canada to Lead an Indigenous Rebellion
Canadian Angels of Mercy – Nurses in Times of Peril
Points of Rebellion: Aboriginals Who Fought for Justice
Lynton Walks on Water
Lynton Curls Her Hair
Lynton and the Vampire at Tagaytay Manor
Lynton Buys a New Cell-Phone and Hears the Voice of Doom
Lynton and Beowulf in the Taal Inferno
Chablis: Avenging Angel for the Forgotten
In the City of Lost Hope
Chablis and the Terrorist
Chablis and the Dildo from Hell
Pursuit
The Disappearance
Lynton and the Ghosts at the Mansion on Belete Drive
Chablis and Lynton in the Room of Doom

J. Wayne Frye

BAD MOON RISING: AMERICAN OUTLAWS OF THE ROARING 1920'S AND 1930'S

PROLOGUE

FRENZY OF VIOLENCE AND MAYHEM

Capitalism does not permit an even flow of economic resources.

With this system, a privileged few are rich beyond conscience,

And almost all others are doomed to be poor at some level.

That's the way the system works, but there are a few people

Who rebel against this inequity in a violent uncontrollable rage

That destroys everything in their path. They are called outlaws.

Outlaws are an enigma, beloved by a few or in some cases, many. The word outlaw comes from two words – *out*, which means not within or someone who is outside. And from the word *law* – which means the principles and regulations established in a community by some authority and applicable to its people. The key here is the word authority. For some of us, myself included, the word authority leaves a bad taste in the mouth, because too often that authority is used for subjugation and regimentation. For example, suppose I ask you to name an institution that is authoritarian, has a dress code, emphasizes silence and order, uses negative reinforcement, makes people walk in lines, forces the loss of autonomy, abridges freedom, allows no input into decision making and sets strict times for walking, talking and exercising. That is a perfect description of life in a prison. Yet, it is also a perfect description of life in typical American schools, which even have metal fences around them now in so many communities.

I was director of an intensive academic support programme for many years in the ghettos of Los Angeles, and I often came into conflict with my superiors, because I believed the people I was hired to help were simply being groomed for life in prisons. Of course, they were African-Americans and Hispanics, so, in a nation that lets whites walk while people of colour are carted off to the slammer, perhaps it was, in its own way, simply a method of saying, "you are second class citizens who will wind up in jail, so we will prepare you for that." This is America, the land with more people in jail than any other nation. It is the only nation that has turned its prisons over to corporations, so it is actually a growth industry that is attracting much investment, as it is clear that America is a country that loves vengeful justice rather than compassionate rehabilitation. It does not embrace the Christian charity of Jesus, but rather is in love with the vengeful justice of the Old Testament practiced by a cruel, unforgiving God.

J. Wayne Frye

BAD MOON RISING: AMERICAN OUTLAWS OF THE ROARING 1920'S AND 1930'S

Executing mentally deficient people, the poor, the minorities and those who often receive inadequate legal representation is common practice in a nation that has refined hypocrisy to an art-form.

In my job as director of the aforementioned programme, I saw the marginalized students I worked with as the victims of a cruel economic system that needs a permanent underclass to serve the needs of the upper class. I was told that the chief thing they needed was discipline and order. To me, that was the last thing they needed. They were outlaws, individuals who had been born into immense poverty in the wealthiest nation on earth, and simply had decided to rail against this unfair system that wants order among the underprivileged, not opportunity. Many of their compatriots had submitted to authority and adapted to the abusive system of inequity - going along to get along, but my charges were the worst of the worst – individuals who actually had the gall to challenge the natural economic order of things.

For example, patriotism is a vital tool in convincing these young impressionable minds that they owe a duty to the very country that is devoted to keeping them in economic slavery. I made it a point to let my charges know that patriotism was used by the corporate run military industrial complex to make them cannon fodder for wars of conquest so defence contractors like Halliburton could make billions destroying places and then reap obscene profits rebuilding what they had destroyed. In the process, the wasted lives of soldieries and civilians were of little consequence when huge profits would be realized so that the stockholders would be rewarded with generous dividends. After all, greed is the driving force in a capitalist society where we are all taught that success is not judged by the content of your character but by the content of your bank account. Success is measured in dollars and cents.

Part of this patriotic indoctrination is making students stand and recite the Pledge of Allegiance every morning just like Hitler required in Nazi Germany. Young minds are fertile ground for instilling patriotic fervour and the belief that your life is not as important as your country and that you should be willing to sacrifice it to defend the illusionary freedom you are brainwashed into thinking you have. In reality, no one could be forced to say the Pledge of Allegiance according to a decision rendered by the Supreme Court, so I distributed pocket cards with the relevant decision in that regards for my students to show anyone who challenged their right of refusal to be brainwashed. Needless to say, I was often not a very popular educator. However, I had a person to whom I reported who always told my detractors, "He may be a radical, but he does a good job. The best thing you can do is leave him alone and do yours."

What is my point? It is simply that I am a person who detests authority too when it is used to cajole, brainwash, manipulate and force adherence to a set of rules that enslaves rather than frees.

BAD MOON RISING: AMERICAN OUTLAWS OF THE ROARING 1920'S AND 1930'S

Now, I am not going to justify the violent behaviour of those termed outlaws by society, but I am going to infer that we need to look at the tenor of the times in which these people lived, and look at the conditions under which they existed.

The pages that follow will offer details on several people who were violent outcasts in society, but again, the time in which they lived were trying and there was not even a modicum of a safety net as the Republicans of those days were no different than they are today. They believed that society owed no one anything and that the natural order of things was for the rich to allow the largesse to trickle down to the middle class and the poor. The more you gave the rich according to this theory, the more they would share with the middle class and poor. Hogwash!

Thanks to the stock market crash of 1929 and the Great Depression, this convoluted way of thinking was arrested by Franklin Roosevelt in 1933, and led to a burgeoning middle class through 1981, when Ronald Reagan introduced trickle down economics which was simply a return to the era from 1921 until 1933, when that theory led to the near destruction of capitalism. This downward trend has continued with only a brief respite until the present day. The near total collapse of the economy under the Bush years was only mildly arrested by the stewardship of Barrack Obama who refused to prosecute the Wall Street manipulators who once again nearly destroyed capitalism with their greed. Then, along came President Trump, which was simply like letting the fox guard the henhouse. The barons of greed will eventually crash the economy again and laugh all the way to the bank, while the American taxpayer picks up the tab for their criminal malfeasance.

Republicans shout the praises of capitalism, but are, in fact, supporters of monolithic, monopolistic corporate theocracy which leads to periodic depressions and recessions. So, we will not explore the laissez-faire economics of probably the two biggest buffoons to ever inhabit the White House, George Bush and Donald Trump, but rather look at what happened as a result of the laissez-faire economics of Harding, Coolidge and Hoover, buffoons in their own right, and how this led to a few men (and women) who became famous outlaws who rebelled in a frenzy of violence and mayhem against an economic order that has always crushed the middle class and poor.

.

CHAPTER 1

ONE THIEF STEALING FROM ANOTHER THIEF

Epitaph on Bonnie Parker's Tombstone:

As the flowers are all made sweeter

By the sunshine and the dew,

So the world is made brighter

By the lives of folks like you.

Quotes about Clyde Barrow:

Marie Barrow (Clyde's sister): "Something awful sure must have

happened to him in prison, because he wasn't

the same person when he got out."

Fellow inmate, **Ralph Fults**, *"I watched Clyde change from*

a schoolboy to a **rattlesnake.***"*

Daniel Penn Quote:

"Prison just made Clyde more determined than ever to get back

at society for all it had done to him."

J. Wayne Frye   11

BAD MOON RISING: AMERICAN OUTLAWS
OF THE ROARING 1920'S AND 1930'S

American prisons today are often corporate run dins of inequity where prisoners are considered subhuman animals who forfeit their right to fair treatment when the jail door slams shut. The USA is consistently chastised by Amnesty International for its penal colony mentality that lets the rich, privileged and well-connected walk while meting out harsh, and often unjust, punishment to those with lower socio-economic status. Of course, the minorities are more likely to go to prison while the whites are given probation or very light sentences. There is a good reason why the USA is often called incarceration nation.

At 17, Clyde Barrow was sent to the cruellest, meanest, vilest prison in all of Texas, and that is saying something for a state that is still considered today the worst place in America to be incarcerated. The journey to that prison was perhaps fore-ordained, as he began an early age to show a propensity toward criminal behaviour.

Clyde Chestnut Barrow (1909-1934) was born into a poor farming family in Ellis County, Texas, just southeast of Dallas. He was the fifth of seven children. When the family farm failed, as many did during the hard times of the 1920's, his family migrated to Dallas as part of the wave of resettlement from the impoverished farms to the urban slum known as West Dallas. The Barrows spent their first months in West Dallas living under their covered wagon. Clyde, who was a small and unassuming boy, attended school until the age of 16 and had ambitions of becoming a musician, learning to play both the guitar and saxophone. However, under the influence of his older brother, Buck, Clyde soon turned to a life of crime. Beginning with petty thievery and then graduating to stealing cars, Clyde soon escalated his activities to armed robbery. By late 1929, at the age of 20, Clyde was already a fugitive from the law, wanted by authorities for several robberies in and around Dallas.

Clyde was first arrested in late 1926, after running when police confronted him over a rental car he had failed to return on time. His second arrest, with brother Buck, came soon after, this time for possession of stolen goods (turkeys). Despite having legitimate jobs during the period 1927 through 1929, he also cracked safes, robbed stores and stole cars.

One cannot discuss Clyde Barrow without the inclusion of Bonnie Elizabeth Parker (1910-1934), because they were so closely entwined that almost every thing they did was a coordinated effort. The five feet tall, beautiful Bonnie Parker was born in Rowena, Texas. After her father died when she was five, the family moved in with her mother's parents. Bonnie did well in school, and excelled at writing poetry. At 16, she married Roy Thornton. In January 1929, Roy returned from one of his many absences, and Bonnie refused to take him back. Roy committed a robbery and went to prison for five years. Bonnie told her mother that the reason she never divorced him was that it would be unfair to divorce him while he was in prison. She worked for a while as a waitress, but the restaurant was a casualty of the Great Depression. She then did housework for a neighbour, Clarence Clay, who was visited by a friend in January of 1930. The friend was a man named Clyde Barrow. When the two met, both were smitten immediately. From then on they were inseparable.

Unfortunately, their courtship was interrupted when Barrow was sent to notoriously cruel Eastham Prison Farm in April 1930 for a string of robberies he had committed prior to meeting Bonnie. While in prison, Barrow used a lead pipe to crush the skull of another inmate, Ed Crowder, a huge, burly man who had repeatedly sexually assaulted the diminutive Clyde. This was Clyde Barrow's first killing. Another inmate took the blame, however because he was a lifer and knew he would never be getting out of prison. Also, while in prison, Clyde convinced another inmate to use an axe to chop off two of his toes in order to excuse him from working hard labour in the fields; Barrow would walk with a limp for the rest of his life as a result. Ironically and unbeknownst to Barrow, his mother had successfully petitioned a release for him that would come six days after the incident.

Paroled on 2 February 1932, Barrow emerged from Eastham a hardened and bitter criminal who vowed that one day he would return to help men escape and kill as many guards as possible in the process. Although it would not be as dramatic as he predicted, it was no idle boast.

J. Wayne Frye

Immediately upon his release, he started on a rambling crime spree, robbing grocery stores and gas stations at a dizzying rate that did not initially involve Bonnie Parker who had remained loyal to him while he was in prison and visited him there regularly. In the crimes, he used a M-1918 Browning automatic rifle that was far more powerful than anything used by most police departments. He was known to judiciously practice his marksmanship, and vowed that he would rather die than ever go back to Eastham.

One day he told a friend, John Phillips, that his goal in life was not to become a famous bank robber, but to exact revenge against the harsh Texas prison system for the abuses he suffered while serving time. He was intent on conducting a raid on Eastham and killing the warden and as many guards as possible.

He and Ralph Fults assembled a rotating core group of associates. They began a series of small robberies with the goal of collecting enough money and firepower to launch a raid of liberation against Eastham. It was not long until Bonnie joined the gang and she and Fults were captured in a failed hardware store burglary, where they intended to take guns and they were subsequently jailed. Fults was prosecuted and tried; he served time and never rejoined the gang. Parker was held in jail until June 17, and she wrote poetry to pass the time. When the Kaufman County grand jury convened, it declined to indict her, and she was released.

BAD MOON RISING: AMERICAN OUTLAWS OF THE ROARING 1920'S AND 1930'S

On April 30 of 1932, Barrow was the driver in a robbery in Hillsboro, Texas, during which the store's owner, J.N. Bucher, was shot and killed. When shown mug shots, the victim's wife identified Barrow as one of the shooters, although he had stayed outside in the car. It was the first time in the crime spree that Barrow was accused of murder.

On August 5, while Parker was visiting her mother in Dallas, Barrow, Raymond Hamilton and Ross Dyer were drinking heavily at a country dance in Stringtown, Oklahoma, the taciturn local sheriff, C. G. Maxwell and his deputy, Eugene C. Moore, approached them in the parking lot. Barrow and Hamilton opened fire, killing the deputy and gravely wounding the sheriff. This was the first time Barrow and his gang killed a lawman; eventually, they reached a total of nine law officers slain. On October 11, they killed Howard Hall at his store during a robbery in Sherman, Texas.

W. D. Jones had been a friend of the Barrow family since childhood. Only 16 years old in 1932, he persuaded Barrow to let him join him and Bonnie. The next day, Jones was initiated into the gang when he and Barrow killed Doyle Johnson, a young family man, while stealing his car in Temple, Texas. Less than two weeks later, on 6 January 1933, Barrow killed Tarrant County Deputy Sheriff Malcolm Davis when he, Parker and Jones wandered into a police trap set for another criminal. The total murdered by the gang since April was five.

BAD MOON RISING: AMERICAN OUTLAWS
OF THE ROARING 1920'S AND 1930'S

So far their robberies had netted less than ten thousand dollars (around $130,000 in today's dollars). Still in the process, they were developing a reputation for brutality. However, things would gradually change as the public began a strange fascination with the two outlaws. The headlines usually read *Bonnie and Clyde*, her name always coming first. The love element began to take hold, so, true to form, the sexually repressed Americans took a prurient interest in the sex lives of these two outlaws, but the truth was that Clyde was likely impotent based upon accounts from several sources. Of course, being impotent does not prevent one from enjoying sexual activities not requiring an erection, but one might simply ask the question that should be asked today in regards to sex. Is it not a private matter and should it not be left that way?

In March of 1933, Buck Barrow was granted a full pardon. Within days, he and his wife Blanche had set up housekeeping with Clyde, Parker and Jones in a temporary hideout at 3347 ½ Oakridge Drive in Joplin, Missouri. According to family sources, Buck and Blanche were there to visit and try to persuade Clyde to surrender to the law.

Buck and Blanche's appeals met with rebuke, and had they been wise enough to leave, perhaps their lives would have turned out differently. However, the next door neighbours were concerned about the suspicious behaviour of the tenants in the apartment. The Barrow gang ran loud, alcohol-fuelled card games late into the night in the quiet neighbourhood. One night, according to Blanche's memoirs, they bought a case of beer and Clyde accidentally discharged his Browning automatic in the apartment while cleaning it. No neighbours went to the house, but one reported suspicions to the Joplin Police Department.

On April 13, local law officers arrived with a search warrant, assuming that there were bootleggers in the apartment. They blocked the garage door just as Clyde, Buck and W.D. entered. Blanche and Bonnie were inside the apartment. When they heard gun shots from outside, Bonnie began shooting from the living room window while Clyde and W.D. were shooting from inside the garage. Buck went up to the apartment to get the girls during a lull in the gunfire. Blanche's dog got scared and ran down the stairs. She went after him but ran into W.D. who had been shot in the right side. Buck went down to the garage to see if Clyde had been shot. Clyde yelled for them to get down there so they could get away. Bonnie went down first. Blanche helped W.D. down the stairs and into the car. She did not see Clyde or Buck. She went around the car and saw the body of Constable Wes Harryman, lying on the garage floor. She saw Buck near the body and heard Clyde yell for them to get into the car. Blanche helped Clyde push the police car out of the way that was blocking their car. The body of officer Harry McGinnis was just outside the garage. Shots started coming from around the corner of the apartment. Clyde was shot. Blanche heard Buck calling for her and ran back to the door where he stood. They got into the backseat with W.D. Bonnie was already in the front seat. Clyde jumped into the driver's seat and hit the gas. They took off down 34th Street to Main and drove like the wind until they got to Oklahoma.

After the smoke cleared and the gang was long gone, the police gathered evidence and everything left behind. Among the items left were 7 weapons, a money bag from a bank in Springfield, Missouri, a guitar, Bonnie's poetry, Blanche and Buck's marriage license, Buck's parole papers, several rolls of film, Blanche's purse, Buck's car and all their clothes.

The film was developed at *The Joplin Globe* and yielded many now-famous photos of Barrow, Parker and Jones clowning and pointing weapons at one another. When the poem and the photos, including one of Parker clenching a cigar in her teeth and a pistol in her hand, went out on the newly installed newswire, the obscure five criminals from Dallas became front-page news across America as the Barrow Gang.

Bonnie and Clyde were avid picture takers.

J. Wayne Frye

BAD MOON RISING: AMERICAN OUTLAWS
OF THE ROARING 1920'S AND 1930'S

Bonnie often carried a sawed-off shotgun.

Found at the scene of the Joplin carnage was Bonnie's poem called *Suicide Sal*, which much to her delight was published in newspapers all across America. She was now a published writer, and she took great delight in her fame, which was only just beginning to capture the interest of the public.

BAD MOON RISING: AMERICAN OUTLAWS
OF THE ROARING 1920'S AND 1930'S

The Story of Suicide Sal

By Bonnie Parker

We each of us have a good "alibi"
For being down here in the "joint,"
But few of them really are justified
If you get right down to the point.

You've heard of a woman's "glory"
Being spent on a "downright cur,"
Still you can't always judge the story
As true, being told by her.

As long as I've stayed on this "island,"
And heard "confidence tales" from each "gal,"
Only one seemed interesting and truthful --
The story of "Suicide Sal."

Now "Sal" was a gal of rare beauty,
Though her features were coarse and tough;
She never once faltered from duty
To play on the "up and up."

"Sal" told me this tale on the evening
Before she was turned out "free,"

J. Wayne Frye

BAD MOON RISING: AMERICAN OUTLAWS OF THE ROARING 1920'S AND 1930'S

And I'll do my best to relate it
Just as she told it to me:

I was born on a ranch in Wyoming;
Not treated like Helen of Troy;
I was taught that "rods were rulers"
And "ranked" as a greasy cowboy.

Then I left my old home for the city
To play in its mad dizzy whirl,
Not knowing how little of pity
It holds for a country girl.

There I fell for "the line" of a "henchman,"
A "professional killer" from "Chi;"
I couldn't help loving him madly;
For him even now for him I'd die.

One year we were desperately happy;
Our "ill gotten gains" we spent free;
I was taught the ways of the "underworld;"
Jack was just like a "god" to me.

I got on the "F.B.A." payroll
To get the "inside lay" of the job;

J. Wayne Frye   23

BAD MOON RISING: AMERICAN OUTLAWS OF THE ROARING 1920'S AND 1930'S

The bank was "turning big money!"
It looked like a "cinch" for the "mob."

Eighty grand without even a "rumble" --
Jack was last with the "loot" in the door,
When the "teller" dead-aimed a revolver
From where they forced him to lie on the floor.

I knew I had only a moment --
He would surely get Jack as he ran;
So I "staged" a "big fade out" beside him
And knocked the forty-five out of his hand.

They "rapped me down big" at the station,
And informed me that I'd get the blame
For the "dramatic stunt" pulled on the "teller"
Looked to them too much like a "game."

The "police" called it a "frame-up,"
Said it was an "inside job,"
But I steadily denied any knowledge
Or dealings with "underworld mobs."

The "gang" hired a couple of lawyers,
The best "fixers" in any man's town,

J. Wayne Frye

BAD MOON RISING: AMERICAN OUTLAWS
OF THE ROARING 1920'S AND 1930'S

But it takes more than lawyers and money
When Uncle Sam starts "shaking you down."

I was charged as a "scion of gangland"
And tried for my wages of sin;
The "dirty dozen" found me guilty --
From five to fifty years in the pen.

I took the "rap" like good people,
And never one "squawk" did I make.
Jake "dropped himself" on the promise
That we make a "sensational break."

Well, to shorten a sad lengthy story,
Five years have gone over my head
Without even so much as a letter--
At first I thought he was dead.

But not long ago I discovered
From a gal in the joint named Lyle,
That Jack and his "moll" had "got over"
And were living in true "gangster style."

If he had returned to me sometime,
Though he hadn't a cent to give,

J. Wayne Frye   25

BAD MOON RISING: AMERICAN OUTLAWS
OF THE ROARING 1920'S AND 1930'S

I'd forget all this hell that he's caused me,

And love him as long as I live.

But there's no chance of his ever coming,

For he and his moll have no fears

But that I will die in this prison,

Or "flatten" this fifty years.

Tomorrow I'll be on the "outside"

And I'll "drop myself" on it today;

I'll "bump 'em" if they give me the "hotsquat"

On this island out here in the bay...

The iron doors swung wide next morning

For a gruesome woman of waste,

Who at last had a chance to "fix it,"

Murder showed in her cynical face.

Not long ago I read in the paper

That a gal on the East Side got "hot,"

And when the smoke finally retreated,"

It was like a black kettle pot.

It related the colourful story

Of a "jilted gangster gal."

J. Wayne Frye

BAD MOON RISING: AMERICAN OUTLAWS
OF THE ROARING 1920'S AND 1930'S

Two days later a "sub-gun" ended

The story of "Suicide Sal."

The garage apartment where the shoot-out occurred

For the next three months, the group ranged from Texas as far north as Minnesota. In May, they unsuccessfully tried to rob the bank in Lucerne, Indiana but did rob the bank in Okabena, Minnesota. Previously they had kidnapped two people, while stealing their car. They usually released their hostages far from the abduction site, sometimes giving them money to help them return home and actually enjoying their company. They did this consistently.

Stories of such encounters made headlines, as did the more violent episodes. The Barrow Gang did not hesitate to shoot anyone, lawman or civilian, who got in their way. Other members of the Barrow Gang known or thought to have committed murders included Raymond Hamilton, W.D. Jones, Buck Barrow and Henry Methvin. Eventually, the cold-bloodedness of their killings soured the public perception of the outlaws as folk heroes for stealing from the banks which the public held in great disdain. Perhaps if they had killed bank presidents rather than lawmen and civilians, they would have continued their status as folk heroes. Bank presidents were held in greater contempt than even politicians, much like today. Putting people on the streets is not a very good way to endear yourself to the public, but that is capitalism at work. Greed is the driving force that motivates bank presidents and also the biggest factor for outlaws; although outlaws are often driven over the edge by an unforgiving economic system, while a bank president stealing is just part of the job. Again, capitalism is nothing more than a licence to steal for many people in a system that is skewed toward unfairness in the market place. The outlaws of the 20's and 30's were, in many cases, simply working to correct this imbalance.

The photos entertained the public, but the gang was desperate and discontented, as described by Blanche Barrow in her account written while imprisoned in the late 1930's. With their new notoriety, their daily lives became more difficult, as they tried to evade discovery. Restaurants and motels became less secure; they resorted to campfire cooking and bathing in cold streams.

While driving with Jones and Parker near Wellington, Texas, Barrow missed warning signs at a bridge under construction and flipped their car into a ravine. Sources disagree on whether there was a gasoline fire or if Parker was doused with acid from the car's battery under the floorboards; nonetheless, Parker sustained serious third-degree burns to her right leg so severe the muscles contracted and caused the leg to "draw up."

Near the end of her life, Parker could hardly walk; she either hopped on her good leg or was carried by Clyde. After getting help from a nearby farm family and kidnapping two local lawmen, the three outlaws rendezvoused with Blanche and Buck Barrow. They hid in a tourist court near Fort Smith, Arkansas, nursing Parker's burns. Buck and Jones bungled a local robbery and killed the town marshal in Alma, Arkansas. With the renewed pursuit by the law, they had to flee despite Parker's grave condition.

On 18 July 1933, the gang checked into the Red Crown Tourist Court south of Platte City, Missouri. It consisted of two brick cabins joined by garages, and the gang rented both. To the south stood the Red Crown Tavern, a popular restaurant among Missouri Highway Patrolmen. The gang seemed to go out of their way to draw attention: Blanche Barrow registered the party as three guests, but owner Neal Houser could see five people getting out of the car. He noted the driver backed into the garage "gangster style," for a quick getaway. Blanche paid for their cabins with coins rather than bills, and repeated that later when buying five dinners and five beers. The next day, Houser noticed that his guests had taped newspapers over the windows of their cabin. Houser told Captain William Baxter of the Highway Patrol, a patron of his restaurant, about the group.

Clyde and Jones went into town to purchase groceries and medicine to treat Bonnie's leg. The druggist contacted Sheriff Holt Coffey, a determined man, who put the cabins under surveillance. Coffey had been alerted by Oklahoma and Texas law enforcement to watch for strangers seeking such supplies. The sheriff called for reinforcements from Kansas City, including an armoured car. At 11 P.M. that night, Sheriff Coffey led a group of officers armed with Thompson submachine guns.

In the pitched gunfight, the Barrow Gang laid down fire and escaped when a bullet short-circuited the horn on the armoured vehicle and the lawmen mistook it for a cease-fire signal. For some unknown reason, postulating mere fright at the prospect of facing the gang, the law enforcement officers did not pursue the retreating Barrow vehicle.

There was mass confusion among the outlaws in the car as Buck had been mortally wounded. With Blanche screaming as Buck was nearly bleeding to death in her arms, Bonnie was breathing heavily. She looked over at Clyde and said, "It's over isn't it, baby?"

Clyde, blood all over him from his effort to help Buck into the car, managed a grin, as he said, "It ain't over yet, baby." Then, Bonnie reached over and placed her hand on his left leg and nodded her head affirmatively. They simply were not done yet.

J. Wayne Frye

BAD MOON RISING: AMERICAN OUTLAWS OF THE ROARING 1920'S AND 1930'S

Although the gang had evaded the law again, Buck Barrow had a gruesome and ultimately mortal bullet wound that blasted a large hole in his forehead skull bone and exposed his injured brain, and Blanche was nearly blinded by glass fragments in both her eyes. Their prospects for evading a manhunt dwindled. Five days of dealing with an agonizing Buck, who was so strong willed he simply refused to die, began to take a toll on all of them.

On July 24, the Barrow Gang was camped at Dexfield Park, an abandoned amusement park near Dexter, Iowa. Although he was sometimes semiconscious, and even talked and ate, Buck's massive head wound and loss of blood was so severe that Clyde and Jones dug a grave for him.

As Buck was dying, Blanche became increasingly distraught and Bonnie actually suggested that Clyde should ease his pain with a well-placed bullet. Before a decision could be made, fate intervened.

After their bloody bandages were noticed by some people at the park, officers determined the campers were the Barrow gang. Approximately one hundred officers and posse members surrounded the group, and the Barrows soon came under fire. Clyde, Bonnie and W.D. Jones escaped on foot. Buck was shot in the back, and he and his wife were captured by the officers. The ensuing melee led to a frenzy of excitement in the small town and the national press soon descended in mass.

*Blanche Borrow is captured while
Buck lies mortally wounded nearby.*

*Buck and Blanche Barrow during happier times. This photo was
taken three days before the shootout that would lead
to Buck's eventual demise from his wounds.*

Buck actually survived for five days before finally succumbing as a result of his wounds. Doctors were amazed at his determination and will to survive. They allowed Blanche to visit him once, but he gradually slipped into a coma after admitting to the killing of Marshal Humphrey in Arkansas. His last words before going into the coma were, "I ain't got no complaints against the laws. They was just doing their jobs."

For the next six weeks, Bonnie, Clyde and Jones were in Colorado, Minnesota and Mississippi, keeping a low profile and pulling only small robberies for survival. They restocked their arsenal when Barrow and Jones burglarized an armoury at Plattville, Illinois on August 20, stealing handguns and a large quantity of ammunition. By early September, they went to Dallas to see their families, perhaps sensing that time was not on their side. Jones parted company with them, continuing to Houston, where his mother had moved. He was arrested there without incident on November 16 and returned to Dallas. Through the autumn, Clyde Barrow executed a series of small-time robberies while Bonnie healed. They were nearly captured in Sowers, Texas and were in a running shootout, both being shot in the leg. The following week on November 28, a Dallas grand jury delivered a murder indictment against Parker and Barrow for the January 1933 killing of Tarrant County Deputy Malcolm Davis; it was Parker's first warrant for murder.

As mentioned previously, Clyde had always vowed to conduct a raid on Eastham Prison. On January 16, 1934, Barrow orchestrated the bold escape of killers Raymond Hamilton, Henry Methvin and several others in the infamous Eastham Breakout that still ranks as one of the greatest prison breaks of all time. The brazen raid generated publicity all across America, and Barrow seemed to have achieved his overriding goal: revenge on the Texas Department of Corrections. During the jailbreak, escapee Joe Palmer shot prison officer Joe Crowson. This attack attracted the full power of the Texas and federal government to the manhunt for Barrow and Parker. As Crowson struggled for life, prison warden, Lee Simmons, reportedly promised him that all persons involved in the breakout would be hunted down and killed. All were, except for Henry Methvin, whose life was traded for turning Barrow and Parker over to authorities.

This is where the revered and renowned Texas Ranger, Captain Frank Hamer, entered the deteriorating picture. He was a determined, dogged, uncompromising man known for an unflinching devotion to duty.

*Captain Fred Hamer set out on a personal vendetta
to capture Bonnie and Clyde.*

BAD MOON RISING: AMERICAN OUTLAWS
OF THE ROARING 1920'S AND 1930'S

Tall, burly, taciturn, Hamer was described as unimpressed by outlaws and driven by an inflexible adherence to right, or what he thought was right. He had acquired a formidable reputation as a result of several spectacular captures and the shooting of a number of criminals. He was officially credited with 53 kills while suffering 17 wounds. Shooting a woman was something many lawmen found abhorrent, but Hamer said, "I have no problem shooting anyone, and that includes Bonnie Parker." Hamer became the constant shadow of Barrow and Parker, living out of his car, just a town or two behind the bandits.

On 1 April 1934, which was Easter Sunday, Barrow and Henry Methvin killed two young highway patrolmen when they happened upon the two men who were sitting on their car running board sipping whiskey. Seeing the two patrolmen pull onto the dirt road where they were parked about 100 feet off the main highway, the two men shot them as they were getting off their motorcycles. Methvin admitted he shot first, leaving Clyde no alternative but to start shooting too as the officer not hit by Methvin went for his gun.

These cold-blooded murders turned what had been an often admiring public against the gang. The killings were recounted in exaggerated detail, affecting public perception of Bonnie and Clyde. The story told by an eyewitness, a farmer, who claimed to have seen Parker laugh while one of the patrolmen lay on the ground as she gave him a coup de grâce was a complete fabrication in all likelihood, as Methvin later said she was asleep in the back seat of the car and took no part in the killings. The eyewitness's ever-changing story was soon discredited, but the massive negative publicity, against Parker in particular, increased the public clamour for an end to the gang.

On 21 May 1934, four posse members from Texas were in Shreveport, Louisiana when they learned that Barrow and Parker were going to Bienville Parish that evening with Methvin. Barrow had designated the residence of Methvin's parents as a rendezvous in case they were separated, and Methvin did get separated from the pair in Shreveport. The full posse, consisting of Captain Hamer, Dallas County Sheriff's Deputies Alcorn and Hinton (both of whom knew Barrow and Parker by sight), former Texas Ranger Manny Gault, Bienville Parish Sheriff Henderson Jordan and his deputy, Prentiss Oakley, set up an ambush at the rendezvous point along Louisiana State Highway 154, south of the little town of Gibsland. Hinton recounted that their group was in place by 9:00 P.M. on the 21st and waited through the whole next day (May 22) with no sign of the outlaw couple.

At approximately 9:15 A.M. on May 23, the posse, concealed in the bushes and almost ready to concede defeat, heard Barrow's stolen Ford V8 approaching at a high speed. The posse's official report had Barrow stopping to speak with Methvin's father, who had been planted there with his truck that morning to distract Barrow and force him into the lane closer to the posse. The lawmen opened fire, killing Barrow and Parker while shooting a combined total of about 130 rounds. Barrow was killed instantly by Oakley's initial head shot, but Hinton reported hearing Parker scream as she realized Clyde was dead.

Bonnie and Clyde were shot more than fifty times each, so certainly there was no attempt whatsoever at offering them the chance to surrender. Undertaker C. F. "Boots" Bailey had difficulty embalming the bodies because of all the bullet holes. The temporarily deafened officers inspected the vehicle and discovered an arsenal of weapons, including stolen automatic rifles, sawed-off semi-automatic shotguns, assorted handguns, and several thousand rounds of ammunition, along with 15 sets of license plates from various states. Just like today, I am sure that the NRA was delighted that all present were exercising their 2nd Amendment rights to be packing.

Word of the bloody ambush quickly got around when Hamer, Jordan, Oakley, and Hinton drove into town to telephone their respective bosses. A crowd soon gathered at the ambush spot. Gault and Alcorn, left to guard the bodies, lost control of the scene. One woman cut off bloody locks of Parker's hair and pieces from her dress, which were subsequently sold as souvenirs. Hinton returned to find a man trying to cut off Barrow's trigger finger. Welcome to America, where a chance to make money is never squandered. This was capitalism at work in all its gory glory.

BAD MOON RISING: AMERICAN OUTLAWS
OF THE ROARING 1920'S AND 1930'S

One person described the scene as follows: "When I got there nearly everyone had begun collecting souvenirs such as shell casings, slivers of glass from the shattered car windows, and bloody pieces of clothing from the garments of Bonnie and Clyde. One eager man even tried to cut off Clyde's left ear."

Clyde's body was placed in the car along with Bonnie's and the car was towed to town. An autopsy was performed in the combination furniture store and funeral parlour. A huge throng of people emerged outside the parlour, estimated by authorities at well over 10,000 in a town with a population of 2000. Typical of the culture of greed in America, restaurants and bars started doubling their prices to take advantage of the large number of people pouring into town.

Henry Barrow was summoned to identify his son's body, and he sat down on a sofa, head in hands weeping uncontrollably. Two people who had been kidnapped previously by Bonnie and Clyde also identified the bodies.

Bonnie and Clyde wished to be buried side by side, but the Parker family would not allow it. Mrs. Parker wanted to grant her daughter's final wish, to be brought home, but the mobs surrounding the Parker house made that impossible. More than 20,000 attended Bonnie Parker's funeral. Flowers were delivered from all over America, and two of the arrangements came from well-known outlaw gangsters Pretty Boy Floyd and John Dillinger. Bonnie was buried at Fishtrap Cemetery originally, but

J. Wayne Frye

her body was moved to another cemetery in nearby Dallas in 1945.

Clyde's funeral in Dallas attracted a smaller crowd estimated at maybe 5000. He was buried in Western Heights Cemetery in Dallas, next to his brother, Buck. Ironically, both Bonnie and Clyde had insurance policies that were paid out to their families. As a result of that, all insurance policies in the USA today have criminal activity exclusions. Though there were huge rewards offered for the capture or killing of Bonnie and Clyde, none of the rewards were ever paid out.

All the people present at the shooting had different accounts of what happened, so no concrete evidence exists to support any of their contentions. Lingering questions remain about what really happened. One newspaperman said, "The demise of these two notorious outlaws was typical of how all outlaws meet their end. They lived by violence and died by violence. Yet, there was something about these two's bravado that many Americans admired. Hey, they robbed banks, and Americans as a result of the depression hold outlaws in higher regards than banks."

"I see her falling out of the open door, a beautiful and petite young girl who is soft and warm, with hair carefully fixed, and I smell a light perfume against the burned-cordite smell of gunpowder, the sweet and unreal smell of blood". (Ted Hinton's lucid and lurid recollection of Bonnie Parker's death in the book, *AMBUSH*.)

BAD MOON RISING: AMERICAN OUTLAWS
OF THE ROARING 1920'S AND 1930'S

The mortician found it almost impossible to keep embalming fluid in the bodies as they were so riddled with holes it kept seeping out. He finally used glue to seal up some of the wounds so the bodies would retain fluid. As a child, I remember seeing the death car as it was exhibited at the opening for the movie *The Bonnie Parker Story* with Dorothy Provine. The movie was pretty boring, but the car generated a lot of excitement at the Sunset Theatre in the small town of Asheboro, North Carolina.

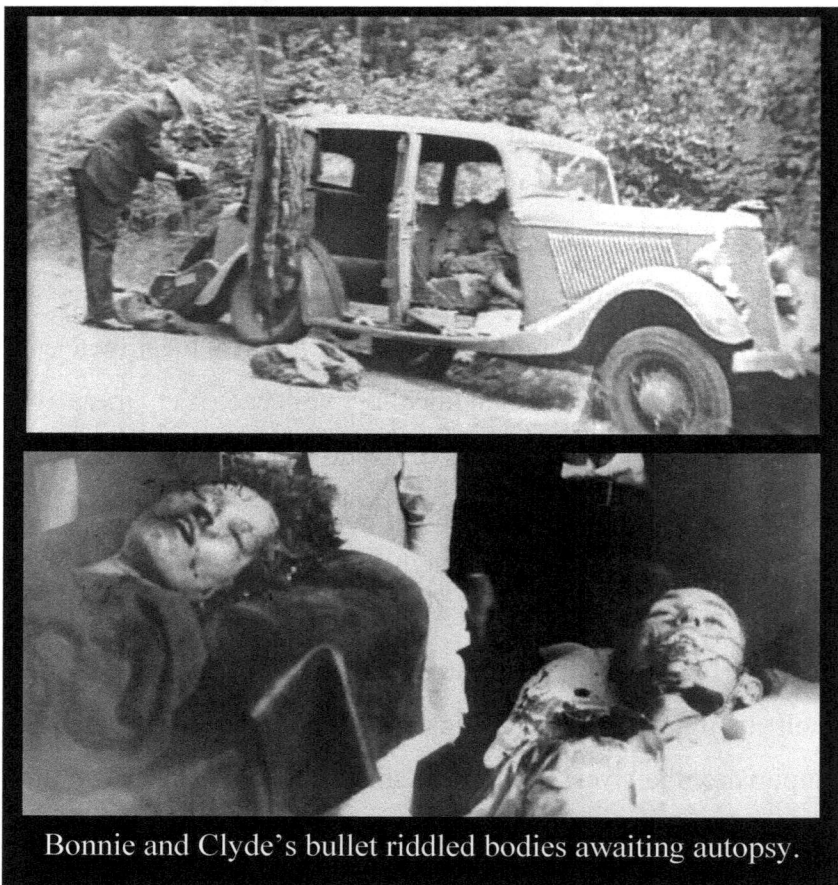

Bonnie and Clyde's bullet riddled bodies awaiting autopsy.

BAD MOON RISING: AMERICAN OUTLAWS
OF THE ROARING 1920'S AND 1930'S

Blanche never carried a gun. Convicted of attempted murder, she served six years. In February 1935, Dallas and federal authorities conducted a harbouring trial in which 20 family members and friends of the outlaw couple were arrested and jailed for the aid and abetment of Barrow and Parker. All twenty either pleaded or were found guilty. The two mothers were jailed for 30 days; other sentences ranged from two years imprisonment to one hour in custody for teenager Marie Barrow, Clyde's sister. Blanche Barrow's injuries left her permanently blinded in her left eye. After the 1933 shootout at Dexfield Park, she was taken into custody on the charge of assault with intent to kill. She was sentenced to ten years in prison but was paroled in 1939 for good behaviour. She returned to Dallas, leaving her life of crime in the past, and lived with her invalid father as his caregiver. She married Eddie Frasure in 1940, worked as a taxi cab dispatcher and a beautician, and completed the terms of her parole one year later. She lived in peace with her husband until he died of cancer in 1969. Warren Beatty approached her to purchase the rights to her name for use in the 1967 film *Bonnie and Clyde*. While she agreed to the original script, she objected to her characterization in the final film, describing Estelle Parsons' Academy Award winning portrayal of her as "screaming horse's ass." Despite this, she maintained a firm friendship with Beatty. She died at the age of 77 on Christmas Eve, 1988, and was buried in Dallas's Grove Hill Memorial Park under the name Blanche B. Frasure.

BAD MOON RISING: AMERICAN OUTLAWS
OF THE ROARING 1920'S AND 1930'S

W.D. Jones avoided capture and made his way to Houston, Texas where he got a job picking cotton. He was discovered by a field hand who overheard him talking in his sleep about Bonnie and Clyde. When arrested, he claimed to have been kept a prisoner by Bonnie and Clyde, serving as a sex surrogate for Bonnie since Clyde was impotent. He was eventually convicted of one murder and given a fifteen year sentence. He served only six years. He resurfaced in 1967 after the famous movie with Warren Beatty and Faye Dunaway came out, doing many television interviews. He was killed in 1974 by the jealous boyfriend of a woman he was trying to help out. Gang member Henry Methvin was convicted of murder and served fifteen years. Shortly after release from prison in 1948, he stepped or was pushed in front of train. Barrow cohorts, Raymond Hamilton and Joe Palmer, both were convicted of murder and in an extreme act of irony were both electrocuted on the same day in 1935.

Frank Hamer returned to a quieter life as a freelance security consultant and a strike breaking goon for oil companies. He made headlines again in 1948 when he and Governor Coke Stevenson unsuccessfully challenged future U.S. President, Lyndon Johnson's vote totals during the election for the U.S. Senate. He died in 1955 at age 71.

The death car can be seen today at Whiskey Pete's casino in the little town of Primm, Nevada. I recall seeing it, and as people strolled by I realized that all things are but fading memories,

J. Wayne Frye

because as I stood there looking at the car, I heard a young woman say to her male companion, "Who the hell were Bonnie and Clyde?"

The tumultuous lives of Bonnie and Clyde have been romanticized and glorified. Several movies have been made, the most popular one being Warren Beatty's 1967 *Bonnie and Clyde*. Though somewhat accurate, it took considerable creative licence with the story.

The Trail's End
(Also know as The Story of Bonnie and Clyde)

You've read the story of Jesse James
of how he lived and died.
If you're still in need;
of something to read,
here's the story of Bonnie and Clyde.

Now Bonnie and Clyde are the Barrow gang
I'm sure you all have read.
how they rob and steal;
and those who squeal,
are usually found dying or dead.

There's lots of untruths to these write-ups;
they're not as ruthless as that.
their nature is raw;

J. Wayne Frye   43

BAD MOON RISING: AMERICAN OUTLAWS
OF THE ROARING 1920'S AND 1930'S

they hate all the law,

the stool pidgeons, spotters and rats.

They call them cold-blooded killers

they say they are heartless and mean.

But I say this with pride

that I once knew Clyde,

when he was honest and upright and clean.

But the law fooled around;

kept taking him down,

and locking him up in a cell.

Till he said to me;

"I'll never be free,

so I'll meet a few of them in hell."

The road was so dimly lighted

there were no highway signs to guide.

But they made up their minds;

if all roads were blind,

they wouldn't give up till they died.

The road gets dimmer and dimmer

sometimes you can hardly see.

But it's fight man to man

J. Wayne Frye

BAD MOON RISING: AMERICAN OUTLAWS OF THE ROARING 1920'S AND 1930'S

and do all you can,

for they know they can never be free.

From heart-break some people have suffered

from weariness some people have died.

But take it all in all;

our troubles are small,

till we get like Bonnie and Clyde.

If a policeman is killed in Dallas

and they have no clue or guide.

If they can't find a fiend,

they just wipe their slate clean

and hang it on Bonnie and Clyde.

There's two crimes committed in America

not accredited to the Barrow mob.

They had no hand;

in the kidnap demand,

nor the Kansas City Depot job.

A newsboy once said to his buddy;

"I wish old Clyde would get jumped.

In these awfull hard times;

we'd make a few dimes,

J. Wayne Frye

if five or six cops would get bumped."

The police haven't got the report yet
but Clyde called me up today.
He said, "Don't start any fights;
we aren't working nights,
we're joining the NRA."

From Irving to West Dallas viaduct
is known as the Great Divide,
where the women are kin;
and the men are men,
and they won't "stool" on Bonnie and Clyde.

If they try to act like citizens
and rent them a nice little flat,
About the third night;
they're invited to fight,
by a sub-gun's rat-a-tat-tat.

They don't think they're too smart or desperate;
they know that the law always wins.
They've been shot at before;
but they do not ignore,
that death is the wages of sin.

J. Wayne Frye

BAD MOON RISING: AMERICAN OUTLAWS
OF THE ROARING 1920'S AND 1930'S

Some day they'll go down together

they'll bury them side by side.

To few it'll be grief,

to the law a relief

but it's death for Bonnie and Clyde.

(Below is another poem that is of recent vintage, and written by an author I won't name. Bet you probably can figure out who is.)

Outlaws – Billy the Kid and Clyde Barrow Meet Ghost Riders

Billy rode on a pinto horse.

Billy the Kid I mean.

And he met Clyde Barrow riding

In a little gray machine.

Billy drew his bridle rein,

And Barrow stopped his car.

And the dead man talked to the living man

Under the morning star.

Billy said to the Barrow boy,

"Is this the way you ride

In a car that does its ninety per

Machine guns at each side?"

"I only had my pinto horse

And my six-gun tried and true.

J. Wayne Frye

BAD MOON RISING: AMERICAN OUTLAWS
OF THE ROARING 1920'S AND 1930'S

I could shoot but they got me,
And someday they'll get you, too!"

"For the men who live like you and me
Are playing a losing game.
And the way we shoot, or the way we ride
Is all about the same."

"And the like of us may never hope
For death to set us free,
For the living are always after you
And the dead are after me."

Then out of the East arose the sound
Of hoof-beats with the dawn, but nothing to see.
Old Billy pulled his rein and said,
"I must be moving on, I got ghost riders after me."

Why does the public grasp so tightly to the stories of outlaws and look upon them as heroic? It is simply that the "outlaws" defy authority, and it titillates our sense of adventure to daydream about being outlaws, too; people who defy the norms of society and stand out as individuals unwilling to bend to the control of a society that, from the time an individual is born, brainwashes them into obedience to an ideal that is illusionary at best. Force children to say the pledge of allegiance and instil patriotism.

J. Wayne Frye

BAD MOON RISING: AMERICAN OUTLAWS
OF THE ROARING 1920'S AND 1930'S

Preach the virtues of capitalism and develop robot-like workers to serve the almighty corporation. Praise the military and create future soldiers to die in wars of conquest to secure natural resources for those same corporations, whose C.E.O.'s never have any children fighting for America in some foreign land. This is the society that the outlaws of the 20's and 30's saw through. They might not have been articulate enough to postulate society's ills that drove them over the edge, but, deep down, they knew that there was something wrong with a nation that only allowed the good things to flow to the top while disregarding those in the middle and at the bottom of the economic ladder.

The simple truth is that Americans are probably some of the most oppressed people in the world, and they do not even realize it. They wave the flag and praise Jesus while both the government and the church brainwash them into blind obedience. The government says the poor are poor because of laziness, and rather than blaming the rich for their plight, the middle class has been propagandized into believing it is the welfare queens who are using their tax dollars egregiously, rather than the tax-dodging corporations and privileged class. Meanwhile, the church tells the poor not to worry, as in the sweet hereafter; they will walk roads paved with gold in the land of milk and honey.

The banks and Wall Street barons of greed crashed the economy in 1929 and did it again in 2009. The reaction of the aggrieved in 1929 spawned some dedicated outlaws who said they would not suffer the indignity heaped upon them by an uncaring, alien government and economic system that used and abused the poor. In 2009, people had been so conditioned and brainwashed into complacency that they simply rolled over and accepted their fate with no protest while the bankers, Wall Street tycoons and insurance company executives laughed all the way to the bank.

In my opinion, if Bonnie and Clyde had not resorted to cold-bloodied murder and stuck to just robbing banks they would indeed be legitimate folk heroes. One of the famous Newton boys' bank robbers, appearing on the old Johnny Carson talk show once said about robbing banks, "Hell, what is the big deal? It is just one thief stealing from another thief." Truer words were never spoken!

CHAPTER 3

NEVER BROUGHT TO JUSTICE

The Street Girl

You don't want to marry me honey,

Though just to hear you ask me is sweet;

If you did you'd regret it tomorrow

For I'm only a girl of the street.

Time was when I'd gladly have listened,

Before I was tainted with shame,

But it wouldn't be fair to you honey;

Men laugh when they mention my name.

Back there on the farm in Nebraska,

I might have said yes to you then,

But I thought the world was a playground;

Just teeming with Santa Claus men.

J. Wayne Frye

BAD MOON RISING: AMERICAN OUTLAWS
OF THE ROARING 1920'S AND 1930'S

So I left the old home for the city,

To play in its mad, dirty whirl,

Never knowing how little of pity,

It holds for a slip of a girl.

You think I'm still good-looking honey!

But know I am faded and spent,

Even Helen of Troy would look seedy,

If she followed the pace I went.

But that day I came in from the country,

With my hair down my back in a curl;

Through the length and the breadth of the city,

There was never a prettier girl.

I soon got a job in the chorus,

With nothing but looks and a form,

I had a new man every evening,

And my kisses were thrilling and warm.

I might have sold them for a fortune,

To some old sugar daddy with dough,

But youth called to youth for its lover,

There was plenty that I didn't know.

Today I am jaded and worn out with dismay.

You see I have scammed and stolen,

J. Wayne Frye

BAD MOON RISING: AMERICAN OUTLAWS
OF THE ROARING 1920'S AND 1930'S

Never thinking about right or wrong,

As I always looked for something golden.

I know the world is a cruel place.

That's why I embraced the wild side of life,

And shouted at authority "this is enough,"

Oh, but along the way, I sowed strife.

This could have been the story of many females in the 1920's, who were forced to use their wiles and sexuality to survive in a world where there was no social safety net. This is the very condition that led to so much lawlessness in the 1920's and early 1930's, when many people simply saw no alternative for survival but to become outlaws fighting a system that was strangling the life out of working men and women. When an animal (and yes, humans are animals) is backed into a corner and left no alternatives, it will fight for survival. That is the natural instinct of beasts and humans. So, was it any wonder that so many girls, like the one mentioned in the above poem, resorted to desperate measures in order to survive? Since Ronald Reagan took office in 1981, there has been a gradual erosion of the social safety net that began with the election of Franklin Roosevelt in 1933. Today, the social safety net is literally being destroyed by a cold hearted poor-hating, wealthy-loving Republican Party and a corporate controlled Democratic Party that is only marginally less cruel in the way the middle class and poor are treated. The world is simply not a very nice place today or yesterday.

J. Wayne Frye

BAD MOON RISING: AMERICAN OUTLAWS OF THE ROARING 1920'S AND 1930'S

Edna "Rabbit" Murray and Volney Davis

Edna "Rabbit" Murray (1898-1966) was a criminal associated with several high-profile gangs in the Depression-era of the early 1930s. Although popularly known to the press as the "Kissing Bandit" for kissing a male robbery victim, she was known in the underworld as "Rabbit" for her skills in breaking out of the penitentiary. She was married to two criminals in the 1920s, but is best known as the lover and crime partner of Volney Davis.

She was born Martha Edna Stanley in Marion, Kansas. She moved with her father to Oklahoma at an early age. As a teenager, she married and had a son. She divorced shortly after the baby's birth and remarried. That marriage also failed.

Murray was working as a waitress when she met robber Volney Davis, who became her lover, but the romance was ill-fated as he was imprisoned for life in 1919. Volney Everett "Curley" Davis (1902 - 1979) was a long-time Oklahoma bandit from the Cherokee Nation and would eventually become an associate of both the John Dillinger, Alvin Karpis and the Barker gang during the 1930's.

J. Wayne Frye

BAD MOON RISING: AMERICAN OUTLAWS OF THE ROARING 1920'S AND 1930'S

Davis was an early member of the Oklahoma-based Central Park Gang, where he first met the Barkers and committed his first major robbery with Arthur "Doc" Barker, when they burglarized St. John's Hospital in Tulsa. The night watchman was killed during the robbery. Barker was arrested about 5 months later for the murder; however, Davis evaded authorities for nearly a year before he was captured. He was sentenced to life imprisonment for his role in the robbery, and thus Edna was again left in a lurch with a small child. Davis briefly escaped from the state penitentiary in McAlester, Oklahoma, participating in a mass escape with several other convicts by using ropes and a ladder to climb over the wall but was recaptured almost two weeks later.

Meantime, Edna moved to Kansas City, Missouri where she joined her younger sister Doris, who was living with criminal, Emory Connell. Murray met and married Connell's partner, jewel thief Diamond Joe Sullivan. Sullivan was convicted of murder in 1924 and was executed. Thus, it appears a dark cloud had formed over Edna when it came to marriage. After Sullivan's death, she met and married another criminal, Jack Murray. On 1 October 1925, Edna and Murray were sentenced to 25 years for a Kansas City, Missouri hold-up. It was this crime that earned Edna the nickname "The Kissing Bandit," after she supposedly kissed the victim of the robbery. On 2 May 1927, Edna escaped from Missouri State Penitentiary and remained free until arrested in

Chicago on 10 September 1931. She made a one-day escape from prison on 4 November 1931, and then a third escape on 13 December 1932, having sawed through the bars of her cell, assisted by another prisoner who escaped with her. Thus, she acquired the nickname "Rabbit" for her ability to escape incarceration and hop away into the sunset.

She joined up with her old heartthrob, Volney Davis again, who had also escaped from prison, himself, in 1932. The two continued their crime spree and later settled down in Aurora, Illinois. The couple soon joined up with the Barker-Karpis gang as Edna's sister was living with Jess Doyle, also a member of that gang.

On 23 April 1934, famous bank robbers, John Dillinger, Homer Van Meter and John Hamilton arrived together at Edna Murray's home seeking refuge after being ambushed by federal agents and police in the famous Little Bohemia shootout at their hideout in Wisconsin. Hamilton, having been badly wounded, died of his injuries several days later, despite the valiant efforts of Edna to save him. Murray and Davis helped bury Hamilton in an unmarked grave and used lye on his face and hands so no one would know who it was.

On 22 January 1935, Murray was indicted along with several members of the Barker gang for a conspiracy to kidnap wealthy Minnesota banker, Edward Bremerand and ransom him for $200,000. Fleeing the state, she was eventually apprehended in Pittsburg, Kansas while traveling with criminal Jess Doyle in February of 1935.

Murray's brother, Harry C. Stanley, was subsequently arrested for aiding and abetting Murray in early 1935, was fined $1,000 and sentenced to six months imprisonment. The following year, her son, Preston Leroy Paden, was convicted of murder for killing a night watchman in Kansas. He was given a life sentence.

Murray was not found guilty in the kidnapping conspiracy but was returned to prison in Jefferson City, Missouri to finish serving her term for robbery. Volney Davis led FBI agents to Hamilton's grave outside Aurora, Illinois three months later. Edna eventually backed his story up.

Murray was very cooperative with the authorities after her capture and gave evidence against a number of the Barker-Karpis gang's associates, and about corrupt police officers and lawyers. While in prison, she marketed herself as a gangster's moll in a number of newspapers and journals.

Davis and Murray were never charged with the hold-ups he committed while part of the Karpis-Barker Gang. However, they were indicted for the Bremer kidnapping on 22 January 1935. A little over two weeks later, Davis was captured in St. Louis by federal agents on February 6 but escaped from federal custody the next day. He had been traveling under escort to stand trial in St. Paul when their plane was forced to land in Yorkville, Illinois. Once on the ground, Davis knocked out a guard and stole a car.

He evaded capture for nearly four months before being traced to Chicago by the FBI and arrested by famous FBI agent Melvin Purvis. He was eventually returned to St. Paul where he was convicted of kidnapping and summarily sentenced to life imprisonment. Davis cooperated with the government and gave information as well as testified against other members of the gang. Like the rest of the Karpis-Barker Gang, Davis was sent to Alcatraz, where he spent the next several decades. By the time of his release in the late 1950s, however, he was in poor health. Davis married and lived out his life in Guerneville, California. He died in 1979.

Edna Murray was released from the Missouri prison right before Christmas in 1940. She lived out her life in anonymity and died in San Francisco in 1966. Her granddaughter, Pamela Paden Tippet, wrote a book (*Run Rabbit Run: The Life and Legacy of Edna Murray*) about her, which details some of the little known aspects of a woman who went from being a criminal to a dotting grandmother. Like most of us, as we age, the zeal to rebel against authority is quieted, and we accept the fact that the establishment will always criminalize any behaviour that does not reflect the accepted order of things. This is the way of the world where it is the job of law enforcement to keep us in line so that the real criminals, the privileged and government officials, at the top of the economic ladder are never brought to justice.

J. Wayne Frye

CHAPTER 3

YOU DON'T MESS WITH THAT FELLA

Arthur Rimbaud knew it way back in 1883.

He saw how banks robbed the poor every day.

That is why he said, "If it is truth you want to see,

Grab a gun and a rob a bank to be truly free."

The previous chapter dealt with a woman few people would recognize as a famous bank robber, and in this chapter, we are going to discuss someone even more obscure, but the truth is he is the man widely recognized as the father of the modern bank robbery. He refined robbing banks to a fine art and his methods were copied by some of the most famous bank robbers in the history of the "sport." O.K., I am being a bit facetious in calling it a sport, but hey, we admire sports figures who score goals, sink baskets or hit home runs, so why not admire the finesse of a great bank robber?

BAD MOON RISING: AMERICAN OUTLAWS
OF THE ROARING 1920'S AND 1930'S

Herman Karl "Baron" Lamm (1890-1930) was a German-American bank robber. His robberies were famous for the precision in which they were meticulously carried out. Part of his attention to detail was learned as a Prussian soldier before he immigrated to the United States. Lamm believed a heist required all the planning of a military operation. He pioneered the concepts of thoroughly casing a bank and developing escape routes before conducting the robbery. Using a highly refined planning system called "The Lamm Technique," he conducted dozens of successful bank robberies between 1919 and 1930. His bank robbing was not the result of the Great Depression that drove so many to desperate measures, but was simply a chosen lifestyle that he looked upon as perfectly normal for anyone who saw banks as nothing more than monuments to greed that were always taking advantage of poor people. He once said, "Hey, I'm just getting even for all the money the banks have stolen over the years from their customers."

Lamm's superior techniques were studied and imitated by other bank robbers across the country, including the most famous one of the era, John Dillinger.

Lamm was, indeed, a hold-up artist, adapting his military training, his study of tactics, and his precision and discipline into the art of crime. He theorized that a heist required all the planning of a military operation, which included the development of contingency options in the event of unforeseen circumstances.

J. Wayne Frye

BAD MOON RISING: AMERICAN OUTLAWS
OF THE ROARING 1920'S AND 1930'S

Bank robberies, at the time, were largely improvised, resulting in failure most of the time. Lamm sought to take the guesswork out of bank robbing. It all came about when he was arrested in 1917 after a botched hold-up and served a brief stint in a Utah prison, where he developed what became known as the aforementioned "Lamm Technique," in which he pioneered the concept of casing banks beforehand. Despite all the movies depicting gangs like the James' and Dalton's casing banks, in reality, it never happened until Lamm came along. There is an old saying that you are supposed to learn from your mistakes. Well, his mistake got him arrested and he vowed to be more methodical about robbing banks in the future.

His system involved carefully studying a target bank for many hours or days before the robbery, developing a detailed floor plan, noting the location of safes, taking meticulous notes and establishing escape routes. He would occasionally have a man pose as a journalist to better understand the inner workings of the bank. Lamm assigned each gang member a specific job, along with a specific zone of the bank they were charged with surveying and a strict timetable to complete their stage of the robbery. Among the jobs he assigned to his fellow robbers were the lookout, the getaway driver, the lobby man and the vault man. He also put his men through a series of rehearsals, some of which involved using a full-scale mock-up of the interior of the bank. Lamm stressed the importance of timing during these practice runs, and used stopwatches to ensure the proper results were achieved. He only allowed his gang members to stay in a bank for a specific period of time, regardless of how much money they could steal.

Lamm is also credited with devising the first detailed bank robbery getaway maps, which included many alternative routes in case of road blocks. He meticulously developed getaway plans for each of his robberies. Before every heist, Lamm obtained a solid black car with a high-powered engine, and often recruited drivers who had been involved in auto racing. Lamm pasted a chart on the dashboard for the driver, which included block-by-block markings of escape routes. Before each run, Lamm and the getaway driver clocked each route to the second under various weather conditions. Practice runs on the escape routes and alternative routes would often take days to master. Using this system, Lamm and his gang conducted dozens of successful bank robberies, taking more than $1 million (around 15 million in today's dollars). Despite the headlines garnered by the more well-known robbers like Dillinger, Bonnie and Clyde, Baby Face Nelson and Pretty Boy Floyd, Lamm's gang was considered the most efficient bank robbers of the era, and stole the most money by far. The members of his gang included several old-time western outlaws, including a few who had ridden with Butch Cassidy and the Sundance Kid, along with young criminals, some college educated, as he preferred thinkers to thugs.

BAD MOON RISING: AMERICAN OUTLAWS
OF THE ROARING 1920'S AND 1930'S

Occasionally, Lamm included among his partners in crime, the ruthless Harry Pierpont, who was also known for his careful tactical planning.

Indiana is a state that seemed to attract many bank robbers, including Lamm, during this era. Maybe it was because, like today, it was a state where uncaring, self-serving politicians playing the religious card and brandishing hatred for anything that lifted up the poor at the expense of the wealthy is embraced as the American way. It must have given robbers great pleasure to steal from the very heart of a system that chastised the poor for being poor and celebrated the evil of banks that seized people's property with cold hearted consistency, showing no remorse for putting orphans and widows on the streets. In fact, sometimes the robbers were actually applauded as they were robbing banks. On most occasions, the robbers would not take money from depositors who were standing in line out of respect for hard working people.

Despite Lamm's meticulous attention to detail, the old saying, "the best laid plans of mice and men often go awry" proved to be apropos for Lamm in December of 1930. His gang walked into the Citizen's Bank in Clinton, Indiana filled with bravado, as they assumed it would be just another easy heist. The robbery , which netted them over $15,000 (over $200,000 in today's dollars) actually went down with the gangs' usual calculated precision; however, Lamm's kind gesture to a lady held up the escape long enough to sit a series of events in motion that would lead to disaster. After taking the money, Lamm noticed a lady was shivering in fear with a little girl by her side. He walked over and said, "We have no grudge against you ma'am. Don't be afraid." He then patted the little girl on the head and exited. This delay affected the concentration of getaway driver W. H. Hunter, who noticed a local barber approaching the car with a shotgun. The barber was one of thousands of Indiana citizens organized to help police fight a growing number of bank robberies in the state. Now, it is not this author's place to discuss the merits of ordinary citizens helping recover banks' money, when the banks do very little to help out anybody in a world where their greed crashed the economy twice with devastating circumstances, but the public often sides with those who exploit them without rhyme or reason. The driver saw a shotgun in his hand, and assumed the man had been alerted to the robbery. The driver panicked and made a fast U-turn, causing the car to blow a tire after jumping a curb. Lamm and his men seized a second car, but were forced to abandon it after they realized it could go no more than 55 kilometres per hour (35 mph) because it was fitted with a governor, which the car's owner had installed to prevent his elderly father from driving too fast. The gang seized a third vehicle, a truck, but because it had very little water in the radiator, they were forced to seize a fourth car, which had only a small amount of gas in the tank. Lamm and his gang roared out of town, across the nearby

Illinois state line where they were cornered near Sidell, Illinois by over 200 police officers and armed citizens when their car ran out of gas. A massive gun battle ensued in a farmer's cornfield. The first bandit to fall was Hunter, who was wounded and would die a few hours later. Lamm and former Butch Cassidy associate, seventy-one year old G.W. Landy, tried to make their way to a nearby farmhouse, where they hoped to steal a car. As they weaved and bobbed through the corn field, Landy, because of his age was exhausted. Realizing they would have to run through open terrain, they stopped, sat down in furrow in the field and shot themselves in the heads rather than face prison. The two other gang members, Walter Dietrich and James "Oklahoma Jack" Clark, surrendered and were eventually sentenced to life in an Indiana state prison.

This is the only known surviving photo of Herman Karl "Baron" Lamm, alongside the bank where his last heist took place.

Lamm was dead, but unfortunately for banks across America, his superb techniques of robbery were being copied by some of the era's most successful bandits. Yes, there were still undisciplined, unskilled thugs who improvised rather than plan, but the most successful of the robbers were those who studied and adhered to the techniques introduced by Lamm known as the five "P's" – Prior Preparation Prevents Poor Performance. Although they would never admit it, when I was in basic training for the U.S. Army, a special forces sergeant once told me that they planned their raids into enemy territory based on the same five "P's" used by Lamm.

Lamm always recognized that escape was more crucial than entry. In fact, entry was the easy part, because you could just stroll in like any other depositor. He once told Harry Pierpont, "Would you go into a blind alley if you were being chased? Of course you wouldn't. Getting the money is easy. The hard part is getting away with it, and proper planning is essential to getting away as swiftly and smoothly as possible. Banks are the enemy, and preparing a bank robbery is like going into battle. Without a plan, you will, in all likelihood, fail." The truth is that Lamm only failed once, never coming close to being caught in countless hold-ups. Of course in a serious business like bank robbing, one mistake is all it takes.

> The Lamm Bam by J. Wayne Frye ©1996
> *Herman Lamm was always a man with a plan.*
> *"Put the money in the bag" is what he said,*
> *With a Cheshire grin showing white teeth.*
> *"Be smart now folks," he uttered, no ego to be fed.*
> *"Don't follow me or their will be some mighty grief.*
> *Tell your kiddies something when you go to bed.*
> *You survived a Lamm hold up and ain't dead."*

BAD MOON RISING: AMERICAN OUTLAWS
OF THE ROARING 1920'S AND 1930'S

One of Lamm's most ardent admirers was a man named "Slick" Willie Sutton. Willie was born William Francis Sutton, Jr. (1901 – 1980) and was often referred to as the gentlemanly bank robber. During his long criminal career, he stole an estimated $2 million (20 million today), and he eventually spent more than half of his adult life in prison, managing to escape three times. For his talent at executing robberies in disguises, he gained two nicknames, "Willie the Actor" and "Slick Willie." "Slick Willie" also being used as a derogatory moniker for Bill Clinton, based upon his uncanny ability to imitate Slick Willie's smooth style of talking his way out of adverse situations. Sutton is also known as the namesake of Sutton's law, as once when he was asked why he robbed banks, his reply was "Because that's where the money is."

Sutton, although Irish, was born into the robust teaming mean streets of Polish-town (Green Point) in Brooklyn, New York, where his father was a blacksmith. Sutton was a streetwise kid who learned to hustle, and dropped out of school in the eight grade, because he said that teachers could not teach him as much as he could learn on the streets of Brooklyn. Thus, he turned to crime at an early age, but never did he kill anyone in all the years he was a criminal. He is also rumoured to have said, "If you have to kill someone to obtain money illegally, you simply are not a very good criminal." He was a fast-talking, chain-smoking fancy dresser who was so well-versed in the law that in stir he was sometimes called "Willie the Lawyer" by fellow inmates.

BAD MOON RISING: AMERICAN OUTLAWS
OF THE ROARING 1920'S AND 1930'S

He was well-liked by the mafia men who controlled vice in Brooklyn, despite the fact that most of the Irish lived in Manhattan. He was what one Mafioso called, "A straight up guy who knows where to draw the line." Despite his diminutive size, when incarcerated, he did not have to worry about assault because Mafia friends looked after him. Although he knew them, he felt that gangsters like Al Capone and Lucky Luciano, were too prone to violence and created problems for more refined hoodlums. Sutton's affable ways made other gangsters enjoy his companionship. He was always a gentleman, witty and non-violent, which was in stark contrast to most of the other New York gangsters. Mobster Donald Frankos declared that Sutton was so skilled at the heist that he made legendary bank robbers Jesse James and John Dillinger look like amateurs.

Despite his propensity for non-violence, for intimidation purposes, on a job, he carried a Thompson submachine gun. He said, "Charm and personality will not get you the money, but sticking a Thompson in a person's face will." In an interview in the Reader's Digest, Sutton was asked if the guns that he used in robberies were loaded. He responded that he never carried a loaded gun because somebody might get hurt. He was sometimes referred to as a Robin Hood bandit, as he would occasionally, after a successful robbery during the depression, hand wads of cash out to poor people living on the streets, especially in his old Brooklyn neighbourhood.

J. Wayne Frye

BAD MOON RISING: AMERICAN OUTLAWS
OF THE ROARING 1920'S AND 1930'S

When he was robbing a bank and a woman screamed, he would politely tell them to be calm, because he would never hurt a woman. He also carried candy, and when a child would cry, he would hand them the candy, pat them on the head and give them a warm smile.

His robberies were the stuff of legends in the 20's, as like his hero, Baron Lamm, he was meticulous in planning. He began his criminal career in 1919 at the age of 18 when he robbed the office of a friend's father with the help of two of his friends. The trio stole $16,000, but were soon caught. No charges were pressed against them. From 1924-1925, he was an assistant to famed burglar, Eddie Tate, who called him a fast learner with great potential. After his apprenticeship with Tate, he became a prolific burglar in 1930, committing a total of seven burglaries, targeting mostly jewellery stores or banks. He was arrested in 1931, but managed to escape in 1932 using a smuggled gun, which was empty, of course.

His first known use of a disguise was when he dressed as a policeman to rob the Corn Exchange Bank in downtown New York in 1933. The same year he attempted to rob the Corn Exchange National Bank & Trust in Philadelphia dressed as a postman, but an employee foiled the plan. Never one to accept failure, a couple of months later he returned with two accomplices disguised as a policeman and made off with more than $20,000 ($350,000 in today's dollars).

*The Corn Bank in Manhattan that was robbed by Sutton and the
Corn Bank in Philadelphia he also robbed. Sutton said, "I loved
robbing Corn Banks, as they were so nice inside and out."*

J. Wayne Frye

BAD MOON RISING: AMERICAN OUTLAWS
OF THE ROARING 1920'S AND 1930'S

Being an equal opportunity employer, Willie used two women to help him rob the Richmond Hill National Bank in 1933, and followed that with a daring hold-up of J. Rosenthal & Son Jewellery Store when an employee opened the door to receive a telegram from whom else but Willie dressed as a telegram messenger. He got jewellery worth $129,000 ($2.3 million in today's dollars), and opened an account under an assumed name at the Corn National Bank – a branch he never robbed!

Sutton was apprehended on 5 February 1934, and was sentenced to serve 25 to 50 years in the Eastern State Penitentiary in Philadelphia, Pennsylvania, for the machine gun robbery of the Corn Exchange Bank. This would turn out to be his second longest term of incarceration as it was not until April 1945 that Sutton was one of 12 convicts who escaped the institution through a tunnel. He was recaptured the same day, as it appeared his luck was running out. However, there was method to his madness, as he wanted to get a transfer to a prison that would be easier to escape from. Sentenced to life imprisonment as a fourth time offender, Sutton was transferred to the Philadelphia County Prison in Philadelphia, Pennsylvania. In February of 1947, Sutton and other prisoners dressed up as prison guards and carried two ladders across the prison yard to the wall in the darkness. When the prison's searchlights hit him, Sutton calmly shouted, "It's okay!" No one stopped him and his cohorts or bothered to ask what they were doing with the ladder. They all escaped.

He remained at large for a number of years, and finally broke into the FBI's most wanted list. He apparently was robbing banks continuously during this period, but was not identified specifically until an astute FBI agent reviewed the 1950 $64,000 ($650,000 in today's dollars) robbery of the Manufacturers Trust Company and observed that it was a text-book example of Sutton's usual time-tested manner.

In February 1952, Sutton was captured by police after having been recognized and followed by a 24-year-old Brooklyn clothing salesman and amateur detective named Arnold Schuster. Schuster later appeared on several television shows describing how he had assisted in Sutton's apprehension. Albert Anastasia, Mafia boss of the Gambino crime family and admirer of Sutton's, took a dislike to Schuster because he had helped capture someone Anastasia felt was the most affable and skilled bank robber he had ever known. According to Mafia turncoat and government informant, Joe Valachi, Anastasia ordered the murder of Schuster, who was then shot dead outside his home in March 1952.

Sutton went to trial in 1952 for the 1950 robbery of a branch of the Manufacturers Trust Company in Sunnyside, Queens. He received a sentence of 30 to 120 years in the notorious Attica State Prison, and this aging master of escape settled down into life behind bars for the next 17 years, until December 1969, when the same judge who had originally sentenced him to the long term, in response to a motion by Sutton's attorneys, ruled that Sutton's good behaviour in prison and his deteriorating health due to emphysema justified commutation of his sentence to time served. At the hearing Sutton responded, "Thank you, your Honour. God bless you," and wept as he was led out of the court building. In 1970, a separate 30-years-to-life sentence handed down in Brooklyn in 1952 was also commuted on similar grounds, and he was released on parole. Ever the dapper dandy with a golden tongue, Sutton became a lecturer on prison reform and consulted with banks on theft deterrent techniques. He once said on a television talk show, "How ironic that a man who made a living robbing banks, is now making a living teaching banks how not to be robbed." He made a serious of television commercials, including ones for New Britain Bank and Trust Company in Connecticut for their credit card with picture ID on it. His lines were, "They call it the 'face card.' Now when I say I'm Willie Sutton, people believe me."

Sutton died in 1980 from emphysema at the age of 79 in Florida, where he had retired. He dressed well and lived well, some saying that he had a great deal of money stashed away from all his robberies. If he did, it was a secret he took to the grave with him.

A dapper Willie Sutton from the 1930's

New York Times photo of an older Sutton in custody.

One detective said of Sutton – "nicest guy I ever arrested."

An elderly Eddie Sutton doing an anti-smoking TV commercial.

J. Wayne Frye

BAD MOON RISING: AMERICAN OUTLAWS
OF THE ROARING 1920'S AND 1930'S

Sutton was diagnosed with emphysema, and in the last few months of his life he made a very poignant anti-smoking plea, which pointed the finger of condemnation at the corporate criminals who sell death in the form of cancer sticks with absolute impunity, because unlike Sutton, their crimes are never punished, since they represent corporate malfeasance, which is tolerated in the capitalist system which promotes greed as an enviable trait. Having had two parents die from emphysema, his message hit home to me, someone who never took a puff of a cigarette in his life, but still has a spot on his lung caused by second hand smoke exposure. (The video is available on You Tube https://www.youtube.com/watch?v=Lb3Up6SACVc.)

In the video, he says that he is "in purgatory now" because when it is shown he will be dead. He goes on to indict the tobacco company executives for getting away with murdering people. This is standard fare in a nation that never goes after the real criminals. A black man robbing a 7-11 of $50 will get 10 to 15 years in prison, while a white Wall Street banker who crashes the economy by robbing people's pension funds is handed taxpayer money to help bail his failing firm out from the very mess he created. This is the way of crony capitalism, where the Citizen's United Supreme Court decision made it legal for corporations and the wealthy to legally buy politicians. Willie Sutton, with his dying words, provided a profound indictment of this heinous corruption that goes unpunished.

BAD MOON RISING: AMERICAN OUTLAWS
OF THE ROARING 1920'S AND 1930'S

Now, we move from Willie Sutton's gentlemanly bandit to one of the most cold, cruel, heartless gangsters of the era. Vernon C. Miller was known for having a short temper which, when set off, could turn deadly. For Miller, it did not matter whether it was a policeman, a fellow criminal or civilian, because if you crossed him you did so at your peril. He was one of the definitely identified gunman at a shootout that rivalled the gunfight at O.K. Corral, the Kansas City Massacre.

Oddly, he was a former sheriff in Huron, South Dakota. He was credited with heroic actions in World War I and as a law enforcement official. Why this supposed good guy went bad no one has ever been able to discern. He was a victim of his parent's contentious divorce and was left on his own at an early age. By the age of 10, he had dropped out of school. In 1914, he moved to Huron and began working as a mechanic. He joined the Army in 1916 and served on the Mexican border fighting raiding bandits until 1917, when he returned to Huron and married. A month later, he left for France with the military service. He returned to Huron a hero having been a sniper in the 18th regiment where he received a French Croix de Guerre award for bravery. In one battle, his skilled marksmanship was said to have felled 21 men in a five hour period as he kept shooting scouts who were being sent to reconnoitre for a coming large assault on American, French and British positions. It was said, that he smiled with delight at each confirmed kill.

J. Wayne Frye

BAD MOON RISING: AMERICAN OUTLAWS
OF THE ROARING 1920'S AND 1930'S

Vernon was married right before he left for France. (Picture circa 1917)

After his return, he joined the Huron city police force where he worked until 1920, when he resigned. By then, his name was on the ballot as the Republican candidate for Beadle County Sheriff. He won by 41 votes. The community was pleased with his service and Miller was on his way to re-election when his wife, Mildred, fell ill and was rushed to a Rochester, Minnesota hospital. Taking a short leave, Miller went to visit his wife, who was seriously ill and needed funds for the hospital and doctors, (Sounds familiar, as even today, the USA is the only First World country where healthcare is a privilege, not a right.) Fearing for his wife's health, he did what so many in a nation with no compassion for the sick have to do when their backs are against the wall - resort to desperate measures. Deputies discovered $6,000 missing from the county fund and thus a criminal was born. A three-month search ensued, ending when a St. Paul, Minnesota hotel clerk turned him in. Miller pled guilty to embezzling county funds and served two years in the South Dakota penitentiary. While there, he landed a position as the warden's chauffeur and passed his time driving the warden around Sioux Falls until he was paroled. His wife also left him at this time. He was paroled and almost immediately met Vivian Gibson, who joined him in a bootlegging business. The pair became the leading bootleggers in the Minneapolis-St. Paul, Minnesota area and also opened a casino in Montreal, Quebec, which had a reputation for being a fair place where you would never be cheated. In the meantime, Vivian gave birth to a girl.

During the late 1920s, after years of heavy drug abuse and suffering from advanced syphilis, Miller slowly became unhinged, having violent mood swings. He was engaged in an altercation in the streets near his club one evening, wounding two Minneapolis police officers, but the case against him was dropped due to lack of evidence when it was brought out in court that the two officers had been receiving bribes from Miller.

It was in Minneapolis that Vernon met many well known criminals, foremost among them the dapper Machine Gun Kelly. On occasion he would join forces with Harvey Bailey, Tommy Holden, Jimmy Keating, Frank Nash and Machine Gun Kelly for numerous bank hold-ups from the Dakotas to Texas. In 1932, he was part of the crew in the infamous Barker-Karpis gang when they held up the 3rd Northwestern Bank of Minneapolis. The carnage rivalled anything done by the James gang in their infamous Northfield, Minnesota raid of 1876. The Barker-Karpis gang that day was made up of Chopper DeVol, Doc Barker, Fred

BAD MOON RISING: AMERICAN OUTLAWS
OF THE ROARING 1920'S AND 1930'S

Barker, Alvin Karpis, Bill "The Deal" Weaver, Jesse Doyle and Vernon.

The gang had cased the bank for weeks, and felt well-prepared, but as alluded to previously, the best laid plans of mice and men often go awry. They quietly entered the building in pairs from the Central Avenue entrance and the Hennepin Avenue entrance, armed with Thompson sub machine-guns and rifles.

Larry "Chopper" DeVol, carrying a machine-gun, stood in front of the bank, guarding the entrance while Fred Barker and Vernon manhandled the tellers, pushing them toward the vault and demanding it be opened. When a teller insisted he was unable to open the vault, Miller brutally pistol-whipped him, but not before the teller was able to trip the bank's silent alarms. People started to panic, and hysteria broke out with people screaming in fear. Outside, a streetcar had pulled up to let passengers off. The motorman, seeing the robbery in progress, fell to the floor covering his head while the passengers simply sit and gawked with intense interest at the robbery unfolding inside the bank. One passenger was heard to say, "Damn, this is better than going to the movies." All the commotion brought two patrolling police officers to the scene, and as they were pulling up in front of the bank, Chopper DeVol, with complete disregard for any innocent bystanders, sprayed the police car with machine gun fire. Other members of the gang inside broke the bank windows and unleashed a hail of bullets, killing both officers.

BAD MOON RISING: AMERICAN OUTLAWS
OF THE ROARING 1920'S AND 1930'S

It was a wild scene, with customers, bank employees and people on the streets outside screaming and running in panic. The gang had stolen over $100,000, and their brand new Lincoln automobile roared like thunder careening down the street heading toward St. Paul, Minnesota with no cops anywhere in sight, save the two dead ones in front of the bank. The highway they were taking became known in later years at Bank Robbers Row.

As they were speeding away, they got a flat, having, in the wild hail of bullets, shot at their own car. Finally, shredding the rubber, all that was left was the rim, which they drove on until they made it to a prearranged spot where they had stored another car. They piled out and a passing car slowed down to see what was going on. As the car passed by, a paranoid Fred Barker, thinking the driver was trying to copy down their license plate number, pulled out a pistol and opened fire, killing the driver with a well-placed shot to the head.

While they were lying low in separate hideouts, Miller, in his Kansas City hideout, received word from Chicago mobster Louis Stacci that his friend, Frank Nash, had been arrested and was in a holding cell in Kansas City awaiting transfer to Leavenworth Prison. He contacted cohorts and formulated a plan to bust him out during the transfer. The details of the transfer were foolishly broadcast in newspapers and on radio. Unable to contact Machine Gun Kelley, Miller's primary partner for the attempt to free Nash was Arthur "Pretty Boy" Floyd.

BAD MOON RISING: AMERICAN OUTLAWS
OF THE ROARING 1920'S AND 1930'S

The Kansas Massacre, as it came to be called, was nothing out of the ordinary for Miller, who was widely known as a freelance assassin. He was alleged to have been able to sign his name in bullet-holes with a Thompson submachine gun. In fact, in 1930, after a friend Millers named Eugene McLaughlin had been killed by members of Al Capone's gang, Miller tracked down three of the suspects to a resort hotel in Fox Lake, Illinois, got the drop on them, lined them up against a wall and gunned them down. Called the Fox Lake Massacre, this was one event that may well have eventually led to Miller's own demise as upsetting Al Capone was not a smart move.

Prior to the Fox Lake killings, Miller, in an argument over a double-cross from some members of a gang he robbed a bank with, killed Frank Coleman, Mike Rusick and Sammy Stein. With this storied history, Machine Gun Kelley actually admired Miller and would probably have been eager to participate in the attempt to help Frank Nash escape if word had reached him. However, a tough hoodlum and crack shot named Adam Richetti was recruited to assist.

The shootout at O.K. Corral is probably the most discussed five minutes of mayhem in American history. However, what happened in Kansas City on 17 June 1933 certainly rivals that western shootout in its intensity. Although not glorified in movies, as was the O.K. Corral shootout, the Kansas City massacre unfolded with the same type of quiet determination from Vernon Miller and his cohorts as were exhibited by Wyatt Earp, his brothers and Doc Holliday.

Nash's criminal record reached back to 1913, when he was sentenced to life at the McAlester, Oklahoma State Penitentiary for murder. He was later pardoned. In 1920, he was given a 25-year sentence at the same penitentiary for burglary with explosives and later pardoned once again. In 1924, Nash began a 25-year sentence at the U.S. Penitentiary at Leavenworth for assaulting a mail carrier. He escaped a few months later. The FBI launched an intensive search for Nash which extended over the entire U.S. and parts of Canada. Evidence gathered by the FBI indicated that Nash had assisted in the escape of seven prisoners from the U.S. Penitentiary at Leavenworth in December of 1931.

Frank Nash

The investigation also disclosed Nash's close association with Francis L. Keating, Thomas Holden, and several other well-known gunmen who had participated in a number of bank robberies throughout the Midwest. Keating and Holden were apprehended by FBI agents on 7 July 1932 in Kansas City, Missouri. Information gained by the FBI as a result of the apprehension of these two indicated that Nash was receiving protection from his underworld contacts in Hot Springs, Arkansas.

Based on such information, two FBI agents, Frank Smith and F. Joseph Lackey, and McAlester, Oklahoma Police Chief Otto Reed located and apprehended Nash on 16 June 1933 in a store in Hot Springs, Arkansas. The law officers drove Nash to Fort Smith, Arkansas, where at 8:30 that night, they boarded a Missouri Pacific train bound for Kansas City, Missouri. It was due to arrive there at 7:15 a.m. on 17 June. Before leaving, the lawmen made arrangements for Reed E. Vetterli, special agent in charge of the FBI's Kansas City Office to meet them at the train station.

Meanwhile, a number of outlaw friends of Nash's had heard of his capture in Hot Springs. They learned the time of the scheduled arrival of Nash and his captors in Kansas City and made plans to free him. The scheme was conceived and engineered by Louis Stacci who selected Vernon Miller. Miller wanted Machine Gun Kelley but could not locate him, so he made a number of phone calls for assistance in the scheme and wound up with Pretty Boy Floyd and Adam Richetti.

Adam Richetti and Charles Arthur "Pretty Boy" Floyd

On their way to Kansas City, Floyd and Richetti had been detained at Bolivar, Missouri early on the morning of the 16th, when the car in which they were riding became disabled. While the two were waiting in a local garage for the necessary repairs to the car, Sheriff Jack Killingsworth entered the building. Richetti, who immediately recognized the sheriff, seized a machine gun and held the sheriff and the garage attendants against the wall. Floyd drew two .45 calibre automatic pistols and ordered all parties to remain motionless. Floyd and Richetti then transferred their arsenal into another automobile and ordered the sheriff to enter that vehicle. The two, along with their prisoner, then drove to Deepwater, Missouri, abandoned that automobile, and commandeered another. After releasing the sheriff, they arrived in Kansas City about 10:00 p.m. on 16 June. There, Floyd and

Richetti abandoned that automobile and stole another car to which they transferred their baggage and firearms. Finally, that same night, they met Miller and went with him to his home. There, Miller went over the plan to free Frank Nash.

Early the next morning, Miller, Floyd, and Richetti drove to the Union Railway Station in a Chevrolet sedan. There they took up their positions to await the arrival of Nash and his captors. Upon the arrival of the train in Kansas City, Agent Lackey went to the loading platform, leaving Smith, Reed, and Nash in a dining room of the train. On the platform, he was met by Special Agent in Charge Vetterli, who was accompanied by FBI Agent R. J. Caffrey and Officers W. J. Grooms and Frank Hermanson of the Kansas City Police Department. These men surveyed the area surrounding the platform and saw nothing that aroused their suspicion. Special Agent in Charge Vetterli advised Agent Lackey that he and Caffrey had brought two cars to Union Station and that the cars were parked immediately outside.

Agent Lackey then returned to the train and accompanied by Chief Reed, Special Agent in Charge Vetterli, Agents Caffrey and Smith, and Officers Hermanson and Grooms, proceeded from the train through the lobby of Union Station. At the time, both Agent Lackey and Chief Reed were armed with shotguns. Other officers carried pistols. Frank Nash, unaware of the coming attempt to rescue him, walked through Union Station with the above-mentioned officers.

BAD MOON RISING: AMERICAN OUTLAWS
OF THE ROARING 1920'S AND 1930'S

There was a surreal nature to the whole scene, almost like it was in slow motion. Each man walked forward toward the coming carnage as if following a script in a dance of death. The sky was slightly overcast with the sun barely peeping through thick, dark clouds. The humidity was heavy for early morning and it was so quiet you could have heard a pin drop. Although there were other passengers scurrying about the railway station, it seemed as if there was no sound about. Even when they walked out of the station toward the two cars waiting to take the prisoner to Leavenworth Prison in Kansas, 45 minutes away, the people on the streets were eerily quiet. However, the quiet was about to be interrupted with the initial rat-a-tat-tat of machinegun fire from "Pretty Boy."

Upon leaving Union Station, the lawmen, with their captive, paused briefly somewhat baffled by the quiet; but again seeing nothing that aroused their suspicion, they proceeded to Caffrey's Chevrolet. Frank Nash was handcuffed throughout the trip from the train to the Chevrolet, which was parked directly in front of the east entrance of Union Station. Agent Caffrey unlocked the right door of the Chevrolet. When the door was opened, Nash started to get into the back seat; however, Agent Lackey told Nash to get into the front of the car. Lackey then climbed into the back of the car directly behind the driver's seat. Agent Smith sat beside him in the center of the back; and Chief Reed sat beside Smith in the right rear seat.

J. Wayne Frye

BAD MOON RISING: AMERICAN OUTLAWS
OF THE ROARING 1920'S AND 1930'S

At this point, Agent Caffrey walked around to get into the driver's seat. Special Agent in Charge Vetterli stood with Officers Hermanson and Grooms at the right side near the front of the car. A green Plymouth was parked about six feet away on the right side of Agent Caffrey's car. Looking in the direction of this Plymouth, Agent Lackey saw two men run from behind a car. He noticed that both men were armed. At least one of them had a machine gun. Before Agent Lackey had a chance to warn his fellow officers, one of the gunmen shouted, "Up, up!" At this instant, Agent Smith, who was in the middle of the back seat, also saw a man with a machine gun to the right of the Plymouth. Special Agent in Charge Vetterli, who was standing at the right front of the Chevrolet, turned just in time to hear a voice command, "Let 'em have it!"

At this point, from a distance approximately 15 feet diagonally to the right of Agent Caffrey's Chevrolet, an individual crouched behind the radiator of another car opened fire. Officers Grooms and Hermanson immediately fell to the ground. They were dead. Special Agent in Charge Vetterli, who was standing beside Office Grooms and Hermanson, was shot in the left arm and dropped to the ground. As he attempted to scramble to the left side of the car to join Agent Caffrey, who had not yet entered the driver's seat of the Chevrolet, Special Agent in Charge Vetterli saw Caffrey fall to the ground. He had been fatally wounded in the head as brain matter spilled onto the pavement.

Inside the car, Frank Nash and Chief Reed were killed by bullets from the hoodlums' guns. Agents Lackey and Smith were able to survive the massacre by falling forward in the back seat of the Chevrolet. Lackey was struck and seriously wounded by three bullets. Smith was unscathed.

The three gunmen rushed to the lawmen's car and looked inside. One of them was heard to shout, "They're all dead. Let's get out of here." With that, they raced toward a dark-coloured Chevrolet. Just then, a Kansas City policeman emerged from Union Station and began firing in the direction of one of the killers, later identified as Floyd, who slumped briefly but continued to run. The killers entered the car which sped westward out of the parking area and disappeared, having failed in their mission to free Nash, who now lay dead along with the others. The whole affair had taken less than a minute.

The three survivors: Agents Smith, Lackey and Vetterli were uncertain if three or four gunmen staged the assault. From their account, it was apparent that the two Kansas City Police Officers were killed immediately, followed seconds later by Frank Nash and Chief Reed and then by Agent Caffrey, who was taken to a hospital and pronounced dead on arrival.

The FBI immediately initiated an investigation to identify and apprehend the gunmen. The investigation developed evidence that the scheme was carried out by Vernon C. Miller, Adam C. Richetti, and Charles Arthur "Pretty Boy" Floyd. The evidence included latent fingerprint impressions located by FBI agents on beer bottles in Miller's Kansas City home and identified as those of Adam Richetti, thus helping to link the latter to the crime.

Following the Kansas City Massacre, Miller, accompanied by a girlfriend, Vivian Mathias, traveled to Chicago. For a few days, he hid out with a member of the Barker-Karpis gang. From there Miller reportedly went to New York, but on 31 October, returned to Chicago at the apartment of Vivian Mathias. The next day, he escaped a trap set for him there by the FBI. However, Mathias was taken into custody and later pleaded guilty to charges of harbouring and concealing Miller.

On 29 November 1933, during the FBI's search for Miller, his mutilated body was found in a ditch on the outskirts of Detroit, Michigan. He had been beaten and strangled. Information received by the FBI indicated that Miller had been involved in an altercation with Longie Zwillman, head of New Jersey's underworld mob, in Newark; during the argument, Miller's temper flared up and he had shot him. One of Zwillman's associates reportedly retaliated by killing Miller.

News of his death was met with a mixture of emotions in South Dakota. The citizens of Miller's hometown refused to honour a life but praised the Vernon Miller, fearless sheriff and valiant soldier they knew. His wife Mildred, though legally separated since 1929, stuck by him saying, "I don't believe all the things they say about Verne. Because he became involved in a few scrapes nearly every major crime in the country was laid to him. He was wonderful to me and I have nothing against him."

His father made plans for the funeral. Miller, a veteran and American Legion member, was entitled to full military rites. However, the American Legion forbad the Huron post from participating. His father's hometown of White Lake, however, held the memorial service with full military rites. Miller's flag-draped casket was then escorted from White Lake to Huron by uniformed ex-servicemen, all Miller's friends. There, following a ceremony for an overflow crowd, Vernon Miller was buried

Miller was one of many hoodlums from this era who faded into obscurity in the public eye. Maybe if he had a moniker like "Pretty Boy" Floyd, "Machine Gun" Kelly or "Baby Face" Nelson he would have become an icon like they did. Icon or not, he lived up to what one former school chum said of him, "You didn't mess with that fella."

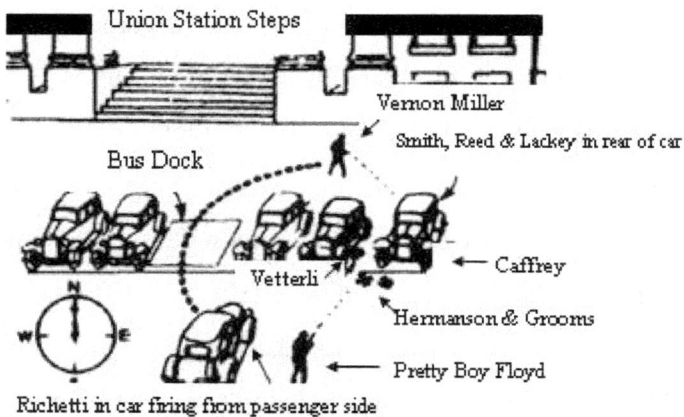

Union Station Steps
Vernon Miller
Smith, Reed & Lackey in rear of car
Bus Dock
Vetterli
Caffrey
Hermanson & Grooms
Pretty Boy Floyd
Richetti in car firing from passenger side

CHAPTER 4

THE LIGHT OF LOVE FOR ETERNITY

I asked God for a bike,

But I know God doesn't work that way.

So, I stole a bike and then asked for forgiveness.

..........Don Corleone in The Godfather

Adam Richetti, about 23 years old at the time of the Kansas City Massacre, began his criminal career with an arrest in Hammond, Indiana on 7 August 1928 for a hold-up that netted him a whopping $25. Richetti was sentenced from one to 10 years in the State Reformatory for that crime. He was paroled in 1930. His next arrest occurred on in 1932 at Sulphur, Oklahoma for bank robbery; he subsequently served a sentence at the State Penitentiary, McAlester, Oklahoma from 5 April 1932 to 25 August 1932, when he was released and placed on bond, which he forfeited.

BAD MOON RISING: AMERICAN OUTLAWS
OF THE ROARING 1920'S AND 1930'S

After fleeing from the Kansas City Massacre, Pretty Boy Floyd and Richetti made their way to Toledo, Ohio, where they met sisters Beulah and Rose Baird in early September 1933. From there the four traveled to Buffalo, New York. On 21 September 1933, Floyd and Beulah Baird and Richetti and Rose Baird, rented an apartment in that city under assumed names. The other occupants of the apartment building considered the two couples very mysterious as they seldom went out. During their occupancy, Floyd reportedly walked from the front to the rear of the apartment almost constantly, an activity that caused much curiosity on the part of the other building occupants. The two couples never visited with any of their neighbours, though they were friendly toward the neighbourhood children who sometimes were permitted to enter the apartment. The women occasionally threw money from the windows of the apartment to the children playing in the street or offered them candy.

In October 1934, the couples agreed to return to Oklahoma. Rose Baird was given a large sum of money to purchase a car, and she bought a Ford V-8 sedan, which was to carry them to the west. The four began the trip early on October 20, with Floyd driving. A few hours later, near Wellsville, Ohio, he skidded into a telephone pole. Floyd and Richetti removed their firearms from the vehicle and remained on the outskirts of the town, while Rose and Beulah Baird took the damaged car into a Wellsville garage for repairs.

J. Wayne Frye

BAD MOON RISING: AMERICAN OUTLAWS
OF THE ROARING 1920'S AND 1930'S

The Wellsville, Ohio Police Chief, J. H. Fultz, following up on reports that two suspicious-looking men were seen on the outskirts of town, found the two resting in a wood tract of land nearby. A gun battle ensued. Chief Fultz apprehended Richetti after Richetti had emptied his gun at the officer. Floyd escaped, but the police chief thought Floyd might have been wounded.

The FBI and local authorities conducted an intensive search for Floyd in eastern Ohio following the above incident. This included interviews of numerous persons in the predominantly rural countryside, including doctors and hospital personnel whom Floyd might approach if, in fact, he was wounded.

A search party was led by famed FBI agent Melvin Purvis, near Clarkson, Ohio. He noticed an automobile move from behind a corn crib on a farm, then the vehicle was driven back to its original position behind the corn crib, and a man whom the officers immediately recognized as Floyd jumped from the car with a .45 calibre automatic pistol in his right hand. They opened fire on him as he ran across a corn field. Hitting him twice in the back, he fell to the ground wounded. When they arrived, he rolled over on his back, looked up at them and said, "I'm done for; you've hit me twice." They took the pistol from his hand and also seized a second gun that he carried in his belt. They stood there about fifteen minutes and watched him die in agony. It was the inglorious end of what was an inglorious journey of a man who had blazed his way into the American gangster history and been a thorn in the side of law enforcement for years. Agent Melvin Purvis lit up a cigar and smiled.

Rose and Beulah Baird, who were in the Wellsville garage awaiting the repair of the wrecked automobile when they overheard the discussion of Richetti's being taken into custody, had left immediately for Kansas City, Missouri. Later they traveled to the home of Floyd's family in Sallisaw, Oklahoma, and attended his funeral, standing by his wife's side.

Adam Richetti, following his apprehension, was returned to Kansas City, Missouri and on 1 March 1935, was indicted by the Jackson County Grand Jury on four counts of murder in the first degree. His trial, predicated on the indictment charging him with the murder of Frank E. Hermanson, one of the police officers killed in the Kansas City Massacre, began in June of 1935. The jury returned a verdict of guilty with the recommendation that Richetti be given the death penalty. He was sentenced to be hanged. Richetti appealed his conviction, but it was affirmed by the State of Missouri Supreme Court in 1938. Subsequently, Richetti's lawyers alleged Richetti to be insane, and a hearing was held at which time his sanity was clearly established. On 31 August 1938, Richetti was again sentenced to death, this time in the gas chamber of the Missouri State Penitentiary at Jefferson City, Missouri. He was executed on 7 October 1938.

Four individuals: Richard Galatas, Herbert Farmer, Louis Stacci, and Frank Mulloy, the investigation disclosed, had engineered the conspiracy to free Nash, and were indicted by a federal grand jury at Kansas City, Missouri on 24 October 1934. In 1935, the four were found guilty of conspiracy to cause the escape of a federal prisoner from the custody of the United States. On the following day, each was sentenced to serve two years in a federal penitentiary and pay a fine of $10,000, the maximum penalty allowed by law.

In one final twist to the tragedy in Kansas City, the FBI Director, J. Edgar Hoover, used the outrage generated by the massacre to lobby Congress for a true national crime-fighting force. Prior to the massacre, FBI agents could not carry weapons without permission and were not even empowered to make arrests. Within months of the Kansas City killings, Congress, in its usual rush to pass legislation in the aftermath of a tragedy without giving serious thought to the consequences, passed a comprehensive crime bill giving the FBI almost unlimited law enforcement powers, placing nearly unbridled power in the hands of J. Edgar Hoover. Ironically, in his own way, Hoover was a hoodlum himself, using his enormous power to investigate politicians and literally blackmail them to get what he wanted. He used his power to destroy the lives of many people who simply wanted a more just country. He also threatened civil rights organization leaders like Martin Luther King with exposure over sexual peccadilloes and his maniacal obsession with communism bordered on paranoia. So fearful of him were politicians that they dared not ever even threaten to remove him as director of the FBI, where his power bordered on the dictatorial.

The demise of Pretty Boy Floyd was particularly gratifying to Hoover, who took credit for his capture and death, despite the fact that Melvin Purvis was the catalyst in the capture of most of the high profile gangsters. The press coverage given Purvis over Floyd infuriated Hoover, but he elected to let Purvis continue as his chief investigator, due to Purvis' tenacity and uncanny acumen in tracking the high profile gangsters.

Charles Arthur "Pretty Boy" Floyd was born on 3 February 1904, to a farm couple in rural Georgia. Floyd was an extremely good child who rarely got into trouble. His family moved when he was 7 to an Oklahoma farm. However, his good image faded rather quickly when at the age of 15 he set off to be a field hand picking crops in Kansas and Oklahoma. It was there that he learned from older men how to drink, carouse and fight.

When Floyd was 20, a local woman captured his heart and quickly became his bride. They bought a house and a baby came shortly thereafter. Arthur Floyd worked hard at being a farmer, but became discouraged, knowing that hard work rarely paid off when the banks owned your house, your car and almost everything else you had. John Hilderbrand, a thief hiding from the police, met Floyd and boasted how he robbed a manufacturing company of $1,900 and would like Floyd to help with thefts of this nature. In August 1925, he kissed his wife and boy and began his career as an outlaw. By the end of August, they robbed a half-dozen food stores and service stations, netting about $600 (Around $8500, today).

In the early days of September, they held up a food store and grossed several thousand dollars. Days later, the thieves bought a new Studebaker and cruised the streets, where they were quickly recognized and arrested. Floyd served five years. During his trial, Floyd received a new nickname. When the clerk described the robbers, Floyd was described as a mere boy, a very pretty boy with apple cheeks. The name "Pretty Boy" stuck, but he hated it.

Two months before Floyd was released from prison, his wife filed for divorce. When he was released on 7 March 1929, he headed for Kansas City. From there, he continued his life of crime. He met Beulah Baird and they became lovers.

A year after his release, Floyd was caught for robbery in Ohio and was sentenced to 15 years in prison. En route to the penitentiary at Columbus, Floyd talked his guards into un-cuffing him so he could use the washroom. Floyd escaped and returned to Kansas City. After reuniting with Beulah, he looked up William Miller (a.k.a. Billy the Baby Face Killer). The two men planned a series of bank jobs in the East and South, but the law caught up with them in Toledo, Ohio. Miller died in the shootout and Beulah was seriously injured. Floyd escaped with several shots to his abdomen. A reward of $6,000 was put up for the capture of Floyd, dead or alive.

Floyd was wanted in numerous cases. In late 1929 he was arrested for vagrancy. (Yes, even back then, being poor was a crime in America as it is today. There is no end to the degradation endured by the poor in the USA.) Two days later, he was arrested in Pueblo, Colorado, and charged with vagrancy again. He was fined $50.00 and sentenced to 60 days in jail. Now, when you are a vagrant, you obviously don't have money to pay a fine, so you are carted off to jail. This was the kind of justice that made Floyd seethe with anger at the injustices of a system where only the rich were treated with any respect. This is probably the reason that he often gave large wads of cash to the poor after a robbery. In fact, his penchant for robbing from the rich (banks) and giving to the poor gave him a moniker he was actually proud of – "The Robin Hood of Cookson Hills."

Floyd, under the alias Frank Mitchell, was arrested in Akron, Ohio, on 8 March 1930, charged in the investigation of the murder of an Akron police officer who had been killed during a robbery that evening. He escaped. The law next caught up with Floyd in Toledo, Ohio, where he was arrested on 20 March 1930. He was convicted of the Sylvania Ohio Bank Robbery and sentenced on 24 November 1930 to 12–15 years in Ohio State penitentiary, but he escaped.

Floyd was a suspect in the deaths of Kansas City brothers Wally and Boll Ash, who were rum-runners. They were found dead in a burning car on 25 March 1931. A month later, members of his gang killed a patrolman and then on 22 July, Floyd killed federal agent Curtis C. Burke in Kansas City, Missouri. In 1932, deputy sheriff Ervin Kelley was killed while trying to arrest Floyd.

Despite his life of crime, Floyd was viewed positively by the general public. When he robbed banks, he allegedly destroyed mortgage documents so the banks would have no records required to foreclose on people. He was often protected by locals in Oklahoma when he was on the run, despite there being large rewards offered for his capture.

Floyd missed his wife and son and decided in 1931 to reacquaint himself with his family. His wife had remarried, but when Floyd showed up, she fell in love with him again and the Floyds disappeared to Fort Smith, Arkansas, using the alias of Mr. and Mrs. Charles Douglas. Soon, the family moved to Tulsa, to take advantage of the better school system. But, trouble loomed. Residents questioned the mysterious couple as the man that resembled Pretty Boy Floyd. Finally, the day came when acting on a tip from a neighbour; the police searched their home in February 1932. The family fled on foot, his wife and son to a bus station and Floyd to Cookson Hills on the Arkansas and Kansas border. His wife and son were caught, but were released.

The Kansas City Massacre on 17 June 1933, would eventually lead to his death nearly a year later. Following the Massacre, the FBI - now incredibly strong with the passing of the Fugitive

Felon Act - searched judiciously for this dangerous criminal. Along with his sidekick, Adam Richetti, Floyd fled to Buffalo, N.Y., and settled under an alias. The two set up housekeeping with Rose and Juanita Baird. Topping the FBI wanted list was bank-robber John Dillinger, followed by Floyd. In October 1934, Dillinger died and Floyd was named Public Enemy Number One. The FBI vowed Floyd would be dead before Christmas and put Melvin Purvis, the man who shot Dillinger, in charge of bringing Floyd down.

Floyd figured there was one way out, leave the country for Mexico, but he wanted to see his wife, son and friends, which was a fatal mistake. As mentioned earlier, on the way there the car slid into the ditch in Ohio. Floyd and Richetti hid in the greenwood while Beulah and her sister Rose traveled to town for repairs. Meanwhile, the police stumbled on Floyd and Richetti. Richetti darted from the brush with Floyd firing his gun. Floyd escaped to the forest beyond, while Richetti was caught.

Roadblocks appeared at all exits. Teams of dogs combed the areas where Floyd vanished. Floyd was tired and hungry. He stumbled on a farm house and a lady, who introduced herself as Widow Condie and she fixed him a meal. Later, her brother agreed to drive Floyd to Clarkson, the nearest town. Along the way, two FBI cars halted when they drove past Floyd. He knew by the way the faces looked his way, it meant trouble. He did not want to get the friendly driver in trouble, so he leaped from the car and headed into a nearby field. A shot was fired and hit Floyd in the right arm and threw him to the ground. He got up and continued to run. Purvis then fired the fatal shot, stood over him and watched him die while he lit a cigar.

After his death, Floyd's body was shipped to Cookson Hills, where the largest funeral in the history of the state was attended by over 20,000 people to honour the Robin Hood of Cookson Hills.

Pretty Boy Floyd with wife and child.
The Ballad of Pretty Boy Floyd
If you'll gather 'round me, children
A story I will tell

BAD MOON RISING: AMERICAN OUTLAWS
OF THE ROARING 1920'S AND 1930'S

'Bout Pretty Boy Floyd, an outlaw

Oklahoma knew him well

It was in the town of Shawnee

A Saturday afternoon

His wife beside him in his wagon

As into town they rode

There a deputy sheriff approached him

In a manner rather rude

Vulgar words of anger

An' his wife, she overheard

Pretty Boy grabbed a log chain

And the deputy grabbed his gun

In the fight that followed

He laid that deputy down

Then he took to the trees and timber

Along the river shore

Hiding on the river bottom

And he never come back no more

Yes, he took to the trees and timber

To live a life of shame

J. Wayne Frye

BAD MOON RISING: AMERICAN OUTLAWS
OF THE ROARING 1920'S AND 1930'S

Every crime in Oklahoma
Was added to his name

But a many a starvin' farmer
The same old story told
How the outlaw paid their mortgage
And saved their little homes

Others tell you 'bout a stranger
That come to beg a meal
Underneath his napkin
Left a thousand-dollar bill

It was in Oklahoma City
It was on a Christmas Day
There was a whole car load of groceries
Come with a note to say

"Well, you say that I'm an outlaw
You say that I'm a thief
Here's a Christmas dinner
For the families on relief"

Yes, as through this world I've wandered
I've seen lots of funny men

J. Wayne Frye

BAD MOON RISING: AMERICAN OUTLAWS
OF THE ROARING 1920'S AND 1930'S

Some will rob you with a six-gun

And some with a fountain pen

And as through your life you travel

Yes, as through your life you roam

You won't never see an outlaw

Drive a family from their home

This author is not trying to be an apologist for criminals, but in a world where more people are robbed with a pen than a gun, it is understandable why praise is often lavished on those who defy laws that are made to make slaves of people, rather than make it possible to live with a modicum of decency. When 1% own more than 80% of Americans at the bottom of the economic ladder, there is something askew, and many people, in desperation, are forced to break the law in order to survive. The rest of the world, although not as bad as the USA in regards to income gaps, is also moving in the same direction, where fewer and fewer own more and more. This disparity is what led to the Great Depression of the 1920's and the economic meltdown of 2009 and it appears nothing has been learned from what occurred as a result of income inequity. Oddly, even a large percentage of the poor actually vote for the very people who enslave them in economic malice. The above ballad was often sung to me by my grandmother, who endured the Great Depression and in her own way was an outlaw against conformity.

J. Wayne Frye

DEATH OF PRETTY BOY FLOYD

In these fields, formerly the site of the Ellen Conkle farm, notorious Depression - Era desperado Charles Arthur "Pretty Boy" Floyd met his death at the hands of federal agents and members of the East Liverpool Police Department on October 22, 1934.

Floyd's criminal career as a bank robber, who reputedly committed a dozen murders, mostly police officers, caused him to be designated "Public Enemy No. 1" only three months earlier by J. Edgar Hoover.

(Continued on other side)

EAST LIVERPOOL HISTORICAL SOCIETY
AND
THE OHIO HISTORICAL SOCIETY

1993   10-15

When, as a young man, I used to drive from North Carolina
To university in Indiana, I passed a sign on an Ohio highway
That struck me as a reminder that sometimes those who
Are branded criminals are like so many of us, wallowing
In the misery of a world where much more is stolen every day
By the pen in the hand of a banker
Than by a gun in the hand of a robber

BAD MOON RISING: AMERICAN OUTLAWS
OF THE ROARING 1920'S AND 1930'S

Although he died before the 1948 Humphrey Bogart movie "Knock on Any Door" in which the line, "Live fast, die young and leave a beautiful corpse" was uttered, Bennie Dickson was the prototype for the young boy who delivered that line in the film. He, along with his 16 year old wife, Stella, blazed onto the crime scene between August 1938 and April 1939 like a comet streaking through the midnight sky. However, that bright comet burned out after only 8 months, but during that 8 months these two, although no Bonnie and Clyde, were actually the last of the Great Depression era criminals, having perhaps been born a bit too late to rise to the grandeur enjoyed by other famous outlaws of that time. However, they did make it to the top of the FBI's Most Wanted list for a brief period.

Bennie (1911-1939) and Stella (1922-1995) Dickson were sweethearts in Topeka, Kansas, and in those days most states allowed marriage at 16, so they eloped when Stella turned 16. After tying the knot of wedlock, they almost immediately began to tie the knot of crime that would bring them fame, but little fortune. They were both described by friend and foe as drop dead gorgeous, many comparing them to movie stars of the day. Bennie was trim, athletic and exuded an air of confidence, while Stella was an attractive young woman mature in appearance far beyond her 16 years. Often described as gingerly gorgeous, she was a fine figure of a woman who turned heads when she would walk down the streets of Topeka.

BAD MOON RISING: AMERICAN OUTLAWS
OF THE ROARING 1920'S AND 1930'S

It is rumoured that they were admirers of Bonnie and Clyde, so, it is no wonder that in 1938 when they were proclaimed public enemies number one and two by J. Edgar Hoover, they probably experienced a bit of ego gratification. However, it is claimed by many who knew them that they were victims of the FBI public relations machine in the 1930's that ignored organized crime, instead focusing on small-time crooks the federal agents knew they could capture, rather than going after the real criminals who did their stealing with a pen rather than a gun. (Sounds a lot like today, doesn't it? Arrest the petty criminal who steals a few hundred dollars while letting the banker, insurance executive or stock manipulator go about their thievery unimpeded.)

When these two came along, the big name criminals had all been killed or carted off to prison. The intervening years, with Franklin Roosevelt's New Deal giving people a hand up, rather than the backhand they had gotten from Herbert Hoover, crime diminished. However, J. Edgar Hoover was always looking for a way to get the FBI in the limelight. Bennie and Stella Dickson were perfect foils for him in his quest to convince the public of the FBI's superior criminal catching skills.

Benny and Stella Dickson, robbing banks, kidnapping motorists, eluding police and displaying extraordinary bravado was tailor made to generate headlines that were so important to massage the enormous ego of Hoover, when he would eventually bring them down. First build them up, then show how proficient the FBI was at bringing criminals to justice.

Bennie's first arrest was when he was 15 years old. There was a beautiful car that attracted his eye, and he simply thought it would be fun to take a ride in it. Unfortunately for Bennie, the owner felt it was stealing, and initiated charges against him, even though he returned the car. Bennie spent 90 days in jail. Shortly after getting out, he punched a cab driver and stole his taxi for another joy ride and two years in the reformatory. According to several sources, it was not Bennie who committed the crime as he was seen at a restaurant when the assault occurred, but the jury, looking at his previous conviction for a similar crime, ignored the testimony of eyewitnesses who saw him at the restaurant. This built a great furry inside Bennie, as he proclaimed, "I ain't guilty of the goddamn crime and that blame jury knows it, but they just see a poor boy they want to railroad, get him off the streets."

As is the norm in the USA, reformatory or prison is not about rehabilitation, it is about meting out punishment in the tradition of the Old Testament that demands an eye for an eye and a tooth for a tooth. That is the same justice system today that does not rehabilitate, but hardens people into criminality with a sternness that makes the USA the number one nation in the world with people incarcerated. There is no room for compassion, and the harsh treatment received by Bennie only served to instil a hatred for those who administered justice with a cold, cruel hand of repression.

BAD MOON RISING: AMERICAN OUTLAWS
OF THE ROARING 1920'S AND 1930'S

Two days after his release from the reformatory, his pent up anger boiled over into a fit of rage when he was denied a job because of his criminal record. He went to a small town in Missouri and robbed a bank. As always, he was not very skilled at getting away with it and was caught the same day. Sentenced to 10 years this time, he served a long stretch, being released in 1937.

A few months after getting out all the stars were perfectly aligned to bring Bennie and Stella together. Perhaps you cannot argue with what is meant to be, once the stars have spoken, it is absolute and final, and when these two met sparks flew that lit a fire neither one could put out.

Stella's full name was Estelle Mae Irwin, but her last name became Redenbaugh when her mother's second husband adopted her. At age 15, Stella was raped and contracted a venereal disease. When word got out, she was shamed and ran away to California, but was caught and forced to return home. Stella and Bennie met at a skating party in Topeka. As alluded to earlier, there was an instant connection and only two months later, with her parents' permission, 15 year old Stella married Bennie.

Stella just wanted a normal life and a family, and she went along with Bennie who promised that, but Bennie convinced the naïve little girl they needed money for that normal life. Thus, she helped him rob the Corn Exchange Bank of Elkton, South Dakota on 25 August 1938, then the Northwest Security

National Bank at Brookings, South Dakota. Each time, they were described as polite robbers who never raised their voices. At times, they carjacked vehicles and kidnapped those in the cars. While the pair never shot anyone, Stella once used a rifle to disable a pursuing police car during a car chase. One of the couple's more memorable exploits occurred in Topeka on 24 November 1938, which was Thanksgiving Day. A day earlier Bennie and Stella had arrived at her mother's, took her for a short drive, returned her home and promised to eat Thanksgiving dinner with her and Stella's stepfather the next day. They spent the night at Ace's Cabins, in East Topeka. They got up early the next day to go for dinner at her parents home without knowing that eight officers from the Topeka Police Department, Shawnee County Sheriff's Department and Kansas Highway Patrol had gone into nearby cabins and the office, waiting for the two to show themselves. Bennie came out carrying two suitcases, when an officer told him to put up his hands.

Bennie, unarmed, grinned at him, dropped the suitcases and dashed for his car, revving up the engine as the officers opened-fire. A total of 48 shots whizzed all about Bennie, with one bullet lodging in his thick overcoat and another grazing his head. The car was riddled with bullets as he drove off in a wild, careening, roaring, hair-raising fury, screeching onto the highway as the calm Stella crawled though a back window to escape on foot.

The officers had been so concentrated on Bennie that they completely overlooked Stella as she was running toward the highway, where she smoothly leaped into the car, as Bennie leaned over to open the passenger door without slowing down. They were so fast and furious that by the time the officers had retrieved their cars, the pair had seemingly disappeared into thin air.

The story was on the front page of newspapers across the Midwest. A few days after the escape, despite the fact they had not fired one single shot at the officers; J. Edgar Hoover insisted the Dickson's be labelled public enemies by the FBI. A few days later, they were at another motel, and being aware they might face the same scrutiny, they rented two rooms, one with a rear exit where they parked their car. When the police arrived, they burst into the wrong cabin only to watch through a rear window as the couple sped into the night. They blasted away in a hail of gunfire, but hit nothing.

The two decided to go their separate ways in order to throw off the police and meet up in St. Louis. To this day, no one has ever found out exactly where Stella stayed while waiting to meet Bennie, as she never revealed that to anyone, perhaps in order to keep from incriminating a friend, but while waiting for her in his hotel room, Bennie got hungry and decided to go to the nearby Yankee Hamburger Shop around 8:00 PM, when four FBI agents told him to put up his hands, then shot him when Bennie reached for a gun, according to newspaper stories. However, this version has often been questioned as years later, a waitress at the restaurant who saw the whole thing unfold through a large plate glass window, said that Bennie ran and without any command, one of the agents shot him in the back and when he fell, the agent walked toward him still firing, one bullet hitting him in the side. Another agent fired, shooting Bennie twice, once in the back and once in a side as he walked toward the prone Bennie. When people arrived on the scene, everyone noticed that Bennie's guns were still in his belt.

Who tipped off the FBI has never been revealed. Freedom of information requests have been honoured, but there is no mention of an informant in any of the documents. There is an indication of a payout of $2500 to a woman simply listed as X in the documents. Could this have been Stella's friend?

There was a huge crowd at Bennie's funeral, primarily because his father was a well-known and highly respected man of the community. Meanwhile, Stella, who had just arrived when she heard the gunshots that killed Bennie and had briefly seen him lying on the ground, made her way to Kansas City, and then to Topeka to see her mother. Encouraged by her mother, who said that Stella's age might keep her from severe punishment, she turned herself in to the FBI in Topeka.

The FBI utilized the death of Bennie and the capture of Stella in an on-going public relations campaign to aggrandize the work of the J. Edgar Hoover at a time when there simply were not many outlaws left. This was great publicity for the FBI at a time Hoover was appealing to the President and Congress for an expanded role for the organization. There was never an inquiry into why Bennie was shot when he never pulled a gun, but that is not unusual when it comes to the actions of police.

Stella confessed to only two bank robberies in a plea deal and was convicted of two counts of bank robbery and sentenced to two concurrent 10-year sentences. During incarceration, she became known for her obstinacy and spent much of her time in solitary confinement. She was released after serving nearly the full term of 10 years and moved to Raytown, Missouri where she married several times and lived an uneventful life. She worked menial jobs and avoided any discussion of her past, with no one apparently knowing who she was as she used the name Stella Mae Irwin. She told a neighbour several times that her failed marriages were because she never really loved but one man her entire life, and he had been killed in a car wreck. She died in 1975. After her death the truth shocked the small town, and the neighbour shared a fact that solidified the love story for all time. It seems that several months before Bennie was killed the two of them had shared a shrimp cocktail, and every New Years Eve, Stella locked up her home and had a shrimp cocktail.

Bonnie and Clyde's gang killed 12 men in a two-year crime spree, but there is no evidence that Benny or Stella ever killed a single person. In fact, there is no evidence that they ever fired a shot at anyone, even when involved in wild chases. An incident in which Stella used a rifle to disable a pursuing police car was the closest they came to harming anyone, and all the people they kidnapped while commandeering their cars, had nothing but nice things to say about the way they were treated.

Despite the death of Bennie, Stella never let go of that love, never let the embers that made the fire blaze die into obscurity. Hers was an affection that spanned across time and found its magnificence in the firmament where two stars twinkled with the light of love for eternity.

CHAPTER 5

Do It You Bastard!

"Stealing is like dancing with the devil,

and it is never a waltz.

It is a wild Charleston,

with the band playing a tune

of foot-stomping, spine-tingling,

heart pounding music that

lights the fires of excitement

in world of pain."

(Gerald Chapman – 1925)

"Death itself isn't dreadful,

but hanging seems an awkward way

of ending the adventure."

(Gerald Chapman after being sentenced

to death for murder in 1925.)

BAD MOON RISING: AMERICAN OUTLAWS
OF THE ROARING 1920'S AND 1930'S

Gerald Chapman (1887 - 1926), affectionately known by many as "The Count of Gramercy Park", "The Gentleman Bandit" and "Gentleman Gerald," held the distinction for over 25 years of making the largest heist in U.S. history ($2.4 million in 1924 which is over $24 million in today's dollars). Today, he is still number eleven on the list of most productive heists in U.S. history.

Chapman led an early Prohibition-era gang from 1919 until the mid-1920's. Although his career as a criminal was short, it was noteworthy. He was also the first criminal to be awarded the title "Public Enemy Number One."

Chapman was born George Chartres, but always preferred the alias, Chapman, in 1887 to Irish parents in the lower east side section of Manhattan. Arrested for the first time in 1902 at age fourteen, Chapman was incarcerated for most of his early adult life. While serving time for bank robbery on a later conviction, he was transferred from New York's Sing-Sing Prison to Auburn State Prison, and became acquainted with highly educated, well-bred Danish-born con-man George "Dutch" Anderson in 1908. Anderson was unusual in many ways. He was from an affluent family in Denmark and went to undergraduate school at Heidelberg University and went to graduate school at Uppsala College, both in Germany. He was working on his Ph.D. in Wisconsin, but dropped out to become a professional criminal, specializing in burglary, robbery and counterfeiting. Chapman

J. Wayne Frye

looked on Anderson as a mentor and a long-running criminal partnership was facilitated.

The Anderson University of Crime had a prize student in Chapman. With time off for good behaviour, Chapman was paroled and Anderson later joined him in New York. Needing a driver to assist in robberies and burglaries, they recruited another Sing Sing alumnus, Charles Loerber, to be their wheelman and pose as their chauffeur while they set themselves up as wealthy businessmen.

The year 1919 marked the opening of the ill-fated Prohibition Era which was forced upon Americans by the finger-pointing moralists who assumed that banning the production, sale and distribution of alcohol would put everyone on the path to heaven. Rather than end drinking, it simply made a majority of Americans criminals as they sought out illicit spirits from a variety of sources. Chapman and Anderson were quick to spot its potential and began a bootlegging businesses in several states. Then, there old friend from Sing-Sing Prison, Charles Loerber suggested robbing mail trucks and armoured cars. New York being home to huge brokerage houses, banks and Wall Street stock brokers there were many available targets.

The U.S. Postal Service had delivery trucks plying through Manhattan and they often carried huge amounts of jewellery, bearer bonds, negotiable securities and cash. Careful research pinpointed a postal delivery truck running regularly along

Leonard Street in downtown Manhattan, and it was known to carry large sums of money and jewels. To get ready for the big robbery, they went to Queens and the Bronx Boroughs to practice by robbing postal trucks with less valuable cargo. However, they, too, were very lucrative.

The set up for the big robbery was pretty simple. With some of the proceeds from the previous robberies, they bought two of the most expensive cars of the day, a Pierce-Arrow and a Packard. Loerber, a skilled mechanic, souped them up to make them fast getaway cars.

They followed the mail truck, pulled in front of it with the Packard, driven by Loerber, to block its path, while Chapman and Anderson pulled alongside the driver's side, jumped out and pulled their guns. They assaulted the driver and guard and then made off with four pouches. They actually could have doubled their take, but did not want to take longer than two minutes to perform the hold-up. No shots were fired and they made off with the equivalent of 24 million dollars, which attracted media attention. This robbery would make Chapman the very first person to wear the moniker, *Public Enemy Number One*. Of course notoriety is a double edged sword, as it also makes you popular with the authorities, who want the notoriety they gain by bringing you down.

Robbing mail trucks was highly lucrative, but it was a federal crime since it involved the U.S. mail, unlike bank robbery which, at the time, was still within state jurisdiction, as the FBI was not even formed.

Rather than lying low, invigorated by their success, the gang began a spree of robberies in upstate New York. Over the next few weeks they pulled one job after another. They robbed five banks and several major stores before opting for another armoured truck heist. This time they decided to try their luck with the American Express Company and they wound up with around $70,000, but a private detective was hired by American Express and he traced them back to Manhattan. Although they had gotten away with $2.4 million in cash (24 million in today's dollars), bonds and jewellery from the initial robbery, it was the $70,000 robbery that would be their undoing and lead to a connection with the initial robbery.

While being interrogated, Chapman pulled off his first of many escapes over the years. When being moved from one floor to another, he was un-handcuffed, and as they walked into a crowded area toward the elevators, he saw an open elevator door and moved swiftly into the waiting elevator just as the door was closing, leaving the dumfounded inspectors aghast at how easily he got away. The elevator operator, frightened, was told to go up one floor. Chapman quickly exited, and went toward an open window but there was no fire escape, so he crawled out on the ledge and hid for two hours while the building was frantically searched. Standing on the ledge, he was noticed by someone in a building across the street who called the authorities. He was retrieved by the police.

A few days later, Anderson was also captured. The two of them were sentenced to 25 years imprisonment and ordered to serve their time at the Atlanta Federal Prison. Charles Loeber, was sentenced to 15 years and after his parole in 1932, simply disappeared into obscurity.

Chapman escaped from the prison on 27 March 1923, knocking out the facility's power in the process. He was wounded and captured a couple of days later in eastern Georgia, but within a week escaped the hospital, adding to his reputation. Anderson broke out of the Atlanta prison on 30 December 1923. The two men reunited, and were suspected by authorities in several hold-ups. This escape led to an orgy of violence, and although there were no eyewitnesses, while in Connecticut on a crime spree, Chapman apparently murdered Officer James Skelly of the New Britain, Connecticut Police Department in a gunfight during a break-in. Though an accomplice was caught and quickly identified Chapman as the perpetrator, authorities initially refused to believe that the notorious bandit had been operating unnoticed in their area. Chapman's role was confirmed by his partner in the crime, who was given a lighter sentence as a result.

Chapman high-tailed it out of town and headed to Indiana, where he was captured in Muncie, after the couple from whom he was renting a room recognized him and contacted authorities.

During his apprehension, Chapman fired at a police officer but missed. President Calvin Coolidge was convinced by Connecticut authorities to reduce the robbery sentence of Chapman in federal prison to time served, so they could try him for first degree murder in that state, which carried the death penalty. Thus, Chapman was handed over to the Connecticut authorities, who were determined to make him pay the ultimate price for his crime.

Hearing of the arrest of his friend in Muncie, Anderson was determined to make the two people who had apparently turned him in pay. The man and woman who turned Chapman into the authorities had been worried about vengeance, and asked for government protection. They were laughed at and ignored in the usual lackadaisical government unconcern. While renting a room at the couple's farm, Chapman had installed a telephone. Now that Chapman was gone, the couple found the phone very useful for taking orders from people buying sacks of dried vegetables from them. Ben Hance answered the phone one day and took an order for some peas and beans. The customer asked him for delivery, so Hance asked his wife to come along. As they turned onto the highway about a kilometre from their farm, a car pulled along side of them and a wild chase ensued with the Hances trying to outrun Anderson who was on the passenger side as the car was being driven by an accomplice, Charlie Wolfe. Wolf cut in front of them, forcing them to stop. Anderson jumped out and unleashed a hail of deadly bullets into the Hance's car with his 45 Colt Revolver. Anderson, who had been passing counterfeit $20 dollar bills, was spotted in Muskegon, Michigan at a hamburger stand by Police Officer Charles Hammond. The two of them had a shoot out in the street, both dying from their wounds.

During Chapman's murder trial in Connecticut, crowds gathered about due to his status as public enemy number 1. The jury deliberated for 11 hours, after which Chapman was found guilty and eventually sentenced to hang. He proclaimed his innocence to the end, asking in his final appeal for justice, not mercy. Chapman was executed by the Connecticut upright jerker on 6 April 1926, a horribly cruel form of death similar to hanging but far more sinisterly evil, which, of course, was par for the course in a nation that believed in an eye for an eye and a tooth for tooth retribution.

Even today, there are those who still believe that Chapman was innocent of the Connecticut murder, as only his partner in the crime was an eyewitness, and he had much to be gained by turning state's evidence on Chapman, who maintained even as he was placed in the aforementioned infamous "upright jerker" that he did not kill the police officer.

The USA, as the only First World nation with a death penalty, has always insisted on Old Testament justice, based on what it perceives as its Christian heritage. Chapman's death was particularly brutal, as Connecticut had abandoned the traditional hanging method for what was considered a more humane method of "torturous death." Instead of standing on a trapdoor and being dropped, a prisoner would stand inside a marked square and the rope was lowered from the ceiling, placed around the prisoner's neck and the prison warden pushed a large metal button which made iron counterweights weighing 600 kilos (around 350 pounds) be released. The dropping of the weights would violently jerk the prisoner into the air, fracturing the neck and bringing instant, painless death supposedly. The only problem was it rarely worked properly, and in Chapman's case, the execution was so badly botched that his neck was not broken, and he spent nine minutes dangling above the assembled witnesses before he finally died. So, as a result of this, and also later botched executions in New York State, the last being a woman, states looked for other methods of execution. Eventually, they came up with the equally sinister and unreliable method, which created a new word in the English language - "electrocution." Somehow, strapping people into an electric chair and letting them ride thousands of volts of electricity into eternity was more humane.

It is extremely ironic that America's first true celebrity gangster is today almost completely unknown, while those who were actually less successful are immortalized in print and on the screen. Although it has never been confirmed, it is rumoured that he said as the noose was put around his neck, "Do it you bastard!"

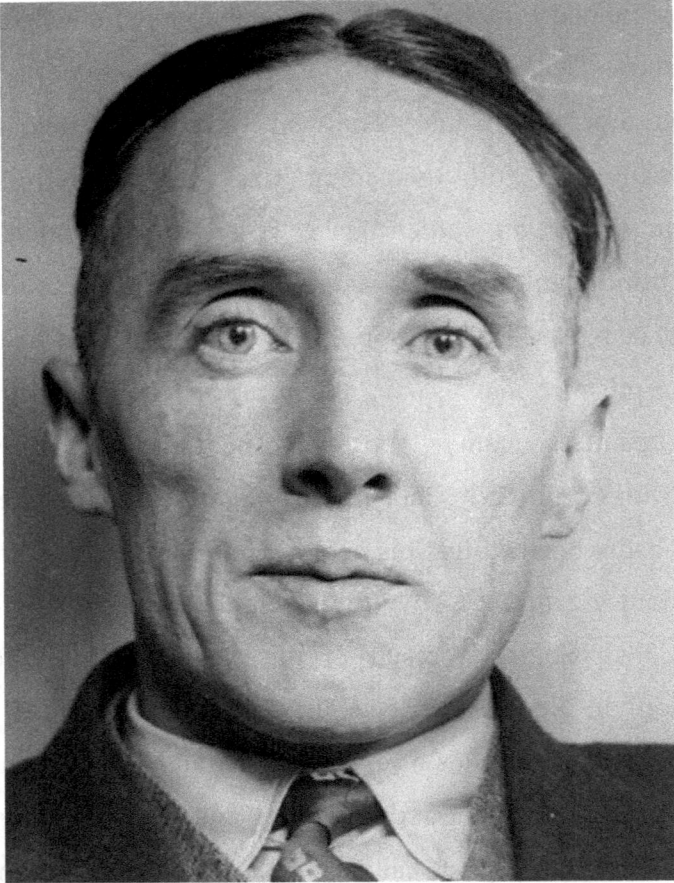

Gerald "The Gentleman" Chapman

CHAPTER 6

TOUGHEST KID ON ANY BLOCK

I sincerely admire I must admit
The man who robs a bank,
'Cause it really takes a lot of grit.

A burglar can slip into a house
With little trouble and then leave
Quiet and unobtrusive as a mouse.

Even soldiers swaggering with rank,
In my opinion can not rival those
Care-free dandies who rob a bank!

Do not lament the money stolen,
For it's one thief stealing from another

J. Wayne Frye

BAD MOON RISING: AMERICAN OUTLAWS
OF THE ROARING 1920'S AND 1930'S

And about that there's something golden.

(Poem by guest Speaker, Wayne Frye, at San Quentin Prisoners' Reunion and Prison Reform Symposium in 1997.)

Frank "The Owl" Banghart (1901–1982) was a well-known American criminal, burglar and prison escape artist. Although a successful robber during the 1920s and early 1930s, he is best remembered for his involvement in the hoax kidnapping of Chicago mobster, Jake "The Barber" Factor, a crime for which he and Roger Touhy were eventually proven innocent after nearly 20 years in prison.

Banghart was born in Berville, Michigan in 1901. He dropped out of college for what he said would offer him more security than a university degree, a career as a professional car thief. He was certainly right, initially at least, as within one year he stole over one hundred cars in the Detroit, Michigan area before his arrest and conviction in 1926. It was while in prison that Banghart acquired his criminal nickname "The Owl" because of his abnormally large eyes.

Banghart escaped from prison after a few months. Escaping from a window washing detail, he leapt three floors from a window he was washing and hopped over the prison's wall, escaping through the marsh on the other side. He got as far as Montana but was recaptured and returned to jail. He made a second escape a year later, but was caught trying to steal a car in Pittsburgh in October 1928. This time, Banghart was escorted

J. Wayne Frye

back to prison by U.S. Marshals. He was taken to a federal building and, left alone in an office for a few minutes, Banghart used a phone to call local police, claiming he was a federal agent who had been assaulted and overpowered by his prisoner, one Basil Banghart. He continued claiming that Banghart had escaped after handcuffing him and described the U.S. Marshal that was escorting him, noting that he was a dangerous, armed felon and a police impostor. When police arrived moments later, they took the escort into custody while Banghart escaped in the confusion.

Banghart was arrested again in February 1930, and was returned the Leavenworth, Kansas prison, but quickly escaped again. He was arrested in Detroit for armed robbery in January 1932 and held in the South Bend, Indiana jail but escaped by throwing pepper in a guard's face, then using the guard's machine gun to shoot his way out.

Banghart headed south and eventually made his way to Chicago, Illinois where he joined up with his old pal, Roger Touhy. Touhy, a veteran bootlegger from the days of Prohibition, was then in the midst of a fierce rivalry between himself and Al Capone associate, Frank Nitti, over control of the Chicago labour union racketeering. .

On 31 January 1933, Jimmy O'Brien was killed by Nitti's gunmen in front of the Garage Nightclub. O'Brien was one of Touhy's union men. A week later, Banghart went to the nightclub, owned by Nitti, where he stepped out of a car and tossed a bomb through the front doors of the club. No one was injured, but the club was heavily damaged.

When the Chicago mob staged the elaborate kidnapping of one of their own members, Jake "The Barber" Factor, in July 1933, it was expected that doing so would postpone his extradition to stand trial for fraud in Great Britain, as well as rid themselves of rival bootlegger Roger Touhy for whom the kidnapping would be blamed. The members of the British consulate refused to believe the story of the kidnapping and won a judgment for Factor's extradition from the United States Supreme Court. In utter desperation, Factor and the Chicago mob sought to make the kidnapping more legitimate by arranging a pickup with the supposed kidnappers. Banghart and his partner Charles "Ice Wagon" Connors were brought into the plan at this point. Hired to be the bagmen, they were told all they needed was to pick up the money, make it look real, and they could keep the ransom money.

On August 15, the two showed up at the scheduled drop on Manheim Road just outside the Chicago city limits. As soon as they arrived, they found 300 Chicago police officers and FBI agents waiting for them. To make matters worse, inside the ransom package was only $500, not the $200,000 promised. They had been double-crossed. Banghart and Connors surprised everyone by escaping after a wild shootout that fortunately killed no one.

Despite being set up, Banghart and Connors did not seek revenge against the Chicago mob and instead went on the run. On 15 November 1933, they teamed with Ike Costner and Ludwig "Dutch" Schmidt to hijack a U.S. mail truck of $100,000 in Charlotte, North Carolina. Banghart and Costner were arrested for that heist. A little later the trial for Factor's kidnapping was being held on 13 February 1934. Facing a very long prison sentence for the Charlotte mail truck robbery, both men agreed to testify for the prosecution. Although Costner had not been involved in the ransom pickup, when Connors was found murdered on 14 March, he took Connors' place and falsely stated that he and Banghart had been hired for the Factor kidnapping by Roger Touhy. When Banghart took the stand, however, he denied these claims and attempted to explain that the kidnapping was staged. Banghart's testimony was largely ignored, and he, along with Touhy and two others, were convicted and received 99-year sentences.

After years of unsuccessful appeals, Banghart and Touhy escaped the Joliet, Illinois Prison along with five other men on 9 October 1942. Soon after their escape, Banghart and Touhy were suspected of taking part in a robbery at Melrose Park, Illinois on 19 December which netted $20,000. Two of the other escapees were killed in a gun battle with federal agents less than two weeks after their escape and the rest were captured on 20 December, 1942. Then Banghart and Touhy were captured.

BAD MOON RISING: AMERICAN OUTLAWS
OF THE ROARING 1920'S AND 1930'S

The convicts were given even longer jail sentences for their escape, and in early 1943 Banghart was transferred, with an escort of 18 federal marshals for fear he might escape again, to what was considered America's escape proof prison, Alcatraz. He spent the rest of his time in the prison kitchen working with former public enemy number 1, Alvin Karpis, in the bakery. In 1954, federal judges declared the Factor kidnapping a fraud and that Banghart and Touhy had most likely been wrongly convicted because of the collusion of the Chicago Mob and corrupt Chicago officials. Eventually his kidnapping conviction was overturned and the mail robbery charges were dropped for time served. He was released the following year at age 60. He lived out his life on a small island in Puget Sound, Washington, apparently never having to work, as he had wisely stashed away some of the robbery money from all those years ago.

Frank "The Owl" Banghart

J. Wayne Frye

BAD MOON RISING: AMERICAN OUTLAWS OF THE ROARING 1920'S AND 1930'S

On 16 December 1959, 22 days after his release from prison on parole, Roger Touhy and his bodyguard were gunned down by mob hit men as they were entering the home of Touhy's sister in Chicago. Touhy and Walter Miller, a retired Chicago police detective, were climbing the steps to the home when two men appeared from the shadows behind them. Touhy and Miller turned, and Miller showed them his police badge and told the men he was a police officer. The two men then pulled shotguns from beneath their overcoats, and fired five shots. Touhy was struck twice, once in each leg above the knee. Miller was struck three times, but managed to draw his revolver and fire three shots at the departing gunmen. While being rushed to a hospital, Touhy told a newsman, "I've been expecting it. The bastards never forget!" Whom he meant was never discovered.

Miller was taken to the hospital, where he eventually recovered. Touhy made it to the hospital but died an hour later. This ended one part of a puzzle that still does not have all the pieces in place.

Women are often looked upon as gangsters' molls, rather than active participants in crimes, but Bonnie Parker and Edna "Rabbit" Murray proved that women could be as effective as men at robbing banks. Another woman, who, although she never actually was directly involve in robbing banks, produced sons who were famous bank robbers, and she became known as the leader of a group called "The Barker Gang."

BAD MOON RISING: AMERICAN OUTLAWS
OF THE ROARING 1920'S AND 1930'S

Kate Barker (1873 - 1935), better known as Ma Barker, was the mother of several criminals who traveled along with them on their crime sprees. After Barker was killed during a shoot-out with the FBI, she gained a reputation as a ruthless crime matriarch who controlled and organized her sons' crimes. J. Edgar Hoover, given to extreme hyperbole to aggrandize himself and the FBI, said of her, "She is the most vicious, dangerous and resourceful criminal brain of the last decade." She has been depicted as a monstrous mother in movies and print. The truth is a bit more nebulous.

She was born in the small town of Ash Grove, Missouri. In 1892. She married George Barker, and they had four sons - Herman (1893–1927), Lloyd (1897–1949), Arthur (1899–1939) and Fred (1901–1935).

◄——— *Ma Barker (circa 1925)*

BAD MOON RISING: AMERICAN OUTLAWS
OF THE ROARING 1920'S AND 1930'S

Barker's sons committed crimes as early as 1910, when Herman Barker was arrested for highway robbery after running over a child in the getaway car. Over the next few years, Herman and his brothers Lloyd, Fred and Arthur were repeatedly involved in crimes of increasing seriousness, including robbery and murder. Herman died on 29 August 1927, in Wichita, Kansas, after a robbery and confrontation with police that left one officer dead. He shot the officer at point blank range in the mouth. He killed himself to avoid prosecution when he was seriously wounded after crashing his car. In 1928, Lloyd Barker was incarcerated in the federal penitentiary at Leavenworth, Kansas, Arthur "Doc" Barker was in the Oklahoma State Prison and Fred was in the Kansas State Prison.

Lloyd   *Arthur*   *Fred*

After Herman's death and the imprisonment of his other sons, Ma's husband, George, gave up on the whole family and quietly removed himself from the scene. The FBI claimed that George left Ma for other reasons: because she had become loose in her moral life and was having outside dates with other men. This from

BAD MOON RISING: AMERICAN OUTLAWS
OF THE ROARING 1920'S AND 1930'S

J. Edgar Hoover, who consistently attacked homosexuality and cross dressers all his life, while he was having relations with his deputy director (a male) and wore high heels and a dress around his house; consequently, one must take every pronouncement from the FBI during his nearly 50 year tenure as its head with a very big grain of salt. That old Shakespearean refrain from Hamlet, "Thou doth protest too much" is often apropos as people who have something to hide engage in subterfuge to cover up what they are really doing or thinking. This has been a pretty consistent pattern for conservative politicians for over 200 years.

Ironically, although he pretended revulsion over his sons' actions, George Barker was not above profiting from his sons' crimes after their deaths by claiming their assets as next of kin. Throughout their criminal careers, George Barker decried their behaviour and actually encouraged the judges in their cases to throw the book at them, while his wife did everything she could to get her sons off, no matter what they had done.

Fed up with George's abusive behaviour, Ma had moved in with a man named Arthur W. Dunlop. She called herself his wife in 1930 when they moved to Tulsa, Oklahoma. In 1931, her son was released from jail. He joined former prison-mate Alvin Karpis to form the Barker-Karpis gang. After a series of robberies, Fred and Karpis killed Sheriff C. Roy Kelly in West Plains, Missouri on 19 December 1931, an act that forced them to flee the territory. Ma and Dunlop traveled with them.

J. Wayne Frye

When Arthur "Doc" Barker was released in 1932, he joined Fred and Karpis. Racketeer, Jack Peifer, suggested that they move to St. Paul, Minnesota, a town which had a reputation for welcoming criminals. In St. Paul, the gang operated under the protection of the city's corrupt police chief and under his guidance, graduated from bank robbers to kidnappers.

While at one hideout, a local resident identified the gang from photographs in the popular *True Detective* magazine and told the police. The police chief tipped off the gang, and they escaped. Wrongly believing that Dunlop's loose lips had given them away, they apparently murdered him while traveling. His naked body, with a single bullet wound to the head, was found in Wisconsin.

During this time, Fred Barker stashed Ma Barker in a variety of hotels and hideouts. The purpose was to keep her from learning much about the gang's crimes, as well as to separate her from the gang's girlfriends, with whom she did not get along. By 1933 most of the gang were back in St. Paul, where they planned and carried out two kidnappings of wealthy local businessmen. After successfully obtaining $100,000 ransom from abducting William Hamm, they then arranged the kidnapping of Edward Bremer, from which they netted a $200,000 ransom. The FBI first connected the gang to the William Hamm kidnapping by using a then new method of latent fingerprint identification. The gang moved to the Chicago, renting apartments for Ma Barker, while they tried to launder the ransom money which was marked.

BAD MOON RISING: AMERICAN OUTLAWS
OF THE ROARING 1920'S AND 1930'S

FBI agents discovered the hideout of Barker and her son, Fred, after Arthur "Doc" Barker was arrested in Chicago on 8 January 1935. A map found in his possession indicated that other gang members were in Ocklawaha, Florida. The FBI soon located the Florida house where the gang was staying after identifying references to a local alligator named "Gator Joe," mentioned in a letter sent to Doc. They had rented the property under the name Blackburn, claiming to be a mother and sons wanting to vacation in a country retreat.

Agents surrounded the house on the morning of 16 January 1935. Unknown to the FBI, Karpis and other gang members had left three days before, leaving only Fred and Ma in the house. Ordered to surrender, Fred opened fire; both he and his mother were killed by federal agents after an intense, hours-long shootout. Allegedly, many local people came to watch the events unfolding, even holding picnics during the gunfire. Both bodies were found in the same front bedroom. Fred's body was riddled with bullets, but Ma appeared to have died from a single bullet wound. According to the FBI's account, a Tommy gun was found lying in her hands. Other sources say it was lying between the bodies of Ma and Fred. Knowing the FBI's penchant for lying, one must be somewhat sceptical in ascertaining just what to believe. Their bodies were put on public display, and then stored unclaimed, until almost a year later, when relatives had them buried in Welch, Oklahoma next to Herman Barker.

J. Wayne Frye

BAD MOON RISING: AMERICAN OUTLAWS OF THE ROARING 1920'S AND 1930'S

House where Ma and Doc were slain.

The popular image of Ma as the gang's leader and its criminal mastermind, portrayed in films is widely regarded as extreme historical embellishment. The suggestion that she participated in the shoot-out in which she died has also been treated with scepticism, based upon the known FBI proclivity for lying at the time to boost the bureau's image. Many, including Karpis, suggested that the many gangland myths were developed and promoted by J. Edgar Hoover and the FBI's Office of Public Affairs. The tougher the criminals were made to look, the more praise received by the FBI, when they were captured.

After Ma's death, Hoover claimed that she enjoyed the lifestyle that was the fruit of her sons' crimes and supposedly had a string of lovers. Neither was anywhere close to the truth.

BAD MOON RISING: AMERICAN OUTLAWS
OF THE ROARING 1920'S AND 1930'S

Although her children were undoubtedly murderers and committed an incredible spree of robberies, kidnappings and other crimes between 1931 and 1935, there is no evidence that Ma Barker was ever their leader or was in any way significantly involved in their crimes. Mrs. Barker certainly knew of the gang's activities and even helped them before and after they committed their crimes. This would make her an accomplice, but there is no evidence that she was ever an active participant in any of the crimes themselves or was even involved in planning them. Her role was in taking care of gang members, who often sent her to the movies while they committed crimes. Alvin Karpis, the gang's second most notorious member, later in life was quoted as saying, "Ma was just an old-fashioned woman who loved her boys, and she was never engaged in any of the crimes." One other gang member said, "Ma couldn't plan breakfast, let alone a criminal enterprise."

The Barker gang member Alvin Francis Karpis (1907 –1979) was nicknamed "Creepy" because of his sinister smile. He was Canadian but became a naturalized American citizen. There were only four "public enemies" ever given the title of "Public Enemy Number 1" by the FBI and he was the only one to be taken alive. The other three, John Dillinger, Pretty Boy Floyd, and Baby Face Nelson, were all killed before being captured. He also spent the longest time as a federal prisoner in Alcatraz Prison, serving twenty-six years.

J. Wayne Frye

BAD MOON RISING: AMERICAN OUTLAWS
OF THE ROARING 1920'S AND 1930'S

Karpis was born in Montreal, Quebec, and was raised in Topeka, Kansas. He started in crime at about age 10, selling pornography and running around with gamblers, bootleggers, and pimps. In 1926, as was the case then and still is today, he was sent as a young boy to a hell-hole of a reformatory in Hutchinson, Kansas, where he was brutalized and abused rather than rehabilitated. He escaped with another inmate, Lawrence De Vol, and went on a year-long crime spree, interrupted briefly while he lived with his parents after De Vol was arrested. After moving to Kansas City, Missouri, he was caught stealing a car and sent back to the reformatory. Transferred to the Kansas State Penitentiary in Lansing, he met Fred Barker, who was in prison for bank burglary, and even before getting out, considered himself a member of the Barker family.

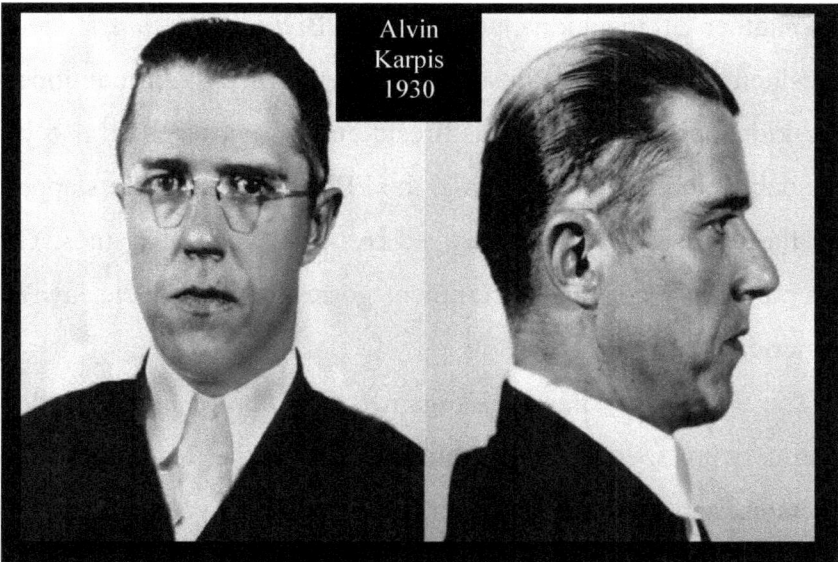

Alvin
Karpis
1930

BAD MOON RISING: AMERICAN OUTLAWS OF THE ROARING 1920'S AND 1930'S

The Barker-Karpis Gang became one of the most formidable criminal gangs of the 1930s. They did not hesitate to kill anyone who got in their way, even innocent bystanders. On 19 December 1931, Karpis and Fred Barker killed Sheriff C. Roy Kelley, who was investigating their robbery of a store in West Plains, Missouri. The gang, including Ma Barker and her domestic partner, Arthur Dunlop, fled to St. Paul, Minnesota.

The group was actually led by Alvin, who had a photographic memory and was described as highly intelligent by all who knew him. In 1933, on the same weekend as the Kansas City Massacre, they kidnapped William Hamm, a millionaire Minnesota brewer. His ransom netted them $100,000. Shortly after this, they abducted St. Paul banker Edward Bremer, whose ransom brought them $200,000. The kidnappings, however, led to the gang's end. The father of the kidnapped Edward Bremer was a friend of President Franklin D. Roosevelt. Roosevelt had even mentioned the kidnapping in one of his fireside chats, and fuelled also by the baby Lindbergh kidnapping, the FBI and local police stepped up their pursuit of those engaged in these types of crimes. Go after the rich, and the government goes after you – the law of America!

The FBI had by this time organized a group of highly skilled agents who specialized in hunting down the leading public enemies, and they had been very effective. The year 1934 alone saw the deaths of John Dillinger, Bonnie and Clyde, Charles

J. Wayne Frye

BAD MOON RISING: AMERICAN OUTLAWS
OF THE ROARING 1920'S AND 1930'S

"Pretty Boy" Floyd, Lester "Baby Face" Nelson, John "Red" Hamilton, Homer Van Meter, Tommy Carroll and Eddie Green.

Just after Ma and Fred's death in a shootout with the FBI on 16 January 1935, Karpis nearly met his own violent end when the FBI located him in Atlantic City, New Jersey. Karpis and Harry Campbell managed to escape, although Karpis' eight-month pregnant girlfriend, Dolores Delaney, was hit in the thigh. She was captured and gave birth to a son, who was adopted by Karpis' parents.

Karpis continued his crimes with others, but had to keep on the move constantly, as he was the fourth and last of the FBI's Public Enemy Number One's, the previous three having been killed. He did manage to pull off a daring crime that was highly unusual for the time, a train robbery in broad daylight which netted him $27,000. After the death of Ma and Fred, Karpis allegedly sent word to FBI chief J. Edgar Hoover that he intended to kill Hoover the way Hoover had killed Ma and Fred. However, as was par for the course with Hoover, it was actually an embellishment of his own created to bring him the attention he craved. According to Karpis, it never happened, and the case of Hoover, this author tends to put more credibility in the criminal Karpis than the fascist-like Hoover.

About this time, Hoover's publicity antics began to annoy some members of the U.S. Senate. The personal low point for Hoover came in April 1936 when he was forced to appear before a U.S.

Senate hearing. Senator Kenneth McKellar of Tennessee, at a time when Southern Senators were less ideologically driven, lambasted Hoover for the performance of the FBI and the fact that Hoover himself had never personally arrested anyone. After the hearing, the egomaniacal Hoover vowed he would capture Karpis personally.

It was not long until the opportunity presented itself. On 1 May 1936, the FBI located Karpis in New Orleans, and Hoover flew there to be in charge of the arrest. As a dozen or so agents swarmed over Karpis' car, Hoover announced to Karpis from a safe distance and behind a large oak tree that he was under arrest. Hoover came out only after all the other agents had seized him. Only then did the agents call to Hoover that it was safe to approach the car. The official FBI version states that Hoover reached into the car and grabbed Karpis before he could reach a rifle in the back seat. In fact, the car, a Plymouth coupe had no back seat. Hoover's egotistical publicity seeking resulted in him prancing around like a peacock before the reporters. Still, the capture of Karpis catapulted Hoover into the public eye and made his name synonymous with law enforcement.

The capture of Karpis actually ended the era of Depression Era gangsters. In addition to those mentioned earlier, others killed violently in the 1930s included Jack "Legs" Diamond, Vincent "Maddog" Coll, Frank "Jelly" Nash and Dutch Schultz. Even the big guy himself, Al Capone, was in Alcatraz ravaged by syphilis which would gradually drive him insane. The era of the charismatic, public attention-getting gangster was over.

Karpis was brought to trial on multiple charges and initially pleaded not guilty, but two weeks later, Karpis worked out a deal through his attorney to plead guilty if the Bremer kidnapping charges were dropped; the court accepted the offer, thus assuring him no death penalty.

Sentenced to life imprisonment, Karpis was incarcerated at the recently constructed Alcatraz federal penitentiary from August 1936 to April 1962. His main job at Alcatraz was working in the bakery. He was far from a model prisoner, frequently fighting with other inmates. Karpis served the longest sentence of any prisoner at Alcatraz, 26 years. In April 1962, with Alcatraz in the process of being closed, he was transferred to McNeil Island Penitentiary in Washington. While at McNeil, Karpis met a young man who actually scared him, and he wrote about him in his autobiography. From his book: "This kid approaches me to request music lessons. He wants to learn guitar and become a music star. He was so lazy and shiftless. The youngster has been in institutions all of his life, first orphanages, then reformatories, and finally federal prison. His mother, a prostitute, was never around to look after him. I decide it's time someone did something for him, and to my surprise, he learned quickly. He has a pleasant voice and a pleasing personality, although he's unusually meek and mild for a convict. He never has a harsh word to say and is never involved in even an argument. Still, there is something scary about him; this little man."

After this prisoner had become somewhat proficient on the guitar, the kid told him he would be bigger than the Beatles. Oh, the kid's name – Charles Manson

Karpis was paroled in 1969 and deported to Canada. He settled in Montreal and wrote his first memoirs in 1971 and published another memoir in 1979. During his first book tour across Canada, Karpis drew big crowds and showed a grand sense of humour. He moved to Spain in 1973 and died there in 1979.

Alcatraz – Home to Alvin Karpis for 26 years.

There are many criminals who are victims of circumstances which lead them into a life outside the law. When I worked with gang kids in South-central Los Angeles, I could often sense that despite their outward veneer of obstinate disregard for the law, deep within, all they wanted was the same opportunities afforded others in a nation that never reaches out with the hand of compassion, but rather looks upon poverty as a disease that spawns criminality that can only be treated with a drug that never cures the problem - severe punishment. I always said that I found more compassion in South-central Los Angeles with the miscreants of mayhem than was evident in the spoiled rich kids of Beverly Hills who were born into privilege and also felt that laws did not apply to them because of their exalted economic status.

Even when gangsters lived the criminal life, there were times, even though maybe brief, when their sense of right and wrong caused them to reach out with some compassion. However, there are some people who it seems are beyond the pale of having even a modicum of a moral conscience. Apparently one of these was a man named Vincent "Mad Dog" Coll (1908 –1932) who was an Irish American mob hit man. Coll proved his callousness when he gained notoriety for the accidental killing of a young child during a mob kidnap attempt.

Coll was born in Ireland, and his family immigrated to the U.S. when he was only one. After settling in the Bronx in 1909, where they remained in poverty, five of Vincent's six siblings died before he was twelve, as in the USA, healthcare, at the time, and even now, is a privilege rather than a right. His mother died of tuberculosis in 1916. Vincent's father had run off years before and was never heard from again. After his mother's death, Vincent's surviving sister tried to raise him in a cold-water flat when Vincent was eleven, but despite her love, there had been too many years of psychological hardship to save him.

BAD MOON RISING: AMERICAN OUTLAWS
OF THE ROARING 1920'S AND 1930'S

Coll simply saw nothing in America that resembled compassion, and he had none himself. At age 12, Coll was first sent to a reform school. After being shuttled between multiple reform schools where he suffered abuse, he developed a reputation for being incorrigible. By the age of 23, he had been arrested a dozen times, but his tough guy persona landed him a job working as an armed guard for the illegal beer delivery trucks of Dutch Schultz's mob. Schultz, Charles Luciano, Bugsy Siegel, and Louis Lepke were all aware of Coll and his reputation for ruthlessness. Schultz was particularly impressed with him. In a tough business, with rival gangs constantly trying to carve out their own territory, Schultz needed ruthless, violent young men with a talent for intimidation and killing. Vincent Coll had all of that in spades and started out as an enforcer for Schultz, when he was still in his mid-teens. Vincent and his older brother Peter were beginning to make names for themselves in the Bronx. Vincent was good-looking, but had a menacing demeanour that seemed to instil fear in people. He favoured tailored suits, silk shirts, double-breasted Chesterfield overcoats and his signature hat, a pearl-grey fedora, always worn at an angle.

As Schultz's criminal empire grew, he employed Coll as an assassin. At age 19, Coll was charged with the murder of Anthony Borello, the owner of a speakeasy, and Mary Smith, a dance hall hostess. Coll allegedly murdered Borello because he refused to sell Schultz's bootleg alcohol. The charges were eventually dismissed. However, Schultz began to see him as a hot-headed liability, when in 1929, without Schultz's permission, Coll robbed a dairy in the Bronx of $17,000. Schultz later confronted Coll about the robbery, but rather than being apologetic, Coll demanded to be an equal partner. Schultz called him an ingrate and declined.

By January 1930, Coll had formed his own gang and was engaged in a shooting war with Schultz. One of the earliest victims was his brother, Peter Coll, shot dead in 1931. Vincent went into a rage. Over the next three weeks he gunned down four of Schultz's men. As the war continued, Vincent and his gang killed approximately 20 of Schultz's men. To finance his new gang, Coll kidnapped rival gangsters and held them for ransom. He knew that the victims would not report the kidnappings to police, as they would have a hard time explaining to the Bureau of Internal Revenue why the ransom cash had not been reported as income.

On 28 July 1931, Coll participated in a kidnapping attempt that resulted in the shooting death of a child. Coll's target was bootlegger Joseph Rao, a Schultz associate who was lounging in front of a social club. Several children were playing outside an apartment house next door. A large touring car pulled up to the curb, and several men pointed shotguns and submachine guns towards Rao and started shooting. Rao threw himself to the sidewalk; however, four young children were wounded in the attack. One of them later died at the hospital. After the killing, New York City Mayor Jimmy Walker dubbed Coll a "Mad Dog." The name stuck.

Coll was arrested and brought to trial in December 1931. He retained the most renowned defence lawyer of the time, Samuel Leibowitz. Coll claimed that he was miles away from the shooting scene and was being framed by his enemies. He added that he would love to tear the throat out of the person who killed the little boy. The prosecution case soon fell apart. Their sole witness to the shooting admitted on the witness stand to having a criminal and mental health record. At the end of December, the judge issued a directed verdict of innocence for Coll.

A few days after his acquittal, Coll married Lottie Kreisberger, a fashion designer, and was hired by mobster Salvatore Maranzano to murder his right-hand man, Charles "Lucky" Luciano. Coll agreed to murder Luciano for a $25,000 payment in advance and a $25,000 payment on completion of the job. On 10 September 1931, Maranzano invited Luciano to visit his office. The plan was that Coll would turn up and kill Luciano. However, Luciano had received a tip-off about this plan, so he instead sent over a squad of his own killers who stabbed and shot Maranzano to death. Coll arrived at the office to kill Luciano, only to learn Luciano had fled the scene. After hearing that Maranzano was dead, Coll immediately left the building, $25,000 richer without having done anything to earn it.

BAD MOON RISING: AMERICAN OUTLAWS
OF THE ROARING 1920'S AND 1930'S

Dutch Schultz, still smarting over the killings of his gang members by Coll, put out a contract on him for $50,000. At one point, Schultz had actually walked into a Bronx police station and offered a house in Westchester to any officer who killed Coll.

A few weeks later, Coll was using a phone booth in a Bronx drug store when three men pulled up in a black limousine. While one waited in the car with the engine running, two others stepped out and walked into the drug store.

One of the gunman looked over at the cashier as he and his partner walked in and said while the two of them pulled out Thompson sub-machine guns from under their overcoats, "keep cool baby." They opened up with a volley of gunfire, obliterating the telephone booth and hitting Coll a total of fifteen times. Coll died instantly.

Dutch Schultz started a tradition when he sent a huge wreath of flowers to the funeral home with a banner that said, "From the boys." After that, it was common for the murderers of fellow gangsters to mock them by sending wreaths to their funerals.

Dutch Schultz continued to operate his rackets for only a few more years. On 23 October 1935, Schultz was killed at the Palace Chophouse in Newark, New Jersey in a hail of gunfire, apparently on orders from Lucky Luciano. Coll's widow, Lottie, was convicted of carrying a concealed weapon and sentenced to six months. She refused to leave prison following her parole, because she feared the people who had killed her husband would also murder her.

The Ballad of Mad Dog Coll

At the age of 8, he was on his own

This little boy had no home.

Listen hear boy, life is a bitch.

Quit your crying and get on with it.

This is the story of Mad Dog Coll,

Just a mean bastard from Donegal.

By the age of 18 his heart was a rock,

He was the toughest kid on any block.

He never thought twice about killing a man,

This kid had grit tough as sand.

Old Dutch Schultz was the king of the Bronx.

He opened the henhouse door to the fox.

He shook Mad Dog's hand and said,

"Kid I'm gonna take you under my wing.

I'll make you richer than your wildest dreams.

Grab your gun and kill me a queen and king."

This is the story of Mad Dog Coll,

Just a mean bastard from Donegal.

By the age of 18 his heart was a rock,

J. Wayne Frye

BAD MOON RISING: AMERICAN OUTLAWS
OF THE ROARING 1920'S AND 1930'S

He was the toughest kid on any block.

Bang, bang, bang with a shot gun,
This boy was having fun.
Never even blinked an eye,
Just smiled, making people die.

The years went by as Mad Dog grew
Swindling and murder was all he knew.
This man was on a dead end run.
On the horizon was the setting sun.

July 28 in 19 hundred and 31
A routine kidnapping went wrong.
There was screaming, people went wild.
Mad Dog shot a 7 year old child.

Salvatore Maranzano, Mafia king of New York,
He wanted to kill Lucky Luciano.
He paid Mad Dog to get it done.
Lucky heard rumours and shot Maranzano down.

Mad Dog had a price on his head.
Old Dutch Shultz wanted him dead.
Went to a drugstore to make a call,

J. Wayne Frye   151

BAD MOON RISING: AMERICAN OUTLAWS
OF THE ROARING 1920'S AND 1930'S

And two Thompson Machine guns made him fall.

This is the story of Mad Dog Coll,

Just a mean bastard from Donegal.

By the age of 18 his heart was a rock,

He was the toughest kid on any block.

(Wayne Frye adaptation of Ballad of Mad Dog Coll

by Rory and the Islanders)

Photo taken at Mad Dog's trial for killing a 7 year old child.

J. Wayne Frye

CHAPTER 7

STORM PALACES OF EXCESS AND DEMAND JUSTICE

It was another Midwest summer day
Under a partly cloudy sky.
I was a new bank teller,
And in came a handsome guy.

At three minutes to noon,
I saw in his hand a gun
Pointed directly at me.
I thought my life was done.

"Put the money in the bag,"
He said through white teeth.
I just did as I was told
To avoid any mischief or grief

J. Wayne Frye 153

BAD MOON RISING: AMERICAN OUTLAWS
OF THE ROARING 1920'S AND 1930'S

But that was not as bad,

As my friend at his desk,

Staring at a sawed off shotgun

Menacingly pointed at his chest.

The man staring at me said,

"I done this before.

Just be cool and I promise

No blood and no gore."

I have a dream almost every night.

I guess it is just my life's lot.

You see, I found out the robbers

Were John Dillinger and Harry Pierpont.

(Wayne Frye ©1992)

Harry Pierpont (1902 - 1934) was born in Muncie, Indiana, and due to his unassuming manner, is best known as John Dillinger's partner and mentor; although, it was always rumoured that he was the real brains of the gang. Described as handsome and soft-spoken, Pierpont was a bright, natural-born leader. Fiercely loyal, he had a reputation of taking care of those around him and not squealing on his friends. He disliked publicity, and was content to let others, especially Dillinger, take credit for the bold bank robberies committed during the daring days when the Dillinger gang wrecked havoc across America's heartland.

J. Wayne Frye

BAD MOON RISING: AMERICAN OUTLAWS
OF THE ROARING 1920'S AND 1930'S

Having attended undergraduate school at Indiana State University in Terre Haute, Indiana, I was able to visit many of the towns associated with Pierpont while there. His name was sometimes even whispered in the 60's and 70's, as if saying it out loud might provoke some type of retribution rained down by those family members who were still about.

The family moved to Indianapolis, Indiana in 1910 where Harry was remembered as an above average student in school. In those days, most poor people stopped their education at the 8th grade and got a job. Harry went to work in an automobile plant, where he was remembered as a hard worker who kept pretty much to himself.

Pierpont's troubles with the police began after an accident in the summer of 1921 in which he received a severe head injury. Of course, there was no such thing as worker's compensation, nor any legal liability on the part of his employer. Like today, if you were poor, you were on your own. The injury caused a change in his demeanour, and he complained of eye problems, dizziness and headaches. Pierpont was constantly sleepy and became maniacally obsessed with firearms to the point that he would constantly fondle them lovingly.

In 1921 at Indianapolis, Pierpont was arrested for carrying a concealed weapon. He was held for ten days and then released for commitment to the state mental hospital. The records there indicate that, after the injury, he became sullen and withdrawn to the point that he shouted his suspicions that there were people out to kill him. His doctors diagnosed him as suffering from dementia praecox of the hebephrenic type (a premature dementia or precocious madness). At the time, it was not known that head injuries could cause or acerbate this condition. The condition is described as a severe chronic, deteriorating psychotic disorder characterized by rapid cognitive disintegration, usually beginning in the late teens or early adulthood.

After nearly a year in the mental institution, Harry was released for a visit in his mother's care around Christmas 1921. On 2 January 1922, Pierpont stole an automobile in Indianapolis and drove to Greencastle, where he robbed the Cook Hardware store, stealing 9 handguns and nothing else. Five days later, he was arrested in Indianapolis for attempted auto theft and battery with intent to kill. The owners of the automobile, Mr. and Mrs. Devine, caught him in the act. Struggling with Mr. Devine, Pierpont fired a gun, slightly wounding him. Mrs. Devine was holding a roast, and hit Pierpont over the head with it. While being held in jail at Terre Haute, Indiana, Pierpont failed in an escape attempt, sawing through the bars of his cell. On 12 March 1922, Pierpont entered the Indiana reformatory for a two to fourteen years sentence for assault and battery with intent to murder, as his mental condition was discounted by the judge. His mother even appealed to the governor for clemency to no avail, even as the warden said to the governor, "He is mad as a hare?"

J. Wayne Frye

Pierpont's mother Lena often visited the superintendent of the prison and told him about Pierpont's mental illness, claiming that he was insane. Sympathetic, the parole board granted him parole on 6 March 1924 with no provision for mental care.

By November 1924, Pierpont was living in Kokomo, Indiana. All of his friends were ex-convicts and within a short time he was implicated as the ringleader in the robbing of several Indiana banks. Newspaper reports indicated there were seven members in all, and all identified Pierpont as their leader. On 26 November 1924, seven men led by Pierpont held up the South Marion State Bank in Marion, Indiana. No one was injured, and not a shot was fired. Pierpont simply walked in and said "hands up," forcing the cashier and bookkeeper into the vault. According to newspaper accounts, the gang had evidently studied the situation, knew the surroundings, and carried out their job with clockwork precision and accuracy. Several customers were standing with money in their hands to deposit, and when one started to hand Pierpont the money, he said, "We're not robbing you, sir. We're robbing the bank."

The abandoned 1924 Nash used in the robbery.

After the robbery, the men jumped into a Nash automobile and sped off. Initial reports indicated that, based on the description of the bandits, they were believed to be the same gang that robbed the Farmers National Bank at Converse, Indiana the week before, the Citizens State Bank, Noblesville, Indiana the week before that, and the South Marion State Bank the week before that.

On 16 December 1924, the same bandits made an unsuccessful attempt to rob the Citizens State Bank again. The bandits' car drove up to the side of the bank and six men leaped to the sidewalk and ran into the building, brandishing revolvers. While three robbers rushed to the rear of the bank to cover officials, the other three ordered several customers and the cashier to hold up their hands. With a revolver near his head, bank President Hiram Dunn touched a button on the floor, which started a burglar alarm. The bandits immediately ran out the door and sped away with nothing for their effort.

Pierpont at the age of 22 was already in a downward spiral as a result of injuries in an accident that caused head trauma.

BAD MOON RISING: AMERICAN OUTLAWS
OF THE ROARING 1920'S AND 1930'S

On 22 December 1924, Pierpont and his gang robbed the John D. Shelby Hardware Store of Lebanon, Indiana of rifles, double barrelled shot guns and fifty boxes of ammunition. The next day, they robbed the Upland State Bank. After getting all the money in sight, they quickly left the bank and hopped into a waiting car. A good description of the men indicated it was the Pierpont gang.

James Robbins of Lebanon, Indiana, was arrested by local police after being seen flashing a large amount of cash two days after Christmas. Robbins confessed to his involvement in the Upland State Bank robbery, the attempted robbery at Noblesville, and the robbery of the Lebanon hardware store. Robbins' confession led to the arrest of the other gang members except for Pierpont, who, knowing his gang had been decimated, recruited other members and on 10 March 1925, walked in with three other men and robbed the New Harmony Bank and Trust in New Harmony, Indiana. The bandits locked the employees and customers into the safe and scooped up $6,000 in cash and $4,000 in bonds from the vault.

Peace officers throughout the Midwest were wired descriptions of the men and advised to take no chances. Guards were placed along every road in southern Indiana with orders to "shoot to kill."

Stopped by Police in Kokomo, Indiana on 22 March 1925, Earl Northern, along with Everett Bridgewater, was arrested by Kokomo, Indiana police on suspicion of possessing a stolen car. They were immediately assumed to be members of the Pierpont gang, and were roughed up by the constabulary as they were carted off to jail, where they were found to be the actual owners of the car and the title in their names was legitimate. No apology was issued and they were sent on their way, as apparently the pursuit of people who robbed corporations warranted unjustified search, seizure and assault in the name of law and order. Ironically, the joke was on the inept police, as they found out the next day that the two men they had let go because they were owners according to the title, in fact, were members of the Pierpont gang. Pierpont met with them and they all had a good laugh.

At 1:30 in the afternoon of 27 March 1925, Pierpont and four others robbed the South Side Bank at Kokomo, Indiana. They made off with a round $10,000. The robbery took less than five minutes, and after cleaning out the bank, the bandits calmly walked to their car.

A string of robberies followed, and at this point, although armed with high-powered weapons, no shots had ever been fired in a Pierpont led hold-up and customers' money was never taken. On occasion, when they came across mortgages, they tore them up, hopefully relieving some poor people of the burden that was putting so many out on the streets with no shelter. In fact, it was the 1920's robberies that led many banks to store mortgages elsewhere to avoid what was referred to as robbing Robin Hoods.

BAD MOON RISING: AMERICAN OUTLAWS
OF THE ROARING 1920'S AND 1930'S

For nearly six months, the wild hold-up carnage continued unabated. However, the gang had been avoiding detection by robbing banks and then heading to a hideout in Detroit, Michigan. The authorities showed up at their home on Lakeshore Drive and arrested Pierpont, along with Thaddeus Skeer and Skeer's girlfriend, Louise Brunner. Pierpont gave his name as Frank Mason, but later in the day admitted his identity. A cache of weapons were found. The three prisoners waived extradition and were carted off to Indiana. It was discovered that the arrests were the result of work by the Pinkerton Detective Agency, the same group that had pursued Jesse James. They were hired by the Indiana Bankers Association, and like their pursuit of the James gang, the pursuit of the Pierpont gang, included a variety of illegal actions and disregard for basic human rights as they steamrolled over any associates of Pierpont, even threatening his mother and father with incarceration.

Pierpont's parents came to Kokomo from their home in Brazil, Indiana and arranged with the firm of Overman, Healy and Bree to defend Harry. Pierpont's attorneys did not yet admit that his name was anything other than Frank Mason, the alias given in Detroit.

On 6 May 1925, Pierpont took the stand and in a surprise defence move, practically admitted to all the evidence contained in a confession by Skeer. Pierpont told of entering and holding up the bank and then fleeing to Fort Wayne, Indiana, where the loot was divided between himself and three others. However, Pierpont stated that Skeer was the planner of the robberies. Pierpont was convicted and sentenced to serve a sentence of ten to twenty-one years and fined $1000.00.

Upon entering the Indiana State Reformatory, he defied authorities by giving the wrong name, refusing to recognize the warden, declining to make a statement or allowing his picture to be taken and spitting on a guard. It was here that he first met John Dillinger and Homer Van Meter. In Pendleton, Pierpont was the convict Dillinger looked up to the most. Pierpont caused so much trouble that he was transferred to the Indiana State Prison at Michigan City within two months, after he attempted to drill through the bars of his cell in an escape attempt. Dillinger and Van Meter were later transferred within the next few years to Michigan City also.

At Michigan City, Pierpont was held in high regard by the other convicts. He soon became the leader of an elite group of former bank robbers. Forever trying to escape, Pierpont constantly fought with the guards and was frequently put in solitary confinement. He was known for his ability to withstand hunger and beatings, as Michigan City was a particularly brutal place. Harry's obstinance won him the respect of all the prisoners, especially from John Dillinger. It was from Pierpont that Dillinger learned the nuances of bank robbery, and with a parole for Dillinger coming up, an escape plan was concocted.

BAD MOON RISING: AMERICAN OUTLAWS
OF THE ROARING 1920'S AND 1930'S

With Dillinger on the outside, he would rob several banks on a list composed by Pierpont and with that money, help finance an escape for a select few.

On 29 December 1930, Pierpont was among a group of 12 men who overpowered a guard and barricaded the doors of their cell block to prevent guards from entering. Pierpont let himself out of his cell with a homemade key. An alarm was sounded and a combined group of city police, fireman and guards were able to force the inmates to surrender.

After the failure, Pierpont began immediate plans on another escape attempt, giving Dillinger another list of banks to rob as well as reliable sources for accomplices. Dillinger wholeheartedly agreed, provided his friend, James Jenkins, be included in the inmates who would break out. By the spring of 1934, the plan was all set.

Michigan City Prison as it appeared in 1933.

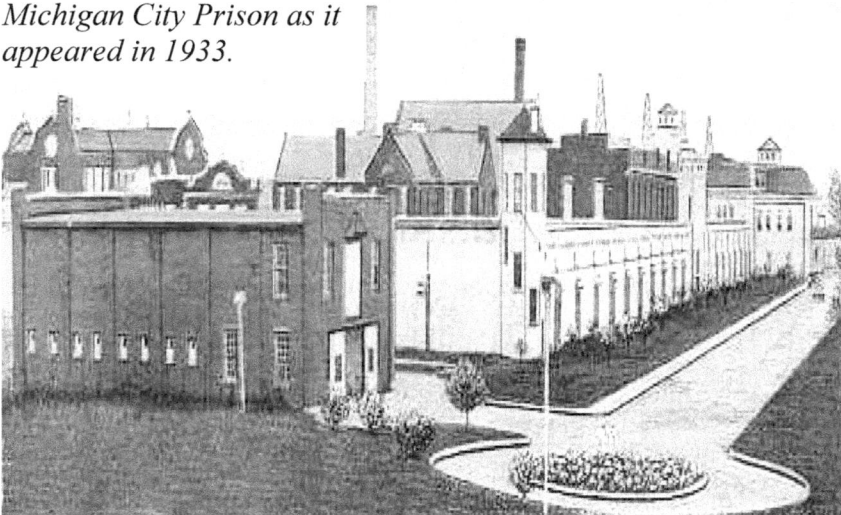

BAD MOON RISING: AMERICAN OUTLAWS
OF THE ROARING 1920'S AND 1930'S

Pierpont was ably aided on the outside by his girlfriend, Mary Kinder, who agreed to help with the break-out if her brother, Earl Northern, was added to the list of escapees. Mary's brother was Pierpont's old partner. Pearl Elliott, called "The Kokomo Madam" who had been involved in Pierpont's Kokomo robbery, was to get money to those who would bribe prison guards.

On 13 September 1933, three loaded revolvers, wrapped in Chicago newspapers, were found near the west wall of the prison. Prisoners Danny McGeogehan, Jack Gray and Eddie Murphy were seen picking them up and were believed to be connected to an escape attempt and ordered immediately into solitary confinement. They were not connected. Dillinger had tossed those pistols over the wall, and they were intended for Pierpont and his conspirators. Pierpont was shocked when he heard what happened, as their plans for a breakout was scheduled, and dependent on them having the guns to facilitate it. Still, he was not deterred. On 25 September 1933, Pierpont and his co-conspirators conferred during the exercise period and decided to crash out on the next day. Each man swore an oath not to be recaptured without a fight.

The next morning, Pierpont, and prisoners Makley, Hamilton, Clark, Dietrich, Shouse, Fox, Burns, and Jenkins escaped using three .45 caliber pistols Dillinger had smuggled into the jail the very day after the other guns were found. Dillinger had spent the summer of 1933 robbing banks throughout Indiana and Ohio to

J. Wayne Frye

raise enough money to smuggle the guns into the prison in boxes of thread sent to the prison shirt factory. At two o'clock that afternoon, Pierpont and Russell Clark told shirt factory superintendent George H. Stevens that one of the officials needed to see him in the basement. Stevens was soon overpowered by the rest of the gang. Walter Dietrich sought out deputy superintendent Albert E. Evans, telling him that a fight was in progress, leading him into the trap as well. Evans was greeted by seven men with pistols and three with clubs. Foreman Dudley Triplett came to the basement for supplies and was soon captured.

Pierpont had received severe punishment at the hands of a marginally sadistic Deputy Evans while in prison, and was prepared to exact revenge. Dietrich stopped him from killing Evans, saying he was a valuable hostage. The convicts, with the hostages, began to walk carefully to freedom. Stevens led the way, with Dietrich on his left side and Hamilton on his right, their guns concealed beneath the stacks of shirts they were carrying. The other men picked up a steel shaft and followed. Though they walked almost the entire length of the prison, the guards and other prisoners paid no attention to what was happening.

When they arrived at the first steel gate, Stevens told guard Frank Swanson to open the gate because the prisoners were armed and would kill the hostages if he did not do so. Swanson was forced to join the procession. After proceeding through a second gate they came to the third gate, where they used the steel shaft as a battering ram. The guard was beaten, and the other guard was forced to open the outer gate.

The prisoners entered the lobby of the administration building, where they herded eight civilian clerks into the vaults. Seventy-two-year-old Finley Carson was shot in the leg and shoulder by Burns for not moving fast enough. Warden Louis E. Kunkel happened upon the group, and he was quickly made a prisoner as well.

Outside the gate, it was every man for himself. It was raining hard. The escaped prisoners ended up splitting into two groups. The first group included Dietrich, James Clark, Fox and Burns. The second group included Pierpont, Hamilton, Russell Clark, Makley, Shouse and Jenkins.

With the alarm sounding, the Dietrich group encountered Sheriff Charles Neel, who had just dropped off some prisoners. Overpowering him, they took his weapons, and forced him to take three of them in his automobile. At a gas station outside the prison, attendant Joe Pawleski was struck over the head by the Pierpont group. The group commandeered another vehicle, releasing two women but forcing the driver to stay with them. They headed out of town, finding an old, seemingly abandoned farmhouse where they hid out through a cold night, contemplating their next move.

J. Wayne Frye

BAD MOON RISING: AMERICAN OUTLAWS OF THE ROARING 1920'S AND 1930'S

The convicts in Sheriff Neel's car purchased gas, but within thirty minutes abandoned the sheriff's car near Wheeler, Indiana, after carjacking another vehicle. The group roared off with the sheriff still their prisoner.

Mary Kinder, around midnight, answered a knock at her door in Indianapolis and found Pierpont standing there smiling. She immediately asked about her brother, Earl Northern. Northern was originally part of the escapee plan, but was ill in the infirmary at the time of the break. Mary had arranged a place for the escapees to stay at the home of her reluctant boyfriend since Pierpont had been in jail. The convicts sent the boyfriend and Mary downtown to buy civilian clothes.

The next day, the convicts were ready to begin robbing banks, only to discover that Dillinger had been arrested in Dayton, Ohio right before the escape. The gang soon hatched a plan to free Dillinger from the Lima, Ohio jail where he was being held. The next evening, the gang was joined by Michigan City parolee Harry Copeland, Dillinger's partner before the arrest, who told the gang he had arranged for a house in Hamilton, Ohio. However, the hideout would not be ready for a few more days but he had found them temporary quarters. When their hideout in Hamilton was ready, the group abandoned their car in Indianapolis and stole another to hide their tracks. Indiana State Police Captain Matt Leach became aware of the theft, and threw up a blockade that almost resulted in the gang's capture. During an attempt to get away from the police, the door of their auto opened and James Jenkins fell out. The gang had to speed on, unable to wait on Jenkins, eventually stealing another vehicle before reaching their Ohio hideout. Jenkins was later killed that evening by a local posse near Beanblossom, Indiana. The gang hid out at the farm of Pierpont's parents, who were now living near Leipsic, Ohio.

Pierpont realized that the group needed more money to break Dillinger out. Makley suggested they rob the First National Bank in his hometown of St. Mary's, Ohio, only a few miles away from Lima. Mary Kinder was in an awkward position with two boyfriends now, but she explained that her allegiance was to Pierpont. Her other boyfriend elected to join the gang and not fight over her. On the morning of October 3, exactly one week after their escape, while the gang began loading into two cars for the robbery, Harry Copeland claimed he was too sick to drive, and Mary Kinder was asked if she would drive the second car for an equal share of the loot.

Makley entered the bank with Pierpont and Clark while Hamilton and Shouse waited nearby. The robbery netted almost $11,000. Mary's other boyfriend, Ralph Saffell, meantime, had managed to send word about what was going on and where they were to the authorities. Pierpont arranged for Dillinger's girlfriend, Billie Frechette, to come to Ohio where he found an apartment in Cincinnati for her and Mary.

BAD MOON RISING: AMERICAN OUTLAWS
OF THE ROARING 1920'S AND 1930'S

Now, it was time for the big breakout. The gang arrived in Lima on Columbus Day. Pierpont, Makley and Clark entered the jail around 6:30 PM while Shouse, Hamilton, and Dillinger's first partner, Harry Copeland, remained outside as a lookout. The gang members introduced themselves to Sheriff Jess Sarber as Indiana State Prison officials there to return Dillinger to Indiana. When Sarber requested their credentials, Pierpont shot Sarber in the abdomen. Makley and Pierpont then beat Sarber and locked his wife and Deputy Wilbur Sharp in the jail cell. Leaving the sheriff for dead, they escaped with Dillinger.

The search for the gang became so intense in Ohio that two days after freeing Dillinger they decided to split into two groups and meet in Chicago.

At about 10:00 PM on 20 October 1933, Dillinger, Pierpont and Dietrich raided the Peru, Indiana police station for guns and bullet-proof vests. Headlines across the country screamed with fear that the Dillinger gang had declared war on the law enforcement, with some predicting the gang would break into the prisons and raise an army to plunder all across America. Typical of the government, fears were stoked and calls to rally around the good guys were ballyhooed as a way to be patriotic. The Indiana National Guard was put at the disposal of the state police, and volunteer posses were formed throughout the state. Meanwhile, the gang was quietly staying in the high rent district of the Windy City (Chicago).

BAD MOON RISING: AMERICAN OUTLAWS
OF THE ROARING 1920'S AND 1930'S

Plans for the gang's first major robbery, that of the Central National Bank in Greencastle, Indiana were prepared and escape routes had been mapped out by Pierpont. Early in the afternoon, a large Studebaker parked on a hill next to the bank. Pierpont headed for one of the cages to change a $20 bill. When the teller told him to go to another window, Pierpont pulled his Tommy gun out, and said, "I prefer this one." The other gang members pulled out their guns and began cleaning money from the vaults. Witnesses clearly identified Pierpont as the leader of the robbers. Five minutes later, the robbery was over, and the gang walked out with $74,000 (1.4 million on today's dollars) in cash and bonds without firing a shot. They were so quiet that no one at the police station across the street knew what had happened.

With the Indiana State Police after them, the gang hid out in Chicago, with Dillinger, Pierpont, Mary Kinder and Billie Frechette sharing an apartment. The gang moved freely about the city. It was there that they hatched the plan to rob a bank in Racine, Wisconsin, despite growing tensions among the gang members. Pierpont, Makley and Mary Kinder drove to the American Bank & Trust Company in Racine. Mary changed a bill while she cased the bank, and the gang then drove around exploring the best getaway routes. Returning to Chicago, Pierpont suggested to the gang that Copeland be dropped as the driver and Shouse put in his place. Shouse had other plans to rob a bank on his own, and Mary Kinder overheard Shouse trying to convince

J. Wayne Frye

others to join him. That evening the gang decided to get rid of Shouse, and the next morning they threw money at him and tossed him out. As he was leaving, Shouse stole Clark's car and headed to California.

The morning of the robbery, the gang read extremely shocking news in the morning Chicago Tribune about Copeland's arrest the evening before, and concerned about him ratting them out, packed up and left their apartment, then headed for Racine, Wisonsin where Pierpont nonchalantly got out of the Studebaker that parked in front of the bank. There was a surreal nature all about, as in so many robberies. Although things were moving along at a rapid pace; they seemed to be in slow motion. There was a band concert down the street in a nearby park, the euphoric sounds filtering up the street toward the bank. The sky was overcast, and as Pierpont walked into the bank he nodded a greeting to an elderly lady who was leaving, smiling at her politely. Each confident stride he took embodied the supreme confidence of a man good at his job, and his job was robbing banks.

Pierpont was carrying a Red Cross poster. He pasted it over the front window to block the view of the teller cages from the street. Dillinger and two others then entered the bank, and Dillinger, every bit as confident as Pierpont, shouted, no barked, "stick 'em up" at one teller who was on the phone. When the teller, Harold Graham, failed to comply, Dillinger shot him in the elbow. As Graham fell, bleeding and in intense pain, he reached under the counter and set off the alarm connected to the police station.

Pierpont, over the screams of the now terrified patrons and employees, calmly ordered everyone in the lobby to lie on the floor while Dillinger marched the bank president, the cashier and his assistant into the main vault at gunpoint. While the cashiers struggled with opening the vault, two police officers responded to the alarm. Pierpont got the jump on one, and Makley wounded the other. With the vault cleaned out, Dillinger and Pierpont rounded up the cops, three female hostages and a bank president as hostages. Using the hostages as shields, the gang marched out to their car, taking a woman, the bank president and an officer with them. Makley, feeling chipper and his adrenalin at soaring heights, cut loose with a barrage of gunfire toward two detectives who had responded with guns drawn. How ironic that law enforcement bursts into action to protect a corporation's money but is always slow to respond when something goes down in a poor neighbourhood. So determined were the officers to recover the corporation's stolen money, they ignored the plight of the hostages and fired bullets into the car as it roared out of town.

A few blocks later, when the car ran into traffic, the bank President was tossed off the running board, tumbling onto the highway and rolling into a muddy ditch. Pierpont shouted at him, "You are where you belong, thief, wallowing in mud."

The gang took the female hostages to the woods where they bound them loosely together around a tree. Pierpont handed them a few hundred dollars and asked them to stay there for twenty minutes before walking to the highway after they unbound themselves.

Many years ago in what almost seems another lifetime, I was in a bank while it was being robbed. As I watched the three men curiously, one of them glanced over at me and said, "What the hell you looking at, dude?"

I smiled at him and said, "Just enjoying watching a bunch of tough hombres taking down a big bad corporation that steals from people every day."

He snickered and replied, "Enjoy yourself, man."

As they ran out the door, while the others were frantically running about, some crying, some still shivering in fear, I took a seat over in the corner and looked all about the elaborate building built with the money the bank paid 3% interest on when you deposited it, but then lent it out at 12%, and asked myself who the real thief was that day. Some wondered the same in Racine, Wisconsin on the day Pierpont robbed that bank.

Due to the unwelcome attention generated by their crimes, the gang and their women took a long vacation at a beach house in Daytona Beach, Florida. However, before long, they were back in Chicago where they robbed the First National Bank in East Chicago, Indiana. Pierpont waited in the car while two others emerged with the money and hostages. They faced several cops who had taken up positions outside. One officer fired at Dillinger, hitting him in the middle of the chest, but failed to injure him, as Dillinger was wearing a bullet-proof vest. Dillinger returned fire, killing the officer. The other officers opened fire as Dillinger and John Hamilton ran for the car. Hamilton was wounded.

Heading out west to lie low, Pierpont, Dillinger, Makley and Clark wound up in Tucson, Arizona. Rolling in cash from all the robberies, they became careless, which led to their being recognized and captured, one by one, during one day in January 1934. All four men and their girlfriends were extradited back to the Midwest; Dillinger to Indiana for the O'Malley's murder, the other three to Ohio.

Testimony from Shouse, one of the first members of the Dillinger gang, helped convict the others. In early March 1934, Pierpont, Makley and Clark were convicted of murder. While Clark got a life sentence, Pierpont and Makley were sentenced to die in the electric chair.

After Dillinger stunned the country by breaking out of the jail at Crown Point, Indiana with a wooden gun on 3 March 1934, it was suspected that he would try to break his pals out of the death house in Columbus, Ohio. Elaborate precautions were taken to keep Pierpont and Makley locked up, on the assumption that Dillinger would show, but he did not, as he had teamed up with Baby Face Nelson and was on a robbing spree.

BAD MOON RISING: AMERICAN OUTLAWS
OF THE ROARING 1920'S AND 1930'S

Makley and Pierpont resorted to other means to get off death row by trying to imitate the wooden gun feat of Dillinger. On 22 September 1934, exactly two months after Dillinger had been killed in Chicago, Pierpont and Makley carved phoney pistols out of soap, and painted them black with shoe polish, and made their move. Brandishing the toys, they managed to get out of their cells and to the main door of the death house before rifle-wielding guards opened fire. Makley was killed outright and Pierpont was riddled with bullets. Although he survived, he was seriously injured.

Pierpont was executed at the Ohio Penitentiary on 17 October, 1934. Still suffering from injuries incurred during his attempted escape, he had to be carried to the electric chair.

Until her dying day, his mother blamed his head injury for Harry's problems with the law. She could not do the same for her other son, Fred, who, despite no head injury was constantly in trouble with the law, too.

Harry Pierpont is a robber who was an anomaly at best. There were times when he exhibited deep concern for the plight of the poor, and would, on occasion, hand over some of his ill gotten gains to them. Still, he was capable of ruthlessness that would sometimes border on the psychotic. How would he have turned out if he had not been injured and suffered head trauma? However, as alluded to earlier, he did have an injury that could partly explain his personality.

J. Wayne Frye

BAD MOON RISING: AMERICAN OUTLAWS
OF THE ROARING 1920'S AND 1930'S

Although they have never personally done me any harm, I must admit to prejudice against banks, as I see them representative of a society where greed is simply destroying the inner soul of a nation that worships at the altar of money. I could never do what Pierpont did. Is it because I am a moral person? I don't think so. I think it is because I fear the police who are paid to keep us in line so those at the top of the economic ladder can live in splendorous luxury unafraid that the rest of us might one day storm their palaces of excess and demand justice.

J. Wayne Frye

CHAPTER 8

HIS LAST ESCAPE

*"There is something about outlaws that reaches deep within us,
and, despite the abhorrent acts done by them, we cannot help but
harbour some admiration for their defiance of authority that most
of us bow to in our everyday lives. We bow not because of a
moral compass that guides us but out of pure, simple,
unmitigated fear of the corporations, the bosses at work, the
government, the militarized police and even God - all those who
rule over us and exert total, complete control of our lives."*

(Wayne Frye Speech, 1986)

Roy G. Gardner (1884 - 1940) was an accomplished American
criminal known for his bravado and ability to escape from
custody. He is said to have been the most hunted man in Pacific
Coast history and in the newspapers was referred to as the
"Smiling Bandit."

His other monikers were "Mail Train Bandit," and the "King of the Escape Artists." He was born in Trenton, Missouri, but was reared in Colorado Springs, Colorado. He was attractive and charming, spending his early manhood as a drifter, learning the various trades. At one time, he was in the U.S. Army but deserted in 1906 and drifted to Mexico.

Gardner began his criminal career as a gunrunner around the time of the Mexican Revolution. He smuggled and traded arms and ammunition to the revolutionary forces until he was captured by General Victoriano Huerta and was sentenced to death by firing squad; however, two hours before his scheduled execution, on 29 March 1909, he broke out of the Mexico City jail along with three other American prisoners. Back in the United States, Gardner became a prizefighter in the Southwest. He was good enough that he became a sparring partner for Heavyweight Champion J. J. Jeffries in Reno, Nevada, during the summer of 1910. Eventually, he ended up in San Francisco, where he gambled all of his boxing money away and then robbed a jewellery store. He was arrested and spent time in San Quentin, but was paroled after he saved a prison guard's life during a riot. He then landed a job as a welder at the Mare Island Navy Yard, married, fathered a daughter, and on Armistice Day in 1918 walked off from his family and began his own welding company.

On a business trip to Mexico, Gardner gambled all his money away at the racetracks in Tijuana. Then on the night of 16 April

1920, outside San Diego, he robbed a U. S. Mail truck of about $80,000 (a little over $1 million today) in cash and securities. The job went smoothly, but he was arrested three days later while burying his loot. He was sentenced to 25 years at McNeil Island Federal Penitentiary for the armed robbery, but vowed he would never serve the sentence. On 5 June 1920, he was being transported by train to the penitentiary by two marshals. Outside Portland, Oregon, he peered out of the train window and shouted, "Look at that deer!" The lawmen looked, and Gardner grabbed one officer's guns from his holster, then disarmed the other at gunpoint, handcuffed the two together, and stole $200 from them. He jumped off the train and made his way to Canada.

He slipped back into the United States the next year, and started robbing banks and mail trains across the country as a lone bandit. Returning to California, on 19 May 1921, he tied up the mail clerk on the train eastbound from Sacramento and robbed the car of $187,000 (over 2 million today). The next morning, he told the mail clerk of another train to throw up his hands or he would blow his head off. When the clerk told him he did not have keys for the safes in the car, Garner very carefully removed two sticks of dynamite from his pocket and blew the safes up. When the train reached Roseville, California, he ran down the tracks with an armful of mail. The home office recognized the gunman as Roy Gardner, the train robber who had gotten away with $187,000 a few days before and now had nearly $70,000 more.

Gardner was recognized at a hotel, and while he was playing a game of cards in a pool hall, federal agents arrived and captured him. He was sentenced to another 25 years at McNeil Island for armed robbery of the mail trains.

Trying to reduce his sentence, he told the Southern Pacific Railroad detectives that he would lead them to the spot where he buried the money from the two robberies. The officers found nothing, and Gardner laughingly said, "I guess I have forgotten where I buried that money." He was heavily shackled on feet and wrists, and was once again transported on a train to McNeil Island, again by two U. S. Marshals, both tried and true veterans. During the journey, Gardner asked to use the bathroom, in which an associate had earlier hidden a .32 calibre pistol. When he came out of the bathroom, Gardner pointed the gun at the officers and ordered another prisoner to handcuff the two lawmen to the seat. He relieved the officers of their weapons and cash before hopping onto another moving train outside Castle Rock, Washington. The largest manhunt in Pacific Coast history ensued. Gardner was described as a dangerous man who would shoot you without hesitation.

He arrived in Centralia, Washington, where he plastered his face with bandages to hide his identity, leaving one eye slit, and told the hotel staff that he had been severely burned in an industrial accident near Tacoma, Washington. The proprietor and the house detective became suspicious, and when the house detective saw a firearm in Gardner's hotel room, he accused him of being the "Smiling Bandit." Gardner fought to get away, but was subdued by the officer and a doctor removed the bandages, confirming his identity. He was sentenced to another 25 years, and heavily chained, was finally brought to McNeil Island.

After six weeks at the penitentiary, Gardner had convinced two other prisoners, Lawardus Bogart and Everett Impyn, that he had paid off the guards in the towers. On Labour Day 1921, at a prison baseball game, he said "now," during the fifth inning when someone hit a fly ball into center field, as the guards in the towers had their eyes on the ball and the runners on base. He, Bogart, and Impyn, ran to the high barbed-wire fence where Gardner cut a hole, and the three men ran to the pasture outside the prison as bullets whizzed about their heads. Gardner was wounded in his left leg, but escaped behind a herd of cattle near timber. He saw Bogart fall, badly wounded. Impyn was shot dead; his dying words were, "Gardner told us those fellows in the towers had been bribed." Bogart later said that Gardner had deceived them and used his companions as decoys to better his chances of escape.

Guards scoured the beaches and confiscated every boat on the shoreline, but were unable to find Gardner, who actually was only about 300 feet from the prison walls in the prison barn, drinking milk from the cows for sustenance. He made it to the nearby ocean and swam to Fox Island, where he lived off fruit in the orchards. Gardener made his way to San Francisco and then Arizona where he committed several crimes. He was captured by train officers during a train robbery in Phoenix in the fall of 1921. He was sentenced to an additional 25 years, this time at Leavenworth Federal Penitentiary. Headlines, after the trial, read: "Gangster Gardner brags that Leavenworth will never hold him."

Now known as the "King of the Escape Artists," Gardner was transferred in 1925 to Atlanta Federal Prison, then the toughest prison in the country, which is saying something about a nation that is filled with prisons where horrid conditions are the norm. The following year, he tried to tunnel under a wall and saw through the bars in the shoe shop. Then in 1927, he led a prison break, during which he held the captain and two guards hostage with two revolvers, but the escape failed and he was placed in solitary confinement for twenty months. When he was released from solitary confinement, he was placed in a mental hospital in Washington, D. C.

In 1929, the warden described Gardner as the most dangerous inmate in the history of Atlanta Prison, and that year Gardner began a hunger strike protesting prison food and threatened suicide. He was then transferred to Leavenworth Annex Prison in 1930, and in 1934 he was transferred to Alcatraz, where he was one of the first hardened criminals incarcerated there. Now, he had gone almost 14 years without a successful escape.

BAD MOON RISING: AMERICAN OUTLAWS
OF THE ROARING 1920'S AND 1930'S

From Alcatraz, there simply was no escape. Gardner's time in Alcatraz coincided with Al Capone's. Capone was an unpopular prisoner. Supposedly, an unidentified inmate once threw a lead pipe at Capone, but Capone was only wounded in the arm because Gardner pushed him out of the way. This endeared him to Capone, who provided him with protection and a variety of benefits the rest of his time there.

During Gardner's time in Alcatraz, he worked and supervised at the mat shop with Ralph Roe and they planned an escape, but Gardner was paroled and released in 1938 after his appeal for clemency was approved. In 1939, the now mellowing with age Gardner published his autobiography, *Hellcatraz*. He delivered crime lectures and made re-enactments of crimes on film about how a person cannot beat the law. Gardner worked as a film salesman and an exposition barker. In 1939 a movie called *I Stole a Million* was based on his life. It was released on Christmas day. It was a box office flop.

On the evening of 10 January 1940, in a run down hotel in San Francisco, an aging Gardner checked in and asked for a room at the end of a hallway on any floor. He had no luggage, but the clerk, having him pay in advance, gave him the key to room 424. He noticed the man avoid the elevator and walk up the stairs. His shoulders were stooped and he looked very tired. Another guest passed him in the hallway, said hello, but got no response. Gardner went into his hotel room, wrote a note and attached to the door. The next morning, the maid saw the note that read, "Do not open door. Poison gas. Call police." He had sealed the door from the inside and then killed himself by dropping cyanide into a glass of acid and inhaling the poison fumes. Roy Gardner had made his last escape.

Roy Gardner (Circa 1925)

CHAPTER 9

MORAL BANKRUPTCY OF A NATION

Can you hear the rat-a-tat-tat, rat-a-tat-tat?

No, I ain't talkin' 'bout no gangsta rap,

Those guys today singing in the hood,

I'm talking about gangsters from long ago,

Ones that let their machine guns hum and flow.

One of 'ums name is like a tune.

Rolls off your lips like sweet honey

With a cadence tried and true,

Giving it to you right in the belly,

A cool daddy named Machine Gun Kelley.

Today's gangstas use a machine gun tongue,

Not realizing all the real gangsters are dead.

J. Wayne Frye

185

BAD MOON RISING: AMERICAN OUTLAWS
OF THE ROARING 1920'S AND 1930'S

Yeah, they bit the dust way back then.

Sadly, today's youth are way too content,

Having 'gangstas with names like 50 cent.

He robbed and he jumped and he gutted.

He murdered and cheated and lied.

Rat-a-tat-tat was sweet music to his ears.

Filled with bravado, machine gun in hand

This is the dude spread fear across the land.

He paid for crimes without pleasure,

When G-men took his measure.

He survived a living hell called Alcatraz.

This man loved the rat-a-tat-tat so cold,

Gun in hand, Machine Gun Kelley so bold.

*(From *Poems on the Run with a Machine Gun*

by J. Wayne Frye, © 1995)

George Francis Barnes Jr. (1895-1954) is a pretty sedate name, but Machine Gun Kelly, has a cavorting cadence to it that flows like thunder in a raging storm. Born in Memphis, Tennessee back when it was just a sleepy Mississippi River delta town, George's nickname came from his favourite weapon, a blazing, burping Thompson submachine gun. His most infamous crime was the kidnapping of oil tycoon and businessman Charles F. Urschel in July 1933 for which he, and his gang, collected a $200,000 ($3.7

million in today's dollars) ransom. Their victim had methodically collected and left considerable evidence that assisted the subsequent FBI investigation that eventually led to Kelly's arrest in Memphis, Tennessee, on 26 September 1933. His crimes also included bootlegging and armed robbery.

During the Prohibition era, Kelly worked as a bootlegger. After several run-ins with the police, he left town and headed west with his girlfriend. To protect his family and escape law enforcement officers, he changed his name to George R. Kelly. He was arrested in Tulsa, Oklahoma, for smuggling liquor onto an Indian Reservation in 1928 and sentenced to three years in prison. He was reportedly a model inmate and was released early. Shortly thereafter, Kelly married Kathryn Thorne, who purchased Kelly's first machine gun and went to great lengths to make him known as Machine Gun Kelly in order to make him sound more sinister.

The truth is that Kelley was all name and no brains in most cases. He actually was not a very good criminal, and for all but one crime and a tough sounding name, he may well have faded into history and never even been mentioned among the likes of Dilligner, Pierpont, the Barkers and Bonnie and Clyde.

Kelly's last and most famous criminal activity proved disastrous when he kidnapped a wealthy Oklahoma City resident, Charles F. Urschel and his friend, Walter R. Jarrett. Urschel, having been blindfolded, made note of evidence about his experience including remembering background sounds, counting footsteps and leaving fingerprints on surfaces. This proved invaluable for the FBI in its investigation, as agents concluded that Urschel had been held in Paradise, Texas, based on the sounds Urshel remembered hearing while he was being held hostage.

An investigation conducted at Memphis disclosed that the Kelly's were living at the residence of J. C. Tichenor. Special agents from Birmingham, Alabama were immediately dispatched to Memphis, where, in the early morning hours of 26 September 1933, a raid was conducted. George and Kathryn Kelly were taken into custody by FBI agents and Memphis police. Caught without a weapon, tough guy Machine Gun George Kelly allegedly shouted, "Don't shoot, G-Men! Don't shoot, G-Men!" as he meekly surrendered to FBI agents. The term, which had applied to all federal investigators, became synonymous with FBI agents. The couple was immediately removed to Oklahoma City.

Even his arrest did not turn out well publicity-wise for Kelley at the time, as it was overshadowed by the escape of ten inmates, including all of the members of the future Dillinger gang, from the penitentiary in Michigan City, Indiana, that same night. On 12 October 1933, George and Kathryn Kelly were convicted of kidnapping and sentenced to life imprisonment.

The kidnapping of Urschel did make Kelley's name endure for a few reasons besides his moniker: his trial was the first federal criminal trial in the United States in which film cameras were allowed; the first kidnapping trial after the passage of the so-called Lindbergh Law, which made kidnapping a federal crime; the first major case solved by J. Edgar Hoover's newly named FBI; and the first prosecution in which defendants were transported by airplane.

Machine Gun Kelly spent his remaining 21 years in prison. Because of his name, during his time and his meek manner at Alcatraz, he got the nickname "Pop Gun Kelly." This was in reference, according to a former prisoner, to the fact that Kelly was a model prisoner and was nowhere near the tough, brutal gangster his wife made him out to be. He spent 17 years on Alcatraz Island, working in the prison industries, and boasting of and exaggerating his past escapades to other inmates, and was quietly transferred to Leavenworth Kansas Penitentiary in 1951. He died of a heart attack at Leavenworth on 18 July 1954, his 59th birthday. Oddly, his tombstone does not mention his preferred name, but simply says, George B. Kelley 1954.

Kathryn Kelly was released from prison in 1958 and lived in anonymity in Oklahoma under an assumed name, dying in 1985 at the age of 84 quietly in her sleep, maybe gently floating off into eternity with the angels singing a cadence of rat-a-tat-tat as she was greeted by her one love, Machine Gun Kelly.

Kelly is an example of how a name can make a man, or a girl. Picking a baby's name is often said to be a predictor of future success. Of course, many times a name reflects the arrogance of a parent who wants the name to reflect on the parent. Take the name Donald Trump picked for his son, Barron. Maybe "Duke" was already taken! The name will always be a problem for him, whether a success or not. The name smacks of arrogance, privilege and wealth, so there is built-in resentment. Machine Gun Kelly did not pick his name – his wife did. It was a name that he simply did not have the ability to live up to.

Machine Gun Kelly on his way to Alcatraz
where the inmates would refer to him as "Pop-Gun Kelly.

Sometimes, people get names they hate. I was thin as a rail in school, so kids would cruelly call me "Weenie," indicating I was as thin as the meat in a hot dog bun. Unfortunately, I no longer have the problem of being thin!

BAD MOON RISING: AMERICAN OUTLAWS
OF THE ROARING 1920'S AND 1930'S

One person who grew to hate his public name was a man named Lester Joseph Gillis, who was called, because of his youthful looks, Baby Face Nelson. Lester (1908-1934), was a ruthless bank robber who entered into a partnership with John Dillinger, helping him escape from prison during the famed Crown Point, Indiana jail break, and was a long-time public enemy number one alongside Dillinger. Nelson was responsible for killing more FBI agents in the line of duty (three) than any other person. Nelson was fatally shot by FBI agents during a shootout called The Battle of Barrington, which ranks alongside the 1986 FBI shootout between FBI agents and two bank robbers in Homestead, Florida as the worst loss of life in a single incident by the FBI.

Lester Gillis seemed doomed from almost the beginning when on 4 July 1916 outside his Chicago, Illinois home, at the age of seven, he was arrested after accidentally shooting a playmate in the jaw with a pistol he had found. Although it was an accident, his poor parents could not afford an attorney to mount a defence, and just like today's USA, sending kids to jail was the norm if poor, because the poor needed punishment, not rehabilitation or psychological help. Some states, like Florida, even today consistently sentence offenders as young as 15 to death. In harsh conditions, Gillis served over a year in the state reformatory, where he grew to obsessively hate authority figures and harbour a growing belief that the law was nobody's friend.

BAD MOON RISING: AMERICAN OUTLAWS
OF THE ROARING 1920'S AND 1930'S

One day, while eating lunch, he accidentally knocked his plate onto the floor. A guard insisted that he lick it up off the floor. Gillis defiantly refused to perform the sadistic request and was so severely beaten by the sadistic guard he required one week's hospitalization. He was forced to serve the full year. After being released, he continued to have scrapes with the law until he was arrested for theft and joyriding at the age of 13, when he received a sentence of 18 months in what the state of Illinois now called a youth penal colony – a better sounding name the officials apparently thought than a youth prison. It simply was a more subdued name for what was a place where brutality was the norm in nation that even today has the highest incarceration rate in the world, and is consistently cited by international human rights organizations, including Amnesty International, as one of the most consistent violators of human rights when it comes to incarceration, especially in the rapidly growing for-profit prisons run by giant corporations.

While in jail (excuse me – a youth penal colony), Nelson became the leader of a prison gang. After he was released, his gang affiliation continued. In 1928, Nelson met and married Helen Wawzynak. The couple had two children. By the time he met Helen, Nelson was working at a gas station in his neighbourhood, which doubled as the headquarters for a group of young tire thieves known as "the strippers." Nelson fell into association with the strippers, and also acquainted himself with a

J. Wayne Frye

number of local criminals, including one who employed him to drive bootleg alcohol throughout the Chicago suburbs late at night.

Within two years, Gillis, now using the name Nelson, and the gang was involved in organized crime, including armed robbery. On 6 January 1930, they forced their way into the home of a magazine executive named Charles M. Richter, who loved to make a public display of his wealth. After tying him up with adhesive tape and cutting the phone lines, they ransacked the house and made off with approximately $25,000 (around $350,000 today) worth of jewellery. Of course, one might argue that anyone stupid enough to have that expensive jewellery lying around is perhaps hanging a target around their necks saying "I am a stupid rich person, please rob me." Much like the Kardashian media darling who was walking around Paris wearing millions in jewellery, there can be little sympathy with someone so audaciously displaying their perceived importance by parading around like a peacock in all their finery. Even the royal leeches in England keep the crown jewels safely locked up and guarded. In March, Nelson and his gang carried out a similar robbery at the bungalow of Lottie Brenner Von Buelow. (There is obviously a rich sounding name if I ever heard one.) This job netted approximately $50,000 worth of jewellery. After the crime, a newspaper wrote – "A bold gang of criminals is plaguing Chicago's finest citizens. Something must be done."

BAD MOON RISING: AMERICAN OUTLAWS
OF THE ROARING 1920'S AND 1930'S

Of course, while the newspapers profusely worried about the pain of losing jewels by Chicago's wealthiest citizens, the poorest ones were going to bed hungry at night, as the rich were dining on caviar and pranced around in their high-priced jewellery that Nelson saw as the geese who were laying his golden eggs, or his diamond eggs!

On 21 April 1930, Nelson robbed his first bank, making off with approximately $4,000, considerably less than he was making boosting jewels from the rich elite of Chicago. A month later, he was back heisting jewels worth $25,000. On October 3, Nelson robbed the Itasca State Bank of $4,600. Three nights later, he stole the jewellery of the wife of Chicago mayor, Big Bill Thompson, valued at $18,000. She described her attacker, saying he had a baby face. The name stuck, although they did not know his last name was Nelson yet. The Chicago Tribune headline was: *Baby Face Jewel Thief Brazenly Steals Mayor's Wife's Jewels.* Nelson was appalled at being called Baby Face, and seeing the headline, slammed the paper down on the kitchen table and said, "I'll machine gun every reporter at the Chicago Tribune."

Nelson had a string of successes that had him and his gang flush with cash, but they began to see themselves as invincible. At a speakeasy roadhouse on 23 November 1930, just outside of Chicago, their luck changed. Nelson and three of his gang were going to rob the gambling proceeds from an illegal backroom casino being run with the full knowledge of the Chicago Police in a fashion that flaunted the laws of Illinois in regards to gambling and the USA in regards to prohibition. As long as the crooked cops got their bribes, nothing was done, and Nelson figured the illegal nature of the establishment made it easy pickings, since the robbery would not even be reported for fear of rousing public indignation over the illegal operation being allowed as a result of a complacent Chicago Police Department.

Again, the scene was almost surreal. Nelson, along with three of his crew, pulled up outside the rear entrance. The driver kept the car running as three men, including Nelson, moved out of the car like gazelles on the open plain, stepping gracefully toward a door where there was a slot that opened and closed to decide whether a person was admissible or not. Baby Face knocked and the slot slid open, a young man peered out and Nelson put the nose of his Tommy Gun into the slot and said, "Open it or I blow your eye balls through the back of your head." As the door eased open, Nelson's two accomplices stepped inside the casino foyer and were met with a hail of gunfire from two guards. The doorman was hit in the back by his own guards and fell to the floor dead. Baby Face stepped into the open doorway and nearly cut the two guards in two with a steady volley of fire. Pandemonium broke out among the customers who were now running toward the front of the casino to seek safety inside the bar at the roadhouse. Nelson noticed three men with guns headed his way and opened up on them with a steady volley. They fell.

One of Nelson's companions was hit in the arm, and the other one had a leg wound. Nelson said, "Let's get out of here," as he looked down at the three men he shot first, and delivered a volley of fire in a coup de grace to the men, who were probably already dead. He then looked over at the three others he had shot sprawled out in agony on the floor in front of him, pulled the trigger again and again and all the gun did was click several times since he was out of bullets. He finally said to the men, "lucky bastards" as he exited.

Apparently frustrated with the failure at the roadhouse, only three nights later, he robbed a tavern and, in the escape, shot a stockbroker who had been sitting at the bar and made the mistake of getting up before the gang had left.

Throughout the winter of 1931, most of the gang were rounded up, including Nelson. The Chicago Tribune referred to their leader as George "Baby Face" Nelson. They were unable to tie any of the murders to him, but the jewel robberies got him one year to life in the state penitentiary at Joliet. Nelson escaped during a prison transfer in February 1932. Through his contacts within the Touhy Gang, Nelson fled west to Reno, where he was harboured by William Graham, a known crime boss and gambler. Using the alias Jimmy Johnson, Nelson went to Sausalito, California, where he worked for bootlegger Joe Parente. During his San Francisco criminal ventures, Nelson most probably first met John Paul Chase and Fatso Negri, who later became close associates. In Reno, Nevada the next winter, Nelson met the vacationing Alvin Karpis, who in turn introduced him to Midwestern bank robber Eddie Bentz. Teaming up with Bentz, Nelson returned to the Midwest the next summer. He committed a major bank robbery in Grand Haven, Michigan on 18 August 1933. The robbery was not lucrative, but it was a smooth operation that convinced Nelson he was ready for bigger things.

Nelson recruited Homer Van Meter, Tommy Carroll and Eddie Green to join what he was calling the gang of all gangs. With these men and two other local thieves, Nelson drove up in front of the First National Bank of Brainerd, Minnesota on 23 October 1933, the car slowly rolling to a stop as four well-dressed men got out carrying sub-machine guns. People on the sidewalk, stopped, gawked in horror, and then began to run frantically in a frenzied retreat from the bank area, aware of what was about to happen. Throughout the crowd, an awareness was shared that Baby Face Nelson was in the group of men about to rob the First National Bank. The operation was smooth and precise, taking less than three minutes for the robbers to steal $32,000 (equivalent to approximately $600,000 in today's dollars). When Nelson emerged and saw the crowd that had observed the robbery milling together across the street, he sent them scurrying by spraying a burst over their heads from his Tommy gun. For good measure, as the car sped away, he sprayed another volley from his gun into the air as he leaned out the car window. He appeared to be having fun.

When the police arrived well after the robbers had made their getaway, people insinuated they had waited because they heard it was the Baby Face Nelson gang and were fearful. Regardless, the police actually did not even bother to chase after the gang.

The Rogue's Gallery of the Accomplices of Baby Face Nelson

Tommy Carroll

Homer Van Meter   *Eddie Green*

Baby Face Nelson

First National Bank in Brainerd, Minnesota (Circa 1931)

After collecting his wife Helen and four-year-old son Ronald, Nelson left with his crew for San Antonio, Texas. Almost immediately upon arrival a local woman tipped off San Antonio police regarding the presence nearby of high-powered Northern gangsters. Two days later, Tommy Carroll was cornered by two detectives and opened fire, killing one policeman and wounding another. All the Nelson gang fled San Antonio. Nelson and his wife went to the San Francisco Bay Area, where he recruited John Paul Chase and Fatso Negri for a new wave of bank robberies the following spring.

John Paul Chase   *Fatso Negri*

On 3 March 1934, John Dillinger made his famous wooden pistol escape from the jail in Crown Point, Indiana. Although the details remain in some dispute, the escape is suspected to have been arranged and financed by members of Nelson's newly formed gang, including Homer Van Meter, Tommy Carroll, Eddie Green, and John "Red" Hamilton, with the understanding that Dillinger would repay some part of the bribe money out of his share of the first robbery. The night Dillinger arrived in the Twin Cities, Nelson and his friend John Paul Chase were driving when they were cut off by a car driven by a local paint salesman named Theodore Kidder. Nelson lost his temper and gave chase, crowding Kidder to the curb. The salesman exited his vehicle to protest, whereupon Nelson shot him dead.

Two days after this, the new gang struck the Security National Bank at Sioux Falls, South Dakota. In the robbery, which netted around $50,000, Nelson severely wounded motorcycle policeman Hale Keith with a burst of sub-machine-gun fire as the officer was arriving at the scene. The six men were soon identified as the Second Dillinger gang, due to Dillinger's extreme notoriety, and this bruised Nelson's ego severely.

The gang robbed the First National Bank in Mason City, Iowa in March and Dillinger and Hamilton were both shot and wounded in the robbery, where they made off with $50,000. On 3 April, federal agents ambushed and killed Eddie Green, though he was unarmed and they were uncertain of his identity. In the aftermath of the Mason City robbery, Nelson and John Paul Chase fled west to Reno, where their old bosses Bill Graham and Jim McKay were fighting a federal mail fraud case. Nelson and Chase abducted and killed the chief witness against the pair, Roy Fritsch.

On the afternoon of 20 April, Nelson, Dillinger, Van Meter, Carroll, Hamilton, and gang associate Pat Reilly, accompanied by Nelson's wife Helen and three girlfriends of the other men, arrived at the secluded Little Bohemia Lodge in a spot called Manitowish Waters, Wisconsin for a weekend of rest. The gang's connection was probably through Dillinger's attorney who frequented it often. They all registered under assumed names. Lodge owner, Emil Wanatka, noticed while playing cards with Dillinger that he had a concealed pistol in a shoulder holster inside his coat, and then observed that Nelson and the others also had shoulder holsters.

The following day, while she was away from the lodge with her young son at a children's birthday party, Wanatka's wife informed a friend, Henry Voss, that she and her husband suspected that the Dillinger gang was at the lodge, and the FBI was subsequently given the tip. Famed FBI Agent Melvin Purvis and a number of agents arrived by plane from Chicago, and with the gang's departure imminent, prepared erratically for the assault on the lodge.

Wanatka offered a one-dollar dinner special on Sunday nights, and the last of a crowd estimated at 75 people were leaving as the agents arrived in the front driveway. A Chevrolet automobile was backing up at the exact time three patrons were exiting the building. The FBI agents mistook them for some of the gangsters and without warning, quickly opened fire on them, instantly killing one and wounding the others, which alerted the real gang members inside the lodge. Adding to the chaos, at this moment, Pat Reilly was returning to the lodge after an out-of-town errand for Van Meter, accompanied by a girlfriend. They sped away quickly under a hail of bullets from the agents.

J. Wayne Frye

BAD MOON RISING: AMERICAN OUTLAWS
OF THE ROARING 1920'S AND 1930'S

Dillinger, Van Meter, Hamilton, and Carroll immediately escaped through the back of the lodge, which was foolishly left unguarded by the incompetent agents, and made their way north on foot through woods and past a lake to the highway where they commandeered a car and a driver.

Little Bohemia Lodge after the raid. It is still in operation today.

Nelson, who had been outside the lodge in the adjacent cabin, characteristically attacked the raiding party head on, exchanging fire with Purvis, before retreating into the lodge under a return volley from other agents. From there he slipped out the back and fled in the opposite direction from the others. Emerging from the woods ninety minutes later, a few kilometres from Little Bohemia, Nelson kidnapped a couple from their home and ordered them to drive him away. Apparently dissatisfied with the car's speed, he ordered them to pull up at a brightly lit roadhouse where the switchboard operator, aware of the ongoing events, quickly phoned authorities to report a suspicious vehicle in front of the lodge. Shortly after Nelson had entered the lodge, taking the owners hostage, as they were preparing to leave, another car arrived with two federal agents, Carter Baum and Jay Newman, along with local constable, Carl Christensen. Nelson quickly opened fire with his automatic pistol, severely wounding Christensen and Newman and killing Baum. With his hostages in tow, Nelson felt he was now home free, but the car had a flat tire and there was no jack. He left the hostages and wandered into the woods where he held a family hostage in their cabin for several days, and for some unknown reason, the FBI never showed up. He took their car and made good his escape.

Three of the women who had accompanied the gang, including Nelson's wife Helen, were captured inside the lodge. They were eventually convicted of harbouring criminals, but released in a couple of months on parole.

With an agent and an innocent bystander dead and four more severely wounded, including two more innocent bystanders, and the complete escape of the Dillinger gang, the FBI came under severe criticism, with calls from the public for Hoover's resignation and a widely circulated petition demanding Purvis' firing. Of course, with Hoover's maniacal penchant for getting incriminating information on politicians and holding it over their heads, especially their liaisons with women, not a one of them uttered anything about him resigning. The reckless killing and wounding of innocents by the FBI was simply ignored.

BAD MOON RISING: AMERICAN OUTLAWS
OF THE ROARING 1920'S AND 1930'S

At the time of the Little Bohemia shootout, Nelson's identity as a member of the Dillinger gang had been known to the FBI for only two weeks. Following the killing of Baum, Nelson became nationally notorious and was made a high-priority target of the FBI.

A day after the Little Bohemia raid, Dillinger, Hamilton, and Van Meter ran through a police roadblock. A ricocheting bullet struck Hamilton in the back, fatally wounding him. Hamilton was secretly buried by Dillinger and others, including Nelson, who had rejoined the gang in Aurora, Illinois.

Tommy Carroll was killed while trying to evade arrest in Waterloo, Iowa. Former gang member Pat Reilly was surrounded as he slept and was captured in St. Paul, Minnesota.

Nelson, Dillinger and Van Meter robbed the Merchants National Bank in South Bend, Indiana. When the robbery began, a policeman directing traffic outside responded quickly to the scene and as he ran toward the bank, gun drawn. He was killed with one shot by Van Meter, who was stationed outside the bank. Also outside the bank, Nelson exchanged fire with a local jeweller, who had shot him in the chest with no effect, as Nelson was wearing a bullet proof vest. As the jeweller retreated into his store under a return volley from Nelson, a man in a parked car was wounded from the wild firing. Nelson also wrestled briefly with a teenage boy, who tackled him to the ground, but Van Meter knocked the kid out with a shift hit on the head from the

J. Wayne Frye

butt of his machine gun. When Dillinger emerged from the bank with sacks containing $28,000, he brought three hostages with him, including the bank president, to deter gunfire from three patrolmen who had taken up positions across the street. The policemen fired nonetheless, wounding two of the hostages before grazing Van Meter as he rushed to Dillinger's side. All this carnage to protect a corporation's $28,000 with total disregard for the human beings that should have meant more the two sacks of money.

This was the last confirmed robbery for all of the known and suspected participants. During the month of July, as the FBI manhunt for him continued, Nelson and his wife fled to California with associate John Paul Chase, who remained with Nelson for the rest of his life. Upon their return to Chicago on July 15, the gang held a reunion meeting at a favourite rendezvous site. When the meeting was interrupted by two Illinois state troopers, Nelson fired on their vehicle with a pistol he had converted into a mini-machine gun, wounding both men as the gangsters fled. On 22 July 1934, Dillinger was ambushed and killed by FBI agents outside the Biograph Theatre in Chicago. The next day the FBI announced that Pretty Boy Floyd was now Public Enemy Number 1. Then, in October, Floyd was killed in a shootout with agents including, Melvin Purvis. Subsequently, J. Edgar Hoover announced that Baby Face Nelson was now Public Enemy Number 1.

BAD MOON RISING: AMERICAN OUTLAWS
OF THE ROARING 1920'S AND 1930'S

In August, Van Meter was ambushed and killed by police in St. Paul, Minnesota, leaving Nelson as the sole survivor of the so-called Dillinger Gang. Nelson and his wife, usually accompanied by Chase, drifted throughout California and Nevada, until they went to the Lake Como Inn in Lake Geneva, Wisconsin for the winter. When the Nelsons and Chase entered, to their surprise they briefly came face to face with two unprepared FBI agents. The fugitives sped away before any shots were fired and armed with a description of the car and its license plate number, agents combed the area, but again, Nelson had eluded capture.

The sweat hum of Nelson's stolen V-8 Ford Roaster was music to the fleeing three's ears as they cruised down Highway 12 toward Chicago, Nelson, always with his seemingly keen ability to sense impending danger, spotted federal agents in a car that breezed past them on the opposite side of the road. The agents also recognized him and immediately made a u-turn. The chase was on fast and furious, but Nelson was playing with them, because his car was much more powerful and he could have floored it at any time and sped off into the sunset. What motivated him to play a sadistic game with the FBI agents has never been known, but for some unimaginable reason he made a wild u-turn, and Nelson wound up in pursuit of the agents' car, as the agents realized that with only pistols, and the likelihood the three were probably armed with machine guns, shooting it out with them was not a good idea. When Nelson's powerful Ford caught up to the agents' weaker auto, Nelson and Chase fired at the agents with blazing machine guns out of their side windows while still roaring down the highway with intensity. A couple who passed the two speeding cars later told authorities that it seemed like something out of a western movie with cowboys chasing each other on horseback and firing wildly at one another, the only difference being these guys were in cars rather than on horseback.

The two agents, looking for cover, turned into a ploughed cornfield and headed for some trees in the distance. To their surprise, Nelson and Chase had stopped the pursuit. They were unaware that their return fire had punctured the water pump of Nelson's Ford. In a dramatic turn of events, with Nelson's Ford rapidly losing power and steam pouring out of the engine, two more agents had shown up and now were pursuing Nelson.

Somehow, they had stopped outside the cornfield and switched drivers. With Helen now driving, she was told by Nelson to turn into a trailer park on their right. The agents followed them into the park, which was filled to capacity with vacationers. They stood in awe of the unfolding scene, as Helen spun the car around and screeched to halt to face the oncoming agents who stopped their car at an angle about 25 metres away. Nelson and Chase popped out of the rear of the car, Tommy guns blazing. Upon both agents exiting their vehicle's passenger side, they took up position behind the open door.

BAD MOON RISING: AMERICAN OUTLAWS
OF THE ROARING 1920'S AND 1930'S

So excited about the unfolding carnage, most of the people in the park did not run from the scene, but stood mesmerized by what they were witnessing. Nelson ordered Helen to take cover in a nearby ditch to their left, then he and Chase moved out in the open, firing at the agents. A single .45 slug from one of the agents hit Nelson in the abdomen, slicing through the liver and pancreas before exiting the lower back. Nelson leaned on the Ford's running board and then wordlessly exchanged weapons with Chase when his machine gun jammed and emptied a complete drum magazine at the agents. Oblivious to his painful and mortal wounds, the determined Nelson complained to Chase that his Thompson sub-Machine gun was not doing its job. Nelson reached into the front seat of the car and picked up a specially modified rapid fire Winchester automatic rifle. Despite his grievous wound, Nelson moved from behind the car and advanced toward the agents while firing the Winchester. Two of his bullets struck on agent dead centre in the chest and stomach, knocking him over. Buckshot pellets from the other agent's shotgun then struck Nelson in the legs and knocked him down. As Nelson struggled to his feet, the upright agent who had been wounded moved to better cover behind a utility pole. As he drew his service pistol, Nelson, gritting his teeth and shouting obscenities, delivered a series of rounds to his chest. The agent fell, mortally wounded. Nelson staggered over to his body, aimed his smoking rifle at the agent for a moment, and then, seeing he

J. Wayne Frye

was dead, limped toward the agents' car. Nelson drove the car over to the disabled Ford. After loading the agents' car with the Ford's guns and supplies, Nelson let Chase get behind the wheel of the agents' car and the two men and Helen fled the scene, with the onlookers in total shock at what they had observed.

Nelson had been shot a total of nine times; a single and ultimately fatal bullet had struck his abdomen and eight shotgun pellets had hit his legs. Later news reports inaccurately gave his number of wounds as seventeen, possibly due to J. Edgar Hoover's tendency to embellish things for public consumption.

Nelson, never once crying with pain simply said to Chase and Helen, "We really stuck it to the FBI today. I'm done for. Take me somewhere and let me die in peace."

As Nelson laid his head in Helen's lap, Chase drove them to a safe house for hoods on Walnut Street in Wilmette, Illinois. Nelson died in bed with his wife at his side that night.

Following a telephone tip from a Chicago Telephone Company employee who was working on telephone lines and saw a body wrapped in a blanket on the ground in front of a church in Skokie, Illinois, the FBI recovered the body of Baby Face Nelson, who was only 25 years old. A sobbing Helen would later say that she had placed the blanket around Nelson's body because, "He always hated being cold."

Newspapers then reported that J. Edgar Hoover had issued a death order for Nelson's widow, who wandered the streets of

Chicago as a fugitive for several days as the U.S.A.'s first female public enemy. Chase was eventually apprehended and served a term at Alcatraz.

After surrendering, Helen served a year in prison for harbouring her husband. She was rarely recognized in later years, living a quiet life, as she and Nelson had been married under his real last name – Gillis, the name that is on his tombstone. However, she never made a secret of who her husband had been, and she never remarried. She died in 1987.

I will not in anyway justify the cruelty exhibited by Baby Face Nelson, any more than I would accept the cruelty sanctioned by war criminals like Dick Cheney and George Bush who claimed the moral high ground while ordering torture, but the difference is that Nelson was in the fight himself, putting his life on the line while people like Bush, Cheney and Trump, born into privilege and always extolling the virtues and greatness of the American capitalist system, never once entertained the thought of going into harms way. These are the people who beat their chests and act tough, but when it comes time to walk the walk rather than talk the talk, they scurry behind their privilege and let others do the fighting and dying.

Baby Face Nelson was a cold bloodied killer, but he was not a hypocrite. In the USA, hypocrites have the reigns of government and pass laws for the citizens, but the legislators are exempted from those laws they pass for the rest of Americans.   This is why

BAD MOON RISING: AMERICAN OUTLAWS
OF THE ROARING 1920'S AND 1930'S

J. Edgar Hoover was, in his own way, just as bad as those he sat out to bring to justice. Who was bringing this hypocrite, who lived a life of lies, to justice? He simply represented the moral bankruptcy of a nation.

J. Wayne Frye

CHAPTER 10

THE DOMINOS WERE FALLING ONE BY ONE

Treacherous sands where death lies in wait
In the middle of nowhere, by hell's open gate
Criminals have walked in this valley's shadow
Unknown and well-known with hearts fallow

Death draws no distinction, partial he's not
He'll take anybody, to their funeral plot
You cannot fight him, you cannot win
He is the ultimate fate of all bad men
(Lament of the Angel of Death, 1995)

Wilbur Underhill, Jr. (1901-1934), often called "Mad Dog" or the "Tri-State Terror," was a burglar and bank robber. He was one of the most wanted bandits in Oklahoma during the 1920's and 1930's and co-led a gang with Harvey Bailey that included many fellow Cookson County, Oklahoma outlaws who emulated their idol from the same place, Pretty Boy Floyd.

Underhill was born in Joplin, Missouri, one of seven children. He, along with his three older brothers, became career criminals, though none gained the notoriety of Wilbur. When Underhill was 12 years old, his brother George killed a local tamale vendor and was sentenced to life imprisonment. Underhill began to show a wild streak soon afterwards, although his mother claimed it was the result of a childhood accident that caused a brain aneurysm.

Underhill committed his first criminal offence by stealing silverware from a neighbour's home. He was warned by the judge and given probation. In 1918, he was convicted of burglary and spent four years in prison. A year after his release, Underhill became locally known as the "Lovers' Lane Bandit," as he would lie in wait until a couple would be undressed and spring upon them and steal their belongings and money, assuming they would be reluctant to report the crime. When his identity became known after being caught by a policeman and his wife posing as lovers, he was carted off to Missouri State Penitentiary for five years.

Underhill was released on parole in late 1926, and on Christmas Eve he and Ike "Skeet" Akins robbed a drug store in Okmulgee, Oklahoma. In the course of the robbery, 19-year-old customer George Fee was killed. They were eventually arrested on 7 January 1927 and charged with murder and armed robbery.

Underhill and Akins were still awaiting trial when they decided to escape from the Okmulgee jailhouse on January 30, using smuggled hacksaws. While Wilbur Underhill successfully eluded authorities, his partner was captured. Three days later, while being brought back to Okmulgee, Akins attempted another escape attempt and was killed.

A day after Akins' death, Underhill robbed a movie theatre for $52 in Pincher, Oklahoma. Confronted by a constable and a deputized civilian, Underhill managed to get a gun away from the constable and killed the civilian. This time, Underhill actually headed out of the country, going all the way to Panama. To his complete surprise, he was greeted by the FBI with extradition papers in hand. He was very quickly convicted of murder and sentenced to life imprisonment on 3 June 1927.

Underhill made several attempts to escape from the Oklahoma State Penitentiary and finally succeeded on 14 July 1931. Twelve days later, Underhill purchased a car in Cherryvale, Kansas under the name Ralph Carraway and robbed a local theatre of $300 that same day. The following month he recruited his young nephew, Frank Underhill, to join him on a new crime spree. On August 12, they robbed a Wichita gas station but got only $14.68. While leaving the scene of the robbery, Underhill crashed into another car and had to have his car towed to a nearby garage and checked into a hotel while awaiting repairs. The next day, Patrolman Merle Colver arrived at the hotel. He had been assigned to check

Wichita hotels for suspicious guests and went to their room to question them. When he knocked on the door, Underhill shot him 3 times in the head, killing him instantly. Fleeing on foot, Underhill became involved in a running gunfight with police. A 2-year-old boy was killed in the crossfire when police fired at Underhill. He was eventually stopped by a lucky shot to the neck. Underhill was caught and again convicted of murder, earning him another life sentence. The 2 year old victim was forgotten!

While an inmate at Lansing State Prison, he participated in a mass escape with 10 other inmates using pistols smuggled in by Frank "Jelly" Nash and headed for Pretty Boy Floyd's old playground, the Cookson Hills, where Underhill and five of the other escaped inmates went on a crime spree lasting a little over six months.

Now, Underhill was ready to move up from the petty crimes he had been committing in the past and take up bank robbing. His first robbery was a bank in Black Rock, Arkansas. The next day, the Kansas City Massacre occurred and many named Underhill as a participant, but he was nowhere near Kansas City when the massacre took place. The gang continued its activities and robbed $11,000 from a bank in Clinton, Oklahoma. Two days later, Underhill apparently acted alone in a bank robbery in Canton, Kansas but rejoined the gang by the time the Bailey-Underhill Gang struck a bank in Kingfisher, Oklahoma on 9 August 1933. By now, the newspapers were calling him the Tri-State Terror.

BAD MOON RISING: AMERICAN OUTLAWS
OF THE ROARING 1920'S AND 1930'S

Underhill decided to cool-off in Texas, so he went to the ranch of Machine Gun Kelly's father-in-law. After a few days, he headed for Kansas, where he robbed a bank in Baxter Springs, Kansas. The Tri State Terror was now on a wild rampage, robbing banks every few days in Kansas, Oklahoma and Arkansas.

Some newspapers outside the tri-state area began using the name "Mad Dog" to describe him. Because of his penchant for being trigger happy other newspapers called him the "Southwest Executioner."

A special task force was formed, and included armoured cars. On November 18, while the task force was still in Cookson Hills, Underhill presented himself at the courthouse in nearby Coalgate and applied for a marriage license under his own name. His fiancée, Hazel Jarrett Hudson, was a sister of the outlaw Jarrett brothers. As part of a wedding present for Hazel, Underhill and several others robbed a Frankfort, Kentucky bank. Now that is what I call an unusual wedding present.

Unlike most of the other bandits of the time, there was little, if any public sympathy for Underhill. In fact, one criminal said of him, "He gives bank robbers a bad name."

FBI Director J. Edgar Hoover, frustrated with the lack of progress from Oklahoma authorities, assigned agent R.H. Colvin to the Underhill case. Colvin soon discovered that Underhill had given his wife's address in Oklahoma City to the minister who married them in order to receive their marriage certificate. Federal agents staked out the home and spotted the newly weds a week later. Agents at the scene called for reinforcements but, by the time they arrived, Underhill and his bride had left to celebrate their honeymoon elsewhere. A few days later, police raided a farm near Konawa, Oklahoma where they knew Underhill was staying. However, Underhill had passed them earlier on the highway and was able to escape before police realized their mistake.

Despite the intensive manhunt, Underhill and his gang continued their robbing spree unabated. They were hitting an average of three banks a week.

On 26 December 1933, Wilbur and Hazel Underhill were having a private drinking party with Ralph Roe and his girlfriend at a rented cottage in Shawnee, Oklahoma. Four days later, a 24-man strike force, including federal agents, state troopers and local police, surrounded the house. The group was led by R.H. Colvin and Frank Smith, the latter a survivor of the Kansas City Massacre. When called on to surrender, Underhill began firing, with the task force returning fire. Typical of the FBI, no consideration was given to the innocent bystanders, who were not as important as Hoover's Bureau getting their man. The other tenants in the cabins were not evacuated before hand or warned. One innocent woman, in a nearby cabin, trying to run away, was apparently mistaken as Underhill's wife and killed by the agents.

Underhill, brave and obviously noble man that he was, deserted his wife and still barefooted and in his underwear, ran from the house attempting to escape. He was hit five times before leaving the yard but ran for another 1000 metres before breaking into a furniture store and collapsing on one of the beds. Ralph Roe, also wounded, was taken into custody with Hazel Underhill. Underhill was taken to McAlester where he remained, handcuffed in his bed, at the prison hospital until his death on 6 January 1934. His last words were "Tell the boys I'm coming home." The Tri State Terror was no more.

Underhill and the agents who got him, apparently showing no remorse for killing an innocent woman.

BAD MOON RISING: AMERICAN OUTLAWS
OF THE ROARING 1920'S AND 1930'S

One by one the miscreants of mayhem were falling now like dominos, and J. Edgar Hoover's ego was expanding like a balloon being filed with helium. Increasingly, his chief agent, Melvin Purvis, was becoming disenchanted with Hoover grabbing all the headlines while Purvis was out there dodging bullets, only to have Hoover show up to be photographed at the scene once the battle was over.

One criminal who was a particular thorn in the FBI's side was Homer Van Meter (1905-1934), an associate of John Dillinger and Baby Face Nelson. Van Meter ran away from his Ft. Wayne, Indiana home in the sixth grade, eventually ending up in Chicago, Illinois, where he worked as a bellhop and a waiter. He was arrested for drunk and disorderly conduct. Of course, since he was poor, rather than give him probation, as they did the more affluent, they carted him off to jail at the age of 14. As soon as he got out, he stole a car and this time got a longer sentence in an adult facility. He had also contracted syphilis.

He was paroled in December 1924. Three months later, he teamed up with an old cellmate to rob the passengers of a train in Crown Point, Indiana. He was caught and convicted of the crime, and received a sentence of 10 to 21 years, to be served in the Pendleton Reformatory. While in Pendleton, he met John Dillinger and Harry Pierpont. He became grand friends with Dillinger, but he and Pierpont developed a hatred for one another that almost bordered on the psychotic.

J. Wayne Frye

BAD MOON RISING: AMERICAN OUTLAWS
OF THE ROARING 1920'S AND 1930'S

When Van Meter's repeated joking and violation of Pendleton rules earned him a transfer to the state prison at Michigan City. Pierpont rejoiced. In January 1926, Van Meter was transported to Chicago to testify in defence of a man wrongly suspected of being his accomplice for a train robbery in Crown Point. He escaped from the marshals escorting him at Union Station, but was quickly apprehended, but undeterred, a week later, after sawing through the bars of his cell; he severely beat a corrections officer but was caught before leaving the prison. As a penalty, he spent the next two months in solitary confinement, where he was severely beaten by prison guards who delighted in torturing prisoners.

Finally, he was released on parole in 1933. On August 18, Van Meter aligned himself with Baby Face Nelson and Tommy Carroll to rob a bank in Grand Haven, Michigan. On October 23, the trio, along with John Paul Chase and Charles Fisher, robbed a bank in Brainerd, Minnesota.

Dillinger broke out of prison in Crown Point, Indiana on 3 March 1934. Dillinger and John "Red" Hamilton later joined Van Meter's gang. On March 6, Dillinger, Nelson, Van Meter, Carroll, Eddie Green and Hamilton robbed the Security National Bank & Trust Company in Sioux Falls, South Dakota. They escaped to their hideout in St. Paul, Minnesota. One week later, on March 13, the men robbed the First National Bank in Mason City, Iowa. On April 12, Dillinger and Van Meter robbed a police station in Warsaw, Indiana, stealing firearms and serveal bullet-proof vests.

Van Meter and the gang became the subject of an intense FBI manhunt. Eddie Green was ambushed and killed by the FBI on April 3. Days earlier, Van Meter, Dillinger, and Dillinger's girlfriend Billie Frechette, had narrowly escaped from police in St. Paul after a gunfight. Later, on April 23, while fleeing from Little Bohemia Lodge, Dillinger, Van Meter and Hamilton were involved in a furiously intense gun battle in Hastings, Minnesota. Hamilton was mortally wounded and died four days later at the house of Volney Davis.

On May 3, Van Meter, Dillinger and Carroll robbed the First National Bank in Fostoria, Ohio, during which Van Meter shot and wounded the local police chief. The three spent most of May hiding in a woodland cabin near East Chicago, Indiana. On May 24, while driving a red panel truck through East Chicago, Van Meter and Dillinger were stopped by two police detectives. Dillinger was driving, so when the car stopped, Van Meter got out of the car with his Tommy gun blazing death. The officers did not even have time to pull their weapons. On June 7, Carroll was killed in a gunfight in Waterloo, Iowa.

A few days later, in an attempt to conceal their identities, both Dillinger and Van Meter had a famed underworld surgeon, Dr. Loeser, perform plastic surgery on them to alter their appearance so they could go about in public with without being recognized.

Unsatisfied with the results and the pain he was forced to endure, Van Meter attempted to kill Loeser, but was restrained by Dillinger.

On June 30, Van Meter, Dillinger, Baby Face Nelson and an unidentified fourth man robbed the Merchants National Bank in South Bend, Indiana, and I shall cover this robbery in more detail as it is indelibly burned into my mind for a variety of reasons, which I shall share when discussing John Dillinger in another chapter. This was a bank robbery that rivalled the famous James gang raid on Northfield, Minnesota in intensity and is still written about by historians.

Van Meter, his girlfriend, Marie Comforti and Dillinger headed for Chicago, and awhile later Dillinger was hunted down and killed, which Van Meter saw as a warning that he was next. He and his girlfriend immediately fled to St. Paul, Minnesota, where, on August 23, Van Meter while strolling down Marion Street nonchalantly as if he did not have a care in the world was confronted by four police officers, one of whom was Police Chief Frank Cullen. The other one was Detective Tom Brown, along with two other officers, all heavily armed with rifles and Tommy guns. Van Meter had previously helped to fund Brown's bid to become sheriff, as like today's politicians, most were, unfortunately, for sale to the highest bidder. However, Brown had been unsuccessful. By this time, Brown had been demoted and was under investigation for corruption and allegations that he had been an willing accomplice to the Barker-Karpis gang kidnappings.

Van Meter ignored a command to stop and fled into a nearby alley, where he fired twice on the officers with a pistol. Chief of Police Frank Cullen, armed with a rifle, to his credit, held his fire as a bystander walked into the line of fire, but the remaining officers opened fire on Van Meter, who fell, mortally wounded. However, as he lay on the ground breathing heavily, Brown continued to fire at Van Meter; the impact of the bullets ripping off some fingers on his right hand. One person who witnessed it said that Van Meter was simply used for target practice as he was prone on the ground.

Van Meter's girlfriend said that he was carrying over $10,000 on him when he left their apartment. A little more than one thousand dollars was found on him.

There are number of theories about who betrayed Van Meter to the authorities, some even suggesting that it was Baby Face Nelson, who detested Van Meter. However, the truth is that the betrayer's identity is not really important. What is important is that which was alluded to previously, the dominos were falling one by one, and next on the list was the biggest domino of all – John Dillinger.

CHAPTER 11

EVEN UP THE SCORE

You can only wallow in misery so long.
Poverty is the trigger of crime.
Damn U.S. government and corporations,
Tell ghetto youth their lives ain't worth a dime.

Tell you what mister, I got some news.
Man named John Dillinger was full of anger,
And he roared through the Midwest long ago,
Telling the government, "here comes danger."

He was one man who really knew the score.
Keep messing around catering to the rich,
And mark my words you politicians
People like Dillinger will make your life a bitch.

J. Wayne Frye   225

BAD MOON RISING: AMERICAN OUTLAWS OF THE ROARING 1920'S AND 1930'S

He told a man, "I rob banks for a living,

What do you do?"

Keep it up America with injustice, and you'll make more

Dillinger's who'll give you your due!

(Wayne Frye – Vancouver Poetry Slam © 2004)

John Herbert Dillinger (1903 -1934) was accused of robbing 24 banks and four police stations in a frenzy of violence that has seldom been matched. In the heyday of the gangster era, when the breaking down of the capitalist system that is designed to allow money to always flow to those at the top, pushed more people into desperation that at any time in U.S. history, Dillinger was the most notorious of all gangsters who simply decided that a corrupt system with no heart could only be matched by equally heartless people who would go to the source of most of the misery, the banks. He loved publicity and the media exaggerated accounts of his bravado and colourful personality, styling him as a Robin Hood figure, which moved a government that could not allow any challenge to the economic order to go after him with a vengeance. Ironically, it was the success of Dillinger and other outlaws that led to the founding of the FBI, led by a criminal in his own right, J. Edgar Hoover, who used Nazi-like methods for nearly 50 years to maintain his position of power and squash descent by the American people through intimidation and fear.

I am amazed at how many of my generation actually believe that the beatings they received from their parents were character builders. How do you build character through a beating? I am proud to say I had parents who did not believe that spanking was the way to teach the difference between good and bad. I received no spankings from my father, and only one from my mother that is indelibly burned into my mind even at my advanced age. She told me she would take me to the movie, if I did not ask for any concessions, and this was back when a box of popcorn was five cents, but stubborn me, I asked for a popcorn when we went in, and when we got home, my mother popped me on the butt about three times, saying, "I told you not to ask for anything to eat." When I became a parent who, by the way, never spanked his kids, I always told my children when I took them to the movies, "Ask for any concessions and we will never go to the movies again." So, certainly my one little spanking (no, it did not even hurt) had a lasting effect. In fact, my oldest son once told my mother, "Grandmother, you know what? You are the reason we can never get anything to eat when we go to the movies."

Not long before her death, my mother said to me, "Wayne I regret a lot of things, but you know when I told you not ask for anything to eat at the movies and you did, I really should never have slapped your butt that night when I got you home." With tears in my eyes, I hugged her and said, "Mother, I have done much worse as a father. You have nothing to be ashamed of."

What is the point of this personal tale? Simply that John Dillinger's father was actually a physical abuser of his son, who said to the media once, "I can't understand how he turned out like he did, because I always believed you spared the rod that you spoiled the child, and I never once spared the rod. I had too often beat that boy into submission?"

Were the beatings justification for John's criminality? I am not a psychologist, but I do believe childhood traumas can make us lean one way or the other in the grand scheme of things. We are all the sum total of our life experiences, and John's childhood was one of marginal poverty and marginal parenting. Also, Dillinger's mother died when he was four, and by all accounts she was a doting mother who lavished attention on her son.

Dillinger's sister, Audrey, was 14 years older than he was and she cared for her brother for several years until their father remarried. It has been reported that Dillinger initially disliked his stepmother, but he eventually came to fall in love with her. Yes, I mean romantic love and the two actually began a romantic relationship that lasted 3 years.

As a teenager, Dillinger was constantly in trouble with the law for fighting and petty theft. He exhibited what was called by his teachers, bewildering behaviour and would bully smaller children. He quit school in the 8th grade to work in an Indianapolis, Indiana machine shop. Although he worked hard at his job, he would be out late most nights partying.

His father feared that the city was corrupting his son, prompting him to move the family to the small town of Mooresville,

Indiana, in 1921 just when John turned 18. Dillinger's wild and rebellious behaviour was unchanged, despite his new rural life. In 1922, he was arrested for auto theft, and his relationship with his father deteriorated more, as even though he was 19 then, the physical abuse continued, as apparently John would not hit back, when his father utilized violence.

His troubles led him to enlist in the United States Navy, where he was a fireman assigned aboard the battleship USS Utah, but he deserted when his ship was docked in Boston. He received a dishonourable discharge and said, "The damn Navy is worse than my dad with all its rules and regulations. Never been so glad to be free in all my life."

Dillinger then returned to Mooresville, where he met Beryl Ethel Hovious. The two were married on 12 April 1924. He attempted to settle down, but he had difficulty holding a job and his marriage was tumultuous.

Finally giving up on finding a job, he began planning a robbery with his friend Edward Singleton. The two robbed a local grocery store, stealing $50. While leaving the scene, they were recognized by a man who reported them to the police. The two were arrested the next day. Singleton pleaded not guilty, but after Dillinger's father (the local Mooresville Church deacon) discussed the matter with the prosecutor, his father convinced Dillinger to confess to the crime and plead guilty without retaining a defence attorney, insisting to his son that Jesus would be by his side through it all. Dillinger was convicted of assault and battery with intent to rob, and conspiracy to commit a felony. He expected a lenient probation sentence as a result of his father's discussion with the prosecutor, but instead was sentenced from 10 to 20 years in prison for his crimes. Meanwhile, Singleton, who pleaded not guilty and had an attorney, was given a two year sentence. As John was being led away in handcuffs, he stared at his dad and said, "Where's Jesus?"

While in prison from 1924 to 1933, Dillinger became more and more embittered and embraced the criminal lifestyle. Upon being admitted to the prison, he looked at a guard and said, "You got your hands full. I will be the meanest bastard you ever saw when I get out of here." His physical examination upon being admitted to the prison showed that he had gonorrhoea. The treatment for his condition was extremely painful, and the medical staff seemed to take delight in seeing him suffer. The guards were also brutal, using their night sticks often to hit him in the testicles and back of the thighs. He became embittered against a society that would allow such brutality. Also, his long prison sentence when he assumed pleading guilty would lead to mercy, made his anger at the law grow into a near mania. While in prison, he befriended other hardened, seasoned criminals like Harry Pierpont, Charles Makley, Russell Clark, and Homer Van Meter, who taught him how to be a successful criminal. The men planned heists that they would commit soon after they were released. In fact, it became a mental exercise to plan out elaborate robberies almost nightly. Dillinger was a devoted student of inmate Herman Lamm's fine-tuned, meticulous bank-robbing system and used it extensively throughout his bank-robbing career.

His father, with remorse over asking him to trust in Jesus and plead guilty, launched a campaign to have him released and was able to get 188 signatures on a petition. Dillinger was paroled on 10 May 1933, after serving nine and a half years of what should have been no more than a two year sentence, which would have led to parole in six months. Despite being released, his bitterness had grown to the point that he was about to unleash hell upon the banks and a society that he saw as corrupt and uncaring. Dillinger's stepmother became sick just before he was released from the prison, and died as he was making his way home to the first woman he had been romantically involved with, a woman who had genuinely shown him the love he so desperately needed. He was now even bitterer as he looked down at her and said, "They even kept me from holding her hand when she was dying. I'll get those bastards, every one of them."

Released at the height of the Great Depression, Dillinger had little prospect of finding employment. Anyway, if you were lucky enough to get a job, once an employer knew you were an ex-con, you were shown the door in a country that always makes you pay for your mistakes ad infinitum. Thus, he immediately returned to crime, this time with a wild, unrestrained vengeance.

On 21 June 1933, he robbed his first bank, taking $10,000 from the New Carlisle National Bank, in New Carlisle, Ohio. Even today, there seems to be a sense of pride that Dillinger picked this town for his first bank robbery, as it is mentioned in tourist guides. Although the bank building has been torn down, there is a commemorative marker on the street corner.

The bank building as it appeared in 1955.

On August 14, Dillinger robbed a bank in Bluffton, Ohio. Tracked by police from Dayton, Ohio, he was captured and later transferred to the Allen County Jail in Lima, Ohio to be indicted in connection with the Bluffton robbery. After searching him, the police discovered a document which appeared to be an escape plan. They demanded Dillinger tell them what the document meant, but he refused as it was a plan he had conceived to free Harry Pierpont and seven others he had met while in prison. Dillinger had friends smuggle guns into their cells, with which

J. Wayne Frye

they escaped, four days after Dillinger's capture. The group, known as "the First Dillinger Gang," included Harry Pierpont, Russell Clark, Charles Makley, Ed Shouse, Harry Copeland and John "Red" Hamilton. Pierpont, Clark, and Makley arrived in Lima on October 12, where they impersonated Indiana State Police officers in uniforms they had stolen from a warehouse, claiming they had come to extradite Dillinger to Indiana. When the sheriff, Jess Sarber, asked for their credentials, Pierpont shot Sarber between the eyes, then released Dillinger from his cell. The four men escaped back to Indiana, where they joined the rest of the gang.

Dillinger is known to have participated in twelve separate bank robberies, between 21 June 1933 and 30 June 1934. Yes, you read that correctly. He actually robbed two banks some days.

Without love there is no life. Love is the glue that binds two people in the euphoria of affection, and that goes for the non-criminal and criminal alike. Dillinger was not given to sentimentality, but in the presence of a woman named "Billie," his hardened persona subsided into an interior of peace and harmony.

Mary Evelyn "Billie" Frechette (1907 -1969) was an American Métis (a person of mixed American Indian and Euro-American ancestry) singer, waitress and eventual convict and lecturer who spent what she said was the most exciting, love filled six months of her life with John Dillinger.

BAD MOON RISING: AMERICAN OUTLAWS
OF THE ROARING 1920'S AND 1930'S

She was born in Neopit, Wisconsin at the Menominee Indian Reservation. Her mother was French and Native America and her father French, which may have accounted for the perfect blend to make her so beautiful.

Billie Frechette with John Dillinger (1934)

Billie in 1933 before she met Dillinger.

BAD MOON RISING: AMERICAN OUTLAWS
OF THE ROARING 1920'S AND 1930'S

John Dillinger and Billie Frechette

Photos taken at Lake Michigan Boardwalk photo booth (1934)

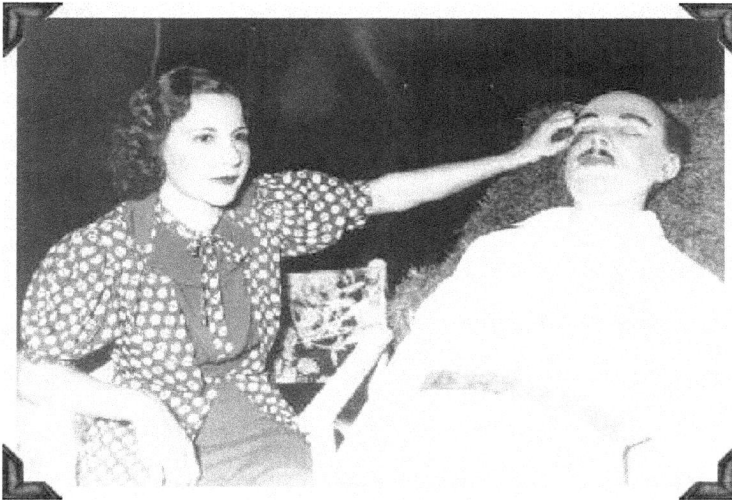

After she was released from prison in 1936, Billie, along with members of the Dillinger family, including his deeply religious father, had no trouble, in the great American way, embracing greed. Using his fame, they made a pile of money touring the country with a show called "Crime Did Not Pay," where Billie, above, does a soliloquy with an actor posing as the dead body of her beloved. The tour lasted for five years.

J. Wayne Frye

BAD MOON RISING: AMERICAN OUTLAWS
OF THE ROARING 1920'S AND 1930'S

Billie met John when she was singing in the Olympic Lounge on the bottom floor of the Clark Apartments. She knew who he was, and took an instant liking to a man she called, "extremely polite and well-mannered – a real gentleman."

Clark Apartments where Billie was singing
in the Olympic Lounge

Billie was actually married to a man named Wally Sparks at the time, but he was in Leavenworth, serving a term for robbery, so she apparently was attracted to the type man who played on the wild side. She had never been in trouble herself, and was a woman known for her immense kindness, as she had moved to Chicago from the Indian Reservation to care for her sick half-sister, but stayed on after she recovered. After touring the country for five years with the play, Frechette returned to the Menominee Reservation, where she had two subsequent marriages. She died of cancer on January 13, 1969, at age 61 in Shawano, Wisconsin. It was rumoured that on her deathbed, she whispered to her cousin, "I'll get to be with Johnny now."

BAD MOON RISING: AMERICAN OUTLAWS
OF THE ROARING 1920'S AND 1930'S

Dillinger, of course, never let love interfere with his profession, robbing banks. He, as the saying goes, "loved his work." He robbed a bank on 15 January 1934 in East Chicago, Indiana, but his luck had temporarily run out as he was captured and imprisoned in what was known as an escape-proof jail, Crown Point Lockup. However, just to make sure that a notorious criminal like Dillinger, whose gang might try to break him out, would not escape, the governor of Indiana called out the National Guard and no less than 20,000 armed men surrounded the jail.

So famous had Dillinger become that the county sheriff, the only female sheriff in the USA, Lillian Holly, posed with Dillinger alongside the county prosecutor, Robert Estill. Talk about stupid! The photo would come back to haunt them.

BAD MOON RISING: AMERICAN OUTLAWS
OF THE ROARING 1920'S AND 1930'S

What really happened is still clouded in mystery even today. In fact, for years, people jokingly referred to Crown Point as CLOWN POINT, based upon the total incompetence of everyone in and around the jail. So humorous was the whole affair that the post office actually delivered mail addressed merely to the CLOWN POINT JAIL.

John Dillinger taught the people at the so-called escape-proof Crown Point Jail a valuable lesson, because they underestimated his brilliance. After planning the escape carefully, he took his time and waited for the right moment. When he was ready, Dillinger remained calm and he made the escape look like child's play. Dillinger used psychology to bluff the guards; he put the image of a real gun into their minds and let them know he meant business. Anyone of those guards could have stopped Dillinger at anytime during the break, but he kept his cool and let them know he was escaping at all costs. Armed with only a piece of wood, and his wits, he fooled the guards. This escape would blast Dillinger to stardom, a super criminal for all times.

It began when Dillinger and fourteen other prisoners were placed in the exercise yard. Sam Cahoon broke Crown Point rules by entering the exercise area when prisoners were present. He was bringing in soap and other supplies for Saturday night baths. At 9:15 A.M., Dillinger struck what appeared to be an automatic pistol in Cahoon's side and ordered him into the cell, stating, "Get in quick or I'll kill you." Then he captured and forced two jail porters into the cell. Dillinger looked down the corridor and saw Ernest Blunk, the fingerprint expert. He commanded Cahoon to call Blunk from the foot of the stairs. Blunk responded, and was easily captured. Cahoon was then locked in the cell with his fellow companions as bait to lure in other guards. One by one Crown Point officials were bluffed into captivity, driven by fear of being shot or perhaps killed.

Dillinger's plan worked like a charm. He had successfully immobilized the entire security of Crown Point armed with a piece of wood and his wits. Dillinger had succeeded in locking up ten guards and a few trustees and took the only master set of keys to the jail with him. To add to Sheriff Holley's embarrassment, Dillinger stole her own personal police car for his escape.

John Dillinger, prisoner Herbert Youngblood, and Earnest Blunk headed for the Main Street Garage. The trio walked behind the Criminal Courthouse building and into the garage. Edwin Saager, a mechanic was busy working on a car when Dillinger came in, and didn't even notice his presence. Leaning on the car, talking to Saager was Robert Volk. He didn't notice anything out of the ordinary either. Dillinger walked up with a machine gun in his hands and asked Saager, "Which is the fastest car?" Saager thought Dillinger was a deputy, so he pointed to Sheriff Holley's black V-8. Dillinger then requested that Saager join the party, but he declined because he was too busy. Dillinger pointed his machine gun and forced Saager into the back seat with

Youngblood. Dillinger and Blunk climbed into the front. Blunk was ordered to drive. As the car pulled out of the garage onto Main Street, Blunk claimed he tried to sideswipe another car to attract attention, and then he ran a red signal light. Dillinger warned Blunk that if he tried that again he would be shot. He advised Blunk to drive the speed limit. He said; "Thirty miles an hour is enough, there's no hurry!" As they passed by the First National and Commercial Bank, Dillinger made a remark that he was tempted to rob the bank, but he had better wait. Blunk noticed how cool and calm Dillinger remained during the entire trip. He told Blunk he wished he could have said goodbye to Sheriff Lillian Holley before he left. Dillinger had Blunk turn at every corner and stick to gravel roads. Blunk remembered that they only passed through one town during the drive, and that was the town of St. John, which was on route 41. As they approached the town, Dillinger told Blunk to stop the car; he jumped out and broke the police spotlight off the side of the vehicle, because every cop in the country would be looking for the car.

Dillinger released Saager and Blunk in a remote area without telephones. He gave them four dollars for carfare, and apologized that he could not give them more, but it was all he could spare. He told them that he would send them something at Christmas. Saager and Blunk were later picked up by farmers passing by. When the two returned to Crown Point, reporters quickly surrounded them for a story. Both Blunk and Saager stated as

Dillinger dashed for freedom, he was singing, "Get Along Little Doggie" and "The Last Roundup." They remarked that he seemed as calm as if he were out for a Sunday afternoon drive with family.

In an interview with reporters, Ed Saager was asked, "Did you see the toy gun at all in the car?" Saager replied, "I just got a glimpse of it, yes. It was made out of wood alright."

Crown Point officials were busy trying to clean up the mess that Dillinger left behind. Everyone at Crown Point was blaming each other for the break. Dillinger had locked up the whole jailhouse before he departed, taking the master set of keys with him. The keys turned out to be the only master set to the jail. Officials had to break their own men out of the jail with welding torches. Sheriff Lillian Holley was sitting on the steps crying, and nobody was guarding prisoners.

The press took a picture of Holley on the stairs and printed the photograph with headlines, which stated, "Sheriff Lillian Holley, the woman he left behind." Holley was so angry that she publicly stated if she could see Dillinger; she would kill him herself.

After Dillinger's famous escape, officials had found an old washboard under the bed of his cell. This was a prop left to stage a scene, and to convince officials that he whittled the wooden gun from the missing top brace of the washboard. This event was staged by Dillinger to protect those who aided his escape and false rumours began that he carved the gun out of wood.

BAD MOON RISING: AMERICAN OUTLAWS
OF THE ROARING 1920'S AND 1930'S

Crown Point made another grave mistake by broadcasting the incorrect license plate number of Sheriff Lillian Holley's car that Dillinger stole. The failure to produce the correct license number was an important factor in Dillinger's escape. This license number belonged to A.C. Mayes of Crown Point. This was a serious error of judgment; Crown Point had placed A.C. Mayes, and any passengers who might be riding in his car in grave danger. News also came out that Sam Cahoon, the turnkey who let Dillinger out, had served two sentences in Crown Point for intoxication, and was not even a guard, but a relative of a guard. Governor Paul V. McNutt called the break inexcusable, and ordered a full-scale investigation. Prosecutor Robert Estill began a full investigation; the results of the inquiry were turned over to the Grand Jury. His duties would diminish considerably as time passed, and he had the good sense to eventually resign. Fingerprint Expert Ernest Blunk was placed on suspension and charged with a felony for aiding Dillinger in his escape, but in fact, there was no proof to substantiate the charges, so he was later exonerated. However, a couple of weeks after Dillinger bluffed his way out of the escape proof jail; Earnest Blunk took a mysterious trip. Upon his return, he told reporters that he went to Indianapolis where he was questioned by Deputy Attorney General Edward Barce, and three state investigators, but state, county and city officials insisted they were unaware of his presence in the State Capital. Many sources believe Blunk met

J. Wayne Frye

with a Dillinger associate and made arrangements to collect money as a payoff for his part in the escape. Relatives of Blunk maintained, after his death, that he was indeed bribed by Dillinger.

There is no solid evidence that a real gun was smuggled into the Crown Point Jail and given to Dillinger and no such gun has ever surfaced, but the wooden gun did show up and is at the Hammond Indiana Museum near the Chicago and Indiana border. During his escape, Police Officer Marshall Keith Leg hesitated for a split second, and began reaching for a nearby black jack. Dillinger warned him by stating, "I don't want to kill you, but one way or another, I'm getting out of here." Believing that Dillinger meant business, Keith Leg reluctantly surrendered. Dillinger also disarmed Warden Hiles, a national guardsman of his .45 automatic pistols.

Dillinger had succeeded in capturing all these men with a piece of wood, but then got his hand on real guns. Still, the mystery remains as to how he actually made the gun out of wood, as there was never any knife found that could have been used in the carving. Of course, that is no proof one did not exist. There was a dismantled wooden wash tub with many pieces of wood missing, so it is likely that would have been where the wood came from. Then, there is the shoe polish which was used to die the wood black. No polish was ever found either, but an analysis of the wood in 1956 confirmed that it was painted with shoe polish.

Not only newspapers in the USA carried the story, but it was front page news all over the world, and as it is today, people worldwide laughed at the inaptitude of America's leaders.

J. Wayne Frye

BAD MOON RISING: AMERICAN OUTLAWS
OF THE ROARING 1920'S AND 1930'S

Dillinger was indicted by a local grand jury, and the Bureau of Investigation (FBI) organized an intensive nationwide manhunt for him. Following the escape from Crown Point, Dillinger reunited with his girlfriend, Billie Frechette, just hours later at her half-sister Patsy's Chicago apartment, where she was staying. According to Billie's trial testimony, Dillinger stayed with her there for almost two weeks, but the two actually had traveled to the St. Paul, Minnesota and moved into the Santa Monica Apartments in nearby Minneapolis as Mr. and Mrs. Carl T. Hellman, and met up with Hamilton (who had been recovering for the past month from his gunshot wounds in the East Chicago robbery), and mustered a new gang, and the two joined Baby Face Nelson, Homer Van Meter, Tommy Carroll and Eddie Green to go on a robbing spree, as within a week after his escape, they robbed a bank in Sioux Falls, South Dakota. A week later they robbed the First National Bank in Mason City, Iowa.

Daisy Coffey, the landlord/owner of the apartments, would testify at Frechette's trial that she spent most evenings during the Hellmans' stay furnishing apartment 310, which enabled her to observe what was happening in apartment 303 (Dillinger's apartment) directly across the courtyard. On March 30, Coffey went to the FBI's St. Paul field office to file a report, including information about the couple's new Hudson sedan parked in the garage behind the apartments. The building was placed under surveillance by two agents, Rufus Coulter and Rusty Nalls, that night, but they saw nothing unusual, mainly due to the blinds being drawn.

The next morning at approximately 10:15 A.M., Nalls circled around the block looking for the Hudson, but observed nothing. He parked, first on the north side of the apartments, then on the west side, at the northwest corner of Lexington and Lincoln Avenues, and remained in his car while watching Coulter and St. Paul Police detective Henry Cummings, pull up, park, and enter the building. Ten minutes later, by Nalls' estimate, Van Meter parked a green Ford coupe on the north side of the apartment building.

Meanwhile, Coulter and Cummings knocked on the door of apartment 303. Frechette answered, opening the door only a small way. She said she was not dressed and to come back. Coulter told her they would wait. After waiting two to three minutes, Coulter went to the basement apartment of the caretakers, Louis and Margaret Meidlinger, and asked to use the phone to call the bureau. He quickly returned to Cummings, and the two of them waited for Frechette to open the door. Van Meter then appeared in the hall and asked Coulter if his name was Johnson. Coulter said it was not, and as Van Meter passed on to the landing of the third floor, Coulter asked him for a name. Van Meter replied, "I am a soap salesman." Asked where his samples were, Van Meter said they were in his car. Coulter asked if he had any credentials. Van Meter said "no," and continued down the stairs. Coulter waited 10 to 20 seconds and then followed Van Meter. As Coulter got to the lobby on the ground floor, Van Meter opened fire on him. Coulter hastily fled outside, chased by Van Meter. Eventually, Van Meter ran back into the front entrance.

Recognizing Van Meter, Nalls pointed out the Ford to Coulter and told him to disable it. Coulter shot out the rear left tire. While Coulter stayed with Van Meter's Ford, Nalls went to the corner drugstore and called first the local police, then the bureau's St. Paul office, but could not get through because both lines were busy. Van Meter, meanwhile, escaped by hopping on a passing coal truck.

Frechette, in her later trial testimony, said that she told Dillinger that the police had showed up after speaking to Cummings. Upon hearing Van Meter firing at Coulter, Dillinger opened fire through the door with a Thompson submachine gun, sending Cummings scrambling for cover. Dillinger then stepped out and fired another burst at Cummings. Cummings shot back with a revolver, but quickly ran out of ammunition. He hit Dillinger in the left calf with one of his five shots. He then hastily retreated down the stairs to the front entrance. Once Cummings retreated, Dillinger and Frechette hurried down the stairs, exited through the back door and drove away in the Hudson.

The couple drove to the apartment of Eddie Green at 3300 South Fremont in Minneapolis. Green called his friend, Dr.

Clayton E. May, at his office in Minneapolis. With Green, his wife Beth, and Frechette following in Green's car, Dr. May drove Dillinger to 1835 Park Avenue, Minneapolis, to the apartment of Augusta Salt, who had been providing nursing services and a bed for May's illicit patients for several years, patients he could not risk seeing at his regular office. May treated Dillinger's wound with antiseptics. Eddie Green visited Dillinger on Monday, April 2, just hours before Green would be mortally wounded by the FBI in St. Paul. Dillinger convalesced at Dr. May's place for five days.

After leaving Minneapolis, Dillinger and Billie traveled to Mooresville, Indiana to visit Dillinger's father. Dillinger spent time contacting several family members, including his half-brother Hubert Dillinger. On April 6, Hubert and Dillinger left Mooresville at about 8:00 P.M. and proceeded to Leipsic, Ohio to see Joseph and Lena Pierpont, Harry's parents. The Pierpont's were not home, so the two headed back to Mooresville around midnight.

On April 7 at approximately 3:30 A.M., they rammed a car driven by Mr. and Mrs. Joseph Manning near Noblesville, Indiana, after Hubert fell asleep behind the wheel. They crashed through a farm fence and tore a path through a corn field about 200 feet into the thick woods of the field. Both men made it back to the Mooresville farm. Swarms of police showed up at the accident scene within hours. Found in the car were maps, a machine gun magazine, a length of rope, and a bullwhip. According to Hubert, his brother planned to pay a visit with the bullwhip to his former one-armed shyster lawyer at Crown Point, Joseph Ryan, who had run off with a retainer after Dillinger fired him.

At about 10:30 A.M.. on April 7, Billie, Hubert and Hubert's wife purchased a black four-door Ford V8, registering it in the name of Mrs. Fred Penfield (Billie Frechette). At 2:30 P.M., Billie and Hubert picked up the V8 and returned to Mooresville.

Now, I realize this seems very detailed and somewhat trite, but the intent is to illustrate the chain of events that would lead to eventual catastrophe, and to show just how these bandits seemed almost mellow in their outlook on life, as if they were seemingly living a normal family type existence in the midst of all this turmoil.

On Sunday, April 8, the Dillinger's enjoyed a leisurely family picnic at the Dillinger family farm while the FBI had the area under surveillance. Oddly, they knew they were being watched, and seemed unconcerned, as they had a small arsenal of weapons nearby, including a box of concussion grenades and an M-2 fifty calibre machine gun that they had stolen from a National Guard Armoury. There were many children about, and John knew the FBI would not risk another incident that would reflect unfavourably on them. The calm, cool demeanour of these outlaws defies convention, as most people would have been frightened so badly that they would have acted irrationally and started trying to escape or grab the arsenal and unleash hell. However, John was playing baseball with the kids, enjoyed a sack race and actively passed out hot dogs and hamburgers.

Later in the afternoon, the group of revellers left in separate cars. Billie drove the new Ford V8, with two of Dillinger's nieces, Mary Hancock in the front seat and Alberta Hancock in the back. Dillinger was on the floor of the car. He was later seen, but not recognized, by two agents. Eventually, Billie dropped off the nieces at their homes. John sat up beside her and placed a machine gun on the passenger side of the car as Billie sped off so fast that the two agents trailing her were startled and when the driver floored the accelerator, the car stalled. Billie and John laughed as they hit the highway at maximum speed, and headed for Chicago. Once again, law enforcement had been made fools of by the devil-may-care attitude of John Dillinger.

The following afternoon, Monday, April 9, Dillinger had an appointment at a tavern at 416 North State Street with someone to talk over a planned bank robbery. Sensing trouble, Billie told John to lie low and she would park the car one block over and go in to see if it was clear for John to enter.

As she went in, John was across the street with his fedora hat pulled low, walking by when he glanced to his left and watched Billie being grabbed and arrested by two FBI agents. John scurried back to the car and sped off. Of course, Billie, loyal to a fault, refused to reveal Dillinger's whereabouts. The two would never see each other again.

Dillinger became despondent after Billie was arrested. The other gang members talked him out of rescuing her. Still, Van Meter knew where they could find bullet-proof vests. Late the next night, Dillinger and Van Meter took Warsaw, Indiana police officer Judd Pittenger hostage. They marched him at gunpoint to the police station, where they stole several guns and bullet-proof vests, then went to Michigan to hide out.

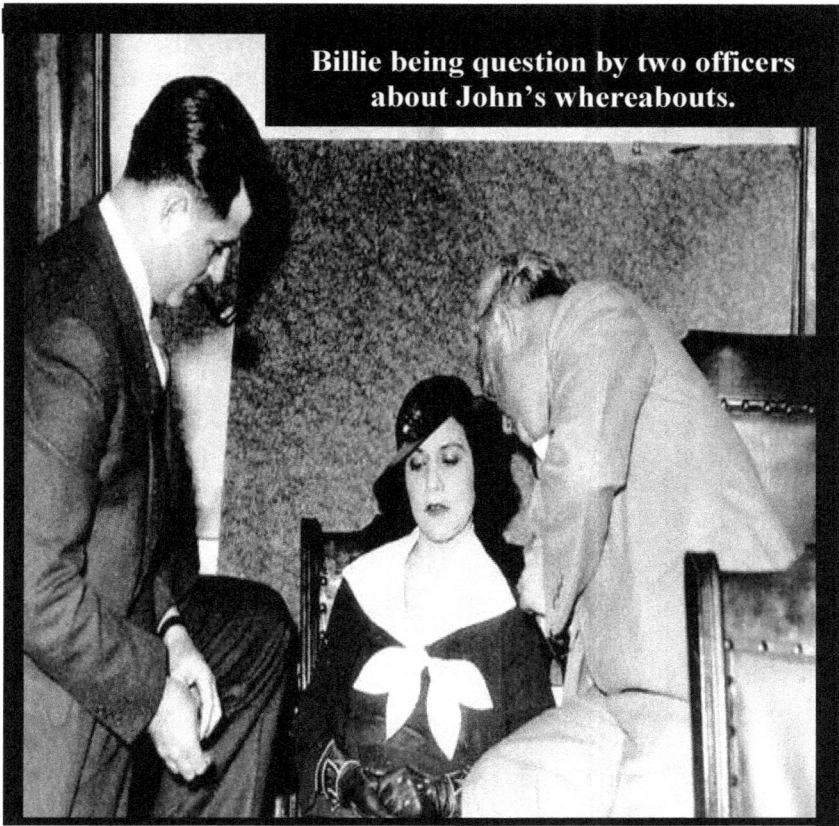

Billie being question by two officers about John's whereabouts.

BAD MOON RISING: AMERICAN OUTLAWS
OF THE ROARING 1920'S AND 1930'S

While in hiding, John kept formulating plans to break Billie out of custody, but the FBI very wisely never let it slip out where she was being held. This led to great frustration on John's part, as he felt powerless to help the woman he desperately loved. Meanwhile, Billie held up under intense FBI questioning, refusing to give any information on John's whereabouts.

John Dillinger is rumoured to have had a dream as he lay in bed one night, contemplating his loss of Billie and how he might somehow facilitate her return. We all have dreams, sometimes nightmares that plague us keep recurring, almost as a sinister premonition is boring into out psyches and reminding us that we are all vulnerable – all at the mercy of fate that will either intervene for good or bad. In his dream, he saw something usual that he could not get off his mind – the feet of ghost-like figures.

The dream consisted of two oblong oval black forms. There were just feet visible and on the ground was a huge spot. The dream was in black and white and it was obviously night-time. He only dreamed it once, but once was enough.

J. Wayne Frye

BAD MOON RISING: AMERICAN OUTLAWS
OF THE ROARING 1920'S AND 1930'S

There is a time at which most of us can reflect back on and realize that was the time everything changed for us. There are certain times that are indelibly branded into our minds, and nothing will make us forget that there was that one time when all the stars in heaven were precisely aligned to deliver us into our fates. For Jesse and Frank James, along with their partners the Younger Brothers and the Millers, the Great Northfield Minnesota Raid that ended in disaster and decimated the gang was the turning point that signalled their end. Go to Northfield, Minnesota today, almost 150 years later, and the townspeople still talk of that day in 1876 when the greatest bank robbery in history signalled the end of Jesse James. I have walked the streets of Northfield, and despite its modernity, the hustle and bustle of cars and pedestrians scurrying about, near the spot where history's most famous robbery took place, you can feel a silence among all the noise, a hush that seems to whirl about and engulf you in another time when all hell broke lose on Division Street. I felt a chill as I trod where Jesse and his gang were met by an aroused townspeople who, for some crazy reason, decided to defend a bank against criminals. In my opinion, they may have picked the wrong criminal to defend, as banks are about as criminal as any robber who ever lived, but history is history and it firmly states that day the people delivered a death blow to the James gang. The same can be said of what happened in South Bend, Indiana on the 30th of June 1934.

J. Wayne Frye

BAD MOON RISING: AMERICAN OUTLAWS
OF THE ROARING 1920'S AND 1930'S

Just like Northfield, I have strolled down the streets of South Bend. The first time I was there I was at Indiana State University and went home with my dear roommate, Brent W. Trump, to visit his parents. I had seen many movies about John Dillinger, but did not know as much about him as I thought I did. As we strolled by a bank building, Brent pointed out a series of bullet holes in the limestone and said, "This is where John Dillinger pulled off his most famous robbery."

Indeed, it is, alongside the Great Northfield, Minnesota Bank Robbery, either the first or second most famous bank robbery in U.S. history. What follows is an account that is as accurate as possible, having been culled from multiple sources. I shall let it unfold in all its glory, because this is more than a story of Dillinger. It is a story about how certain people, good or bad, leave their marks in the annals of time, while most of us simply meekly pass our way humbly through this thing called life. Che Guevara was the world's greatest revolutionary who, badly wounded, sat on the edge of a bed in a small Bolivian village, and as his executioner stood before him with a gun in his hand, shaking with fear, said, "I know you have come to kill me. Shoot coward. You are only killing a man. You cannot kill an idea."

John Dillinger was not only Public Enemy Number 1; he had become a hero for those who felt marginalized in a nation that had let greed destroy hope. While others had bowed before the brutal heartlessness of banks, Dillinger had exacted revenge.

J. Wayne Frye

Dillinger, despondent over Billie Frechette's arrest, sought to relieve his pain the best way he knew how, by robbing a bank. He contacted Homer Van Meter and Baby Face Nelson, and thus, set in motion what would be the gang's Waterloo. They headed toward South Bend, Indiana with supreme confidence, firm in the knowledge that the sleepy little Indiana town had a bank that would be an easy hit. Like the Northfield Minnesota Bank Robbery by the James gang, this would be the Dillinger gang's last hooray.

In early June, Dillinger assembled Homer Van Meter and Baby Face Nelson to discuss what he said would be his last robbery. He was sullen and morose, still desperately missing Billie. Because of the intense manhunt for the gang, finding someone willing to work with them would be difficult, but Nelson said John Paul Chase, Jack Perkins, and then he paused for a long time as Dillinger and Van Meter stared with interest at what other name was on his lips. Then, Nelson blurted it out – "Pretty Boy Floyd."

Floyd was acquainted with Dillinger and Van Meter, but had never worked with them before. Dillinger said, "Floyd, you can get Floyd?"

"Watch me," said Nelson.

They all had a good laugh, and the stage was set for what they assumed would be one of their easiest and most profitable bank robberies. They were mistaken.

BAD MOON RISING: AMERICAN OUTLAWS
OF THE ROARING 1920'S AND 1930'S

Saturday, June 30 was hot, with typical summer Indiana oppressive humidity and overhead was a bright blue cloudless sky. The streets were crowded with shoppers all strolling about near the corner of Wayne and Michigan Streets where the Merchants National Bank stood majestically, glistening in the nearly noonday sun. Across the street was the State Theatre, which was showing the film "Stolen Sweets." South Bend Police Officer, Howard Wagner was directing traffic on the busy street corner. Wagner had kindly taken another man's shift who was on vacation.

The town's assistant postmaster was waiting for Wagner to stop traffic, so he could cross the street and go into the bank to make a huge deposit from the post office. Betty Herbert, who worked in nearby store, was taking an early lunch break. She was also waiting to cross the street. Police detectives, Edward McCormick and Harry Henderson were sitting in their car just up the block, pretty unconcerned about things, but always a little cautious on Saturdays, because businesses made big deposits in the Merchants Bank all day long. They decided to drive up the street about 300 feet, make a right turn and go into Holly's Bar-b-Que for some pork sandwiches.

As they were ordering their sandwiches, a young man named Alex Slaby turned his car right off Michigan Street onto Wayne Street, pulled into a parking lot, got out of his car and was about to experience probably the greatest thrill of his life.

BAD MOON RISING: AMERICAN OUTLAWS
OF THE ROARING 1920'S AND 1930'S

A light brown Hudson Essex Terraplane automobile, the hallmark of luxury in motoring, pulled up beside him as he was getting out. Four serious looking men got out of the car, and Slaby thought he recognized one of them, but he could not place him. The one he recognized was wearing overalls and a straw hat, but had an open overcoat on. Why, he thought was a guy wearing an overcoat in the summertime?

He then noticed that the other men were carrying large pieces of cloth wrapped around something very long. As the men moved out of the parking lot, he noticed the stock of a gun under one of the pieces of cloth.

Slaby was fearful and perplexed. What should he do? If he hollered at the policeman directing traffic or blew his horn, he would alert the robbers and maybe get himself killed for the effort.

"Get the hell outta here," one of the men, who had turned back, shouted to Slaby. When Slaby seemed hesitant, the man said, "Scram!"

Slaby got in his car. He sat there and watched the guy who had talked to him join the other three men, and then he looked to his right and saw that the Hudson's engine was still running. He was suddenly startled when a short man got out and walked up to his passenger's side window, which was rolled down, peered in and said, "You got a problem, boy?"

"No sir," replied Slaby.

BAD MOON RISING: AMERICAN OUTLAWS
OF THE ROARING 1920'S AND 1930'S

Then, the short guy with the baby face said, "Get outta the car, and high tail it outta here, now,"

Slaby jumped out like a jack-rabbit and headed across the street. Baby Face Nelson had elected not to kill him, simply because the noise would have aroused the citizenry and caused pandemonium to break out, something they did not need at this time. Nelson's job was to watch the car and make sure it was ready after the robbery to whisk his comrades away.

The three others turned the corner. Van Meter peeled off and stationed himself against the wall next to the bank, ready to take care of anybody who came along during the robbery. The cloth was still on the Tommy gun, but his finger was on the trigger.

The other two met gang member, John Paul Chase at the front door, and bolted into the bank. "This is a hold-up," one of them shouted, and the two others cut loose with a burst of machine gun fire toward the ceiling. Panic erupted and the customers scurried to the back of the bank as Dillinger and Chase leaped behind the counters and starting bagging money, while Floyd, with a cigar in his mouth stood bold and defiant with his gun scanning all about left to right, right to left.

Outside, people's interest was piqued, but there was no panic, yet. It was more curiosity than anything else. Officer Wagner, more curious than concerned, stopped directing traffic and took quick, even-paced long strides toward the bank to investigate what was causing the noise that sounded like fire-crackers.

J. Wayne Frye

Traffic whistle still in his mouth, Wagner, no doubt, thought it odd that Van Meter was standing there holding a piece of cloth over some object. Just about the time it dawned on Wagner what was happening, before he could reach for his gun, Van Meter flipped the cloth off his Tommy gun and fired one quick burst, hitting Wagner in the chest. Wagner did not fall, but rather, looked down at the holes in his chest with an almost quizzical countenance on his face. Wagner was the standing dead. He staggered back and fell to the pavement.

That one split second when there is no noise, no movement, nothing but the realization that this is a surreal moment that will either kill you or give you a lifetime memory, descended upon all those present. Van Meter, like some great god of war stood there defiant and confident in the knowledge that the gun he held made him nearly invincible. It was the instrument that made him in total command of all he surveyed. Perhaps that confidence explains why an organization like the NRA fights to keep these death dealing guns in the hands of any maniac with the money to buy what was equated with manhood by so many. The vaunted Second Amendment to the Constitution, guaranteeing the right to bear arms was more important than any other right. It was more important than the safety of school children. It was more important than a battered wife. The sanctity of the right to wrap your hands around cold, death-dealing steel was the elixir of life to men of so little courage, only a gun made them whole.

BAD MOON RISING: AMERICAN OUTLAWS
OF THE ROARING 1920'S AND 1930'S

Total chaos was now afoot. Pedestrians frantically ran for cover. Cars slammed on breaks, screeching to a halt to avoid mowing down fleeing pedestrians. The sounds of sirens signalled that things were about to go south, to tumble into an abyss of mayhem.

Inside the bank, things were not much better, as the frightened customers were also in panic mode, shivering, screaming and crying with despair, as the dispassionate robbers seemed cold and callous enough to kill everyone there with no compunction or moral outrage over any indignity that might befall those before them, as these men were cold, calculating and determined to grasp in their hands that treasure of greed called money.

Baby Face Nelson now moved to the edge of the parking lot with his gun also spitting lead indiscriminately in all directions, joining Van Meter in the spaying of the street with firepower.

Jeweller, Harry Berg, observing the commotion from his store, realizing what was happening, reached under the counter and pulled out his hand gun as he watched Nelson standing with his machine gun spitting lead. Oblivious to the futility of the situation, he moved to the door and as Nelson slightly turned his back, he let lose with a shot that slammed into a passing car, then pulled the trigger again and hit Nelson in the back to no avail as he was wearing a bullet proof vest. Nelson was now furious at the audacity of Berg, and the bloodiest chapter in the South Bend book of experience was about to explode with a fury.

J. Wayne Frye

BAD MOON RISING: AMERICAN OUTLAWS
OF THE ROARING 1920'S AND 1930'S

Not sure of where the bullet came from, Nelson simply recklessly fired at every moving thing. He had no idea how many people were firing at him, so he just assumed everyone was.

Berg, the cause of Nelson's wild firing, ducked back into the store for safety, but the carnage Berg had foolishly unleashed to protect a bank's money, was now relentlessly unfolding in the streets of South Bend. One of Nelson's bullets hit an innocent bystander in the leg, and as he slumped over to grab the leg another bullet tore into his stomach. Across the street, store windows were being shattered by the random bullets tearing all about from Van Meter and Nelson. The concrete sidewalk was being shattered by bullets and slices of concrete were penetrating the skin and eyes of frenzied people scurrying about.

High school student, Joe Pawlowski, coming around the corner of Michigan and Wayne to see what all the commotion was about, was somehow missed by Nelson, who now had his back turned to him. Pawlowski, in typical teenage manner, seemed foolishly oblivious to danger. He, not realizing the bank was being robbed, assumed this was some madman on a rampage, standing there at the curb mowing town the town's citizens. He bolted toward Nelson who now had his back completely turned to Pawlowski. He leaped upon his back and began wailing away with fists of fury. Nelson was shocked and confused, and while trying to get the teenager off his back, never faltered in the firing of his gun.

BAD MOON RISING: AMERICAN OUTLAWS OF THE ROARING 1920'S AND 1930'S

Nelson was spinning about wildly, desperately trying to dislodge his assailant, while never letting up with the rat-a-tat cadence of what was music to his ears. He finally dislodged the kid, who stumbled against a store window. Nelson, fired with rage at him, but his anger spoiled his aim and all he did was shatter the window into thousands of shiny little pieces that flew about, some pieces piercing nearby people..

One bullet had passed through Pawlowski's hand, which was probably what saved him. He collapsed unconscious, falling into the display in the window, and Nelson assumed he was dead.

Patrolman Sylvester Zell and another officer, hearing the commotion, were running toward the firing as someone shouted out the open window of a room above the theatre, "Lookout guys. It's a hold-up." The two patrolmen ducked behind parked cars and tried making their way up the street.

While all this was unfolding, the four men inside the bank calmly walked out with three hostage bank employees. As all this mayhem was developing, McCormick and Henderson, the two detectives who just wanted a leisurely lunch were now racing toward their car, but the traffic was too jammed to get the car out. McCormick grabbed a shotgun and bolted toward the bank while Henderson picked up a rifle and was close behind. McCormick arrived just as the robbers were coming out of the bank with the hostages. He took a deep breath and figured from his angle, he had a clear shot at the robbers.

BAD MOON RISING: AMERICAN OUTLAWS
OF THE ROARING 1920'S AND 1930'S

Just as he was about to fire, he realized he had a shotgun and the pellets might hit the hostages. He lowered his gun and watched. Another officer was not as cautious; he fired at Dillinger but hit one of the hostages. However, the hostage was in front of Dillinger, and as he fell, Dillinger was now exposed. The officer fired again, and hit another hostage. Dillinger grabbed the falling hostage, pulling him toward the waiting Nelson in the car, motor revving loudly. The officer, apparently unconcerned about the hostages, in a valiant attempt to save the bank's precious money, fired again, hitting the hostage in the left side, but the bullet passed through him and nicked the side of one of the robbers. Dillinger shoved the hostage to the ground, and fired at him but missed in all the confusion.

All the officers were now moving toward the getaway car. It was like a shootout in the streets of old Dodge City, as all there with guns blazing seemed unconcerned about living or dying. All they wanted was to fire, fire, fire with maniacal mania at one another. The adrenalin was pumping fast and furious, and the amount of carnage unleashed made no difference to any of them. All that mattered was the fury of the moment.

The smell of smoke from all the firing penetrated the humid air and hung like a cloud there in the middle of the street. Bullets were flying about, striking any thing that moved, pounding into cars, shattering windows, bouncing off the sidewalk. This was more than a bank robbery. It was a testament to testosterone.

Dillinger helped the wounded Van Meter into the car, the right side of his head profusely bleeding. As Nelson raced the engine, he shouted to Dillinger, "Get in. Get in."

The car, riddled with bullets, roared out of the parking lot, leaving behind a carnage that would be the stuff of legends. Only two police cars managed to give chase due to all the confusion. Outside of town, they gave up the pursuit as their cars were no match for the swift moving Hudson Terraplane.

The robbers abandoned the car at the Illinois border and made their way back to Chicago. They got an underworld doctor for Van Meter, and his wound healed within a couple of weeks.

Back in South Bend, the town was taking stock of all the damage. Fortunately only one person was killed, but six others were wounded, all bystanders or hostages. The police were once again referred to as clowns. Despite all the firing, they had only hit one robber, but managed to wound several civilians. This was definitely not the South Bend Police Department's finest hour. However, in less than five months four of the five robbers would be dead, and the fifth in jail.

By July 1934, Dillinger had dropped completely out of sight, and the federal agents had no solid leads. He had, in fact, drifted into Chicago where he went under the alias of Jimmy Lawrence, a petty criminal from Wisconsin who bore a close resemblance to Dillinger. Working as a clerk, Dillinger found that, in a large metropolis like Chicago, he was able to lead an anonymous existence for a while. What he did not realize was that the centre of the federal agents' dragnet happened to be Chicago. When the authorities found Dillinger's blood-spattered getaway car from the Merchant's Bank robbery at the Illinois border, they were positive that he was in Chicago.

Dillinger and Van Meter, actually resided together in Chicago and both had plastic surgery to try and disguise themselves. However, Van Meter soured on Chicago and headed for St. Paul, Minnesota where he was killed by an alert policeman, but Dillinger, apparently over the incarceration of Billie Frechette, was enjoying new Chicago female companionship.

Rita "Polly" Hamilton was a former teenage runaway from Fargo, North Dakota. She met Ana Chiolak (alias: Ana Sage) in Gary, Indiana, and worked periodically as a prostitute in Ana's brothel. In the summer of 1934, twenty-six-year-old Hamilton was a waitress in Chicago at the S & S Sandwich Shop. She had remained friends with Sage and was sharing living space with Sage and her twenty-four-year-old son, Steve.

Dillinger and Hamilton, a Billie Frechette look-a-like, met in June 1934 at the Barrel of Fun night club. Dillinger introduced himself as Jimmy Lawrence and said he was a clerk at the Board of Trade. They started dating.

Meanwhile, as Dillinger was enjoying his liaisons with Polly, J. Edgar Hoover put together a special task force headquartered in Chicago to capture Dillinger. The end was coming for John.

BAD MOON RISING: AMERICAN OUTLAWS
OF THE ROARING 1920'S AND 1930'S

On July 21, Ana Sage contacted the FBI. She was a Romanian immigrant threatened with deportation for low moral character, as for some reason, the good old moral USA had a thing about whore houses, which, by the way, many of Hoover's men frequented. Sage had her suspicions that the man Polly was seeing was John Dillinger, and that he would be her ticket to stay in the USA. The FBI agreed that, if the guy was indeed Dillinger, she would be able to stay in the USA. To her ever lasting regret, she did not get it in writing.

She informed the FBI that she, Dillinger and Polly Hamilton would be going to see a movie together on the following day. She agreed to wear an orange dress, so that police could easily identify her. She was unsure which of two theatres they would be attending, the Biograph or the Marbro.

A team of federal agents felt that the Chicago police had been compromised and therefore could not be trusted. Hoover and Purvis also wanted all the credit for the apprehension, anyway. Not wanting to take the risk of another embarrassing escape by Dillinger, they split into two groups. On Sunday, one team was sent to the Marbro Theatre on the city's west side, while another team surrounded the Biograph Theatre at 2433 North Lincoln Avenue on the north side.

Sage, Hamilton and Dillinger were observed entering the Biograph at approximately 8:30 P.M., which was showing the crime film, *Manhattan Melodrama*, starring Clark Gable. When a

FBI agent, who was standing by the box office, signalled Melvin Purvis, who was across the street, that it was definitely Dillinger, the trap was set in motion. They would not risk a gun battle in the theatre, but wait until the three came outside.

Although no one ever admitted it, there was probably a feeling that it was better to kill Dillinger than take him alive. During the stakeout, the Biograph's manager thought the agents were criminals setting up a robbery. He called the Chicago police, who dutifully responded and had to be waved off by the federal agents, who told them that they were on a stakeout for an important target, but were careful not to tell them it was Dillinger, as the Chicago police, even as late as the 1960's and 1970's were notorious for being on the take.

When the film ended, Purvis stood by the front door and signalled Dillinger's exit by lighting a cigar. Both he and the other agents reported that Dillinger turned his head and looked directly at the agent as he walked by, glanced across the street, then moved ahead of his female companions, reached into his pocket but failed to extract his gun, and ran into a nearby alley. Other accounts stated Dillinger ignored a command to surrender, whipped out his gun, then headed for the alley. Agents already had the alley closed off, but Dillinger was determined to shoot it out.

Three men pursued Dillinger into the dark alley and fired. Clarence Hurt shot at him twice, Charles Winstead three times, and Herman Hollis once. Dillinger was hit from behind and fell face first to the ground. He was struck four times, with two bullets grazing him and one causing a superficial wound to the right side. The fatal bullet entered through the back of his neck, severed the spinal cord, passed into his brain and exited just under the right eye, severing two sets of veins and arteries. An ambulance was summoned, though it was soon apparent Dillinger had died from the gunshot wounds. According to investigators, Dillinger died without saying a word.

Typical of FBI recklessness, two female bystanders, Theresa Paulas and Etta Natalsky, were wounded by stray bullets. Dillinger bumped into Natalsky just as the shooting started, but the fact two women were near Dillinger did not deter the agents from gunning him down. Fortunately, neither woman was seriously injured. When they submitted their hospital bills to the FBI, they were turned away.

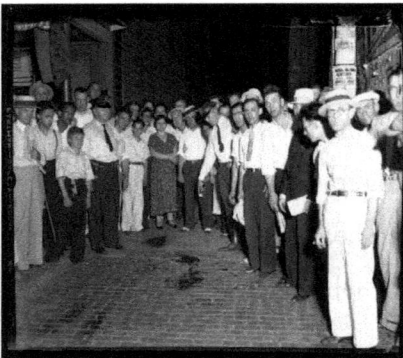

It was uncanny that the very image John Dillinger saw in his nightmare was almost identical to the photo taken by a Chicago Tribune photographer. The only difference was that faces were showing.

People swarmed into the alley, and when told it was Dillinger, some dipped their handkerchiefs and skirts in his blood for what would become treasured souvenirs. There were many photographers suddenly appearing out of nowhere, snapping pictures frantically. This was a monumental event that was the crowning glory in the FBI's pursuit of so many brazen criminals who had captured the public's attention with their bravado.

On my first visit to Chicago from the nearby Indiana university I was attending, I was accompanied by that proverbial older woman all young men dream of when we are at that certain age. She was familiar with Chicago, and assumed we would see all the exciting sites, but the attraction that was first on my list was the Biograph Theatre. With a woman every bit as beautiful as Polly and Ana, I strolled the alley, walked the street and surveyed the scene. I even went to the movies at the Biograph, because the theatre was still in business back then. This, to me, was experiencing history first hand.

Picture taken in 1934 only a few hours before Dillinger was killed.

BAD MOON RISING: AMERICAN OUTLAWS
OF THE ROARING 1920'S AND 1930'S

Today, the Biograph is on the National Registry of Historical
Places and is considered a Chicago landmark. It is run by the
Victory Gardens Organization which puts on plays.

Dillinger's body was available for public display at the Cook
County morgue. An estimated 15,000 people viewed the corpse
over a day and a half. As many as four death masks were also
made. On July 24, the body was returned to Mooresville, Indiana.
It was put on exhibition at intervals during the evening to satisfy
the curiosity of the crowd. The next day at 2 P.M., funeral
services were held at the home of Audrey Hancock, Dillinger's
sister. Thousands attended the burial itself.

He was laid to rest in Crown Hill Cemetery, but his father
noticed something strange when he would visit the grave. Small
pieces of the tombstone would be chipped off. Furthermore, he
and Billie Frechette were making a lot of money touring the
country with the show they had put together to capitalize on
John's fame. What would happen if someone stole John's body?

J. Wayne Frye

BAD MOON RISING: AMERICAN OUTLAWS
OF THE ROARING 1920'S AND 1930'S

The cemetery hired security guards to keep a 24-hour watch on his grave for fear of his gang coming back to take his body, or the public destroying the site. Dillinger's father had the cemetery dig up John's wooden casket and then had it reburied with 4 giant concrete slabs, each reinforced with metal at different depths.

The security details only lasted for awhile, and even today, people are sometimes warned not to chip pieces off his tombstone for souvenirs. The tombstone has had to be replaced four times.

Ana Sage and Polly Hamilton did not wait around the theatre, as they knew John was dead, so they both returned to their respective apartments. True to form, the FBI reneged on their promise to Ana Sage and she was deported back to Romania, where she lived out her life.

Polly Hamilton left Chicago for awhile after Dillinger's death, but returned a short while later and made Chicago her home. She married and lived there until her death in 1969.

John Dillinger was a hero to many, and to others he was nothing but a cold bloodied killer. The truth is he was both. The USA makes heroes out of people who bomb women and children from 80,000 feet, pinning medals on them, while saluting the flag and praying. Why shouldn't Dillinger be a hero then for some? He, as far as is known, never killed innocent woman and children. He was a product of his time, and he saw the banks as bad guys who stole every day from the poor, so he simply decided turn about was fair play to even up the score.

J. Wayne Frye   271

BAD MOON RISING: AMERICAN OUTLAWS
OF THE ROARING 1920'S AND 1930'S

Dillinger with his favourite Tommy gun and the infamous wooden gun used to break out of Crown Point Jail.

J. Wayne Frye

EPILOGUE

BAD MOON RISING

There is an old song about bad times coming
The singer is pleading while the guitar is strumming
You can feel the tension in the air
And you realize that life just ain't fair

You see a bad moon a-rising
You see trouble on the way
You see earthquakes and lightning
You see bad times today

Don't go 'round tonight
It's bound to take your life
There's a bad moon on the rise
As you hear hurricanes a-blowing

J. Wayne Frye   273

BAD MOON RISING: AMERICAN OUTLAWS
OF THE ROARING 1920'S AND 1930'S

You know the end is coming soon

You fear rivers over flowing

You hear the voice of rage and ruin

Don't go 'round tonight

It's bound to take your life

There's a bad moon on the rise

(Adapted by J. Wayne Frye from Bad Moon Rising

by Credence Clearwater Revival)

The USA is a nation that ballyhoos its freedom, but actually stifles decent at almost every turn. The truth is that those who dare exercise independent thought that might run counter to the established norm are branded miscreants who do not appreciate their freedom.

From the Pilgrims who put non-conformists in stocks to Donald Trump's labelling of protestors as un-American, the USA has always been a nation that lives the lie of liberty with no understanding of what freedom really is. A few people in the 1920's and 1930's, when seeing how the real America operated for the benefit of the few at the expense of the many, embarked on a frenzied rebellion against the banks that had bought the government regulators off and caused an economic catastrophe. These people who robbed and plundered were branded outlaws, while the banks, insurance companies and Wall Street stock manipulators were just businessmen who had miscalculated and caused a calamity. Oh, the poor fellas!

BAD MOON RISING: AMERICAN OUTLAWS
OF THE ROARING 1920'S AND 1930'S

The free-wheeling bank robbers of those days, were, as the poem says, facing a bad moon rising, and most, if not all, knew what the final outcome would be – death or prison. Yet, they saw no alternative in a nation that had no safety net to protect the vulnerable. Today, there is one political party hell-bent on dismantling the small safety net enacted by Franklin Roosevelt. The foxes have been put in charge of guarding the henhouse, just as they were in the 1920's. These people really think the government should be run as a business. The purpose of a business is to make money. The purpose of government is to serve the interests of the people, not look at everything with the cold, calculating, perverted, greed-driven logic of a businessperson whose only goal is to maximize profit without concern for the people who are hurt in the process. Government is supposed to be the servant of the people, but in the USA, only those at the top of the economic ladder and corporations are the ones being served.

Why are there not more outlaws standing against tyranny today, like there was in the 1920's and 30's when the government was just as callous as it is now? The sad truth is that the USA has so brainwashed its citizens with propaganda about a Jesus-loving Christian nation, which, in fact, it is the very opposite of everything that Jesus represented, and instilled flag-waving patriotic fervour through indoctrination of children with distorted American history and the robotic like recitation of the Pledge of

J. Wayne Frye

Allegiance to an outright lie, that the people simply line up for their chains.

The police have been militarized to instil fear in all who dare demand some fairness in a nation that has become one of the most oppressive societies in the world. The government has been bought by the highest bidders. The prisons have been turned over to giant incarceration corporations. True capitalism has been subverted to allow monolithic, monopolistic corporations to destroy free enterprise and relegate workers to time-clock punching slaves who live in quiet desperation trying to keep their heads above water while drowning in a raging sea of despair, as the CEO's languish on their yachts sipping cocktails while demanding the workers take wage cuts to keep their companies competitive.

Were the robbers of the 1920's and 1930's miscreants who committed many heinous crimes? Yes, most were, but their crimes often paled in comparison to the crimes of the white collar criminals who then, as they did in 2009 and today, destroyed lives with impunity in the name of free enterprise, because they own the government and use the American taxpayer as a personal ATM machine.

Why are criminals aggrandized? Maybe because they are the only ones brave enough to give the establishment the finger, while the rest of us complacently roll over and accept any indignity without a fight! They have a backbone.

J. Wayne Frye

BAD MOON RISING: AMERICAN OUTLAWS OF THE ROARING 1920'S AND 1930'S

During an abomination called the Vietnam War, while I was bound in servitude to the U.S. Army for two and one-half years, my favourite columnist was Nicholas Von Hoffman, who wrote for the *Washington Post*. In attacking the war for utilizing the poor to fight while the rich, like Bush, Cheney, Trump and a host of other wealthy boys were allowed to take a pass, he said that it was time for the poor who lived disadvantaged lives but were always used as cannon fodder in wars, to hand their rifles to the rich kids of congressmen, senators and high government officials and say, "If it is such a damn noble cause, here are our guns, you go and fight."

Of course, if that was done, there would be no wars, because the rich believe their exalted station in life precludes them from serving their country. Their lives are too valuable to be wasted. One obscure robber from the 1920's, as he was being carted off to jail for stealing $4.50 to buy food for his starving wife and children, served as an inspiration for a song by the Credence Clearwater Rival 50 years later, when he said, "If I was a banker stealing millions, I'd be getting a reward for being a smart businessman, but I ain't no banker, I'm just an iterant field hand with a family to feed. Well, all you hypocrites can go to hell, and I hope that damn money you all worship burns there with you. But I tell you what, mark my words, out there in this here land are a whole bunch of people gettin' fed up, and you can be damn sure there is a bad moon rising!"

J. Wayne Frye

BAD MOON RISING: AMERICAN OUTLAWS
OF THE ROARING 1920'S AND 1930'S

Don't miss these non-fiction works by Wayne Frye, available from Fireside Books.

Canadian Angels of Mercy – Nurses in Times of Peril

Points of Rebellion: Aboriginals Who Fought for Justice

How Hockey Saved a Jew From the Holocaust

Fighting for Justice in the Land of Hypocrisy

References and Bibliography by Chapters
Listed in Order Used

Chapter 1

Toplin, Robert B. History by Hollywood: The Use and Abuse of the American Past (Urbana, IL: University of Illinois, 1996.) ISBN 0-252-06536-0.

Phillips, John Neal (2002). Running with Bonnie & Clyde: The Ten Fast Years of Ralph Fults. Norman, OK: University of Oklahoma Press. ISBN 0-8061-3429-1.

Jones deposition, November 18, 1933. FBI file 26-4114, Section Sub A, pp. 59–62. FBI Records and Information.

Jones, W.D. "Riding with Bonnie and Clyde", Playboy, November 1968. Reprinted at Cinetropic.com.

Parker, Emma Krause; Nell Barrow Cowan and Jan I. Fortune (1968). The True Story of Bonnie and Clyde. New York: New American Library. ISBN 0-8488-2154-8.

Guinn, Jeff (March 9, 2010). Go Down Together: The True, Untold Story of Bonnie and Clyde. Simon & Schuster. pp. 174–176. ISBN 9781471105753..

"The Story of Suicide Sal - Bonnie Parker 1932". cinetropic.com.

"The Story of Bonnie and Clyde". cinetropic.com. - on line compilation.

"Bonnie & Roy." Bonnie and Clyde's Texas Hideout.

"Bonnie and Clyde (Part 1)". American Experience. Season 24. Episode 4. PBS. January 19, 2016.

"Clyde Barrow Death Certificate". "Bonnie and Clyde's Texas Hideout".

Long, Christopher. "Barrow, Clyde Chesnut". Handbook of Texas Online. Texas State Historical Association..

Frye, James Wayne. The Man who Beat Hoover. Essay 1979

Frye, Wayne. Personal interview with Ramseur Rod, 1969

Hinton, Ted and Larry Grove (1979). Ambush: The Real Story of Bonnie and Clyde. Austin, TX: Shoal Creek Publishers. ISBN 0-88319-041-9.

Milner, E.R. The Lives and Times of Bonnie and Clyde. Southern Illinois University Press, 2003. ISBN 0-8093-2552-7. Published 1996.

Moshinskie, James F. "Funerals of the Famous: Bonnie &

Clyde." The American Funeral Director, Vol. 130 (No. 10), October 2007, pp. 74–90.

"Bonnie & Clyde's Demise", Dallas Journal at TexasHideout.

"Skilled Embalmers." Dallas Journal at Texas Hideout.

Texas Country Reporter, May 25, 2013

Toland, John (1963). The Dillinger Days. New York: Random House. ISBN 0-306-80626-6 (1995 Da Capo ed.), p. 83

Sifakis, Carl (2001). The Encyclopedia of American Crime. 2 (2 ed.). New York City, New York: Facts on File. p. 509. ISBN 0-8160-4634-4.

Helmer, William J.; Mattix, Rick (1998). Public Enemies: America's Criminal Past, 1919–1940. New York City, New York: Facts on File. p. 17.ISBN 0-8160-3160-6.

Diehl, William (1991). The Hunt. Ballantine Books. p. 204. ISBN 0-345-37073-2.

Rushville Republican. December 18, 1930. p. 1.

Chapter 2

Newton, Michael. Encyclopedia of Robbers, Heists, and Capers. New York: Facts On File Inc., 2002. ISBN 0-8160-4488-0

Hoover, J. Edgar, "The Kidnapping of Edward Bremer", November 19, 1936

Barker-Karpis gang, Memorandum, July 12, 1937

FBI Barker-Karpis summary, page 13

Smith, Robert Barr The Outlaws: Tales of Bad Guys Who Shaped the Wild West, Globe Pequot, 2013, p,127.

Murray, E, "I Was a Karpis-Barker Gang Moll", Startling Detective Adventures, Oct, 1936

Frye, Wayne. Bang, Bang – Shoot 'um Up Essay 1979

Newton, Michael. The Encyclopedia of Robberies, Heists, and Capers. New York: Facts On File Inc., 2002. (pg. 77) ISBN 0-8160-4488-0

Toland, John. The Dillinger Days. New York: New York Da Capo Press International, Inc., 1995. (pg. 45) ISBN 0-306-80626-6

Ward, David. Alcatraz: The Gangster Years. Berkeley:

University of California Press, 2009. (pg. 92-93) ISBN 0-520-25607-7

Potter, Claire Bond. War on Crime: Bandits, G-Men, and the Politics of Mass Culture. New Brunswick, New Jersey: Rutgers University Press, 1998. (pg. 178) ISBN 0-8135-2487-3

Breuer, William B. J. Edgar Hoover and his G-Men. Westport, Connecticut: Greenwood Publishing Group, 1995. (pg. 195–197) ISBN 0-275-94990-7

Matera, Dary. John Dillinger: The Life and Death of America's First Celebrity Criminal. New York: Carroll & Graf Publishers, 2005. (pg. 283) ISBN 0-7867-1558-8

Chapter 3

Sifakis, Carl (2001). The Encyclopedia of American Crime. 2 (2 ed.). New York City, New York: Facts on File. p. 509. ISBN 0-8160-4634-4.

Helmer, William J.; Mattix, Rick (1998). Public Enemies: America's Criminal Past, 1919–1940. New York City, New York: Facts on File. p. 17.ISBN 0-8160-3160-6. Diehl, William (1991). The Hunt. Ballantine Books. p. 204. ISBN 0-345-37073-2.

Kirchner, L. R. (2003). Robbing Banks: An American History 1831–1999. Book Sales. p. 43. ISBN 0-7858-1709-3.

Burrough, Bryan (2004). Public Enemies: America's Greatest Crime Wave and the Birth of the FBI, 1933–34. New York City, New York: Penguin Group. pp. 17–18. ISBN 0-14-311586-3.

Toland, John (1963). The Dillinger Days. New York City, New York: De Capo Press. pp. 29–31. ISBN 0-306-80626-6.

Coyle, Daniel. The Talent Code. Bantam Books.
p. 160. ISBN 978-0-553-80684-7.

Winston-Salem (NC) Journal, Friday, February 25, 1927, p. 2

Morning Star (Rockford, IL), Wednesday, May 15, 1929, p. 13

Helmer 1998, pp. 165–166

Sutton W, Linn E: Where the Money Was: The Memoirs of a Bank Robber.

Viking Press (1976), p. 160. ISBN 067076115X

Hoffman, William; Headley, Lake (1992). Contract Killer: The Explosive Story of the Mafia's Most Notorious Hitman -- Donald "Tony the Greek" Frankos. Thunder's Mouth Press. New York City, p. 116-118.

Pace, Eric (November 10, 1992). "Peter T. Farrell, 91; Judge Who Presided At the Sutton Trial". The New York Times.

"Sutton Cries for Joy"". The New York Times. December 2, 1969.

"Business: Willie Sutton, Bankers' Friend". Time. October 26, 1970.

Mikkelson, B (November 14, 2008). "Quotes: Willie Sutton". Snopes.com, retrieved July 28, 2015.

Cost and Effect, Kaplan, R.S. and Cooper, R., Harvard Business School Press, Boston MA, 1998, ISBN 0-87584-788-9

Newton, Michael. Encyclopedia of Robbers, Heists, and Capers. New York: Facts On File Inc., 2002.

Merle Clayton Union Station Massacre 1975 BM Bobbs Merrill ISBN 0-672-51899-6

Wayward Soldier: Verne Miller and the Kansas City Massacre – Radio documentary, listen online.

"The Life and Death of Pretty Boy Floyd" Atlas Books, 1998; ISBN 0-87338-582-9

Library of Congress, "End of the trail for desperado Floyd", Library of Congress, 22 October 1934

Fisher, Jeffery S. (1998). The Life and Death of Pretty Boy Floyd. Kent, OH: Kent State University Press. ISBN 978-0-87338-650-0.

Pretty Boy Floyd #29078 Mugshot

Charles "Pretty Boy" Floyd", Biography.com

Wallis, Michael. "Floyd, Charles Arthur (1904–1934)". Encyclopedia of Oklahoma History and Culture. Oklahoma Historical Society.

Arthur "Pretty Boy" Floyd. https://www.fbi.gov/about-us/history/famous-cases/kansas-city-massacre-pretty-boy-floyd

Newton, Michael (2002). The Encyclopedia of Kidnappings. New York: Chekmark Books. p. 158. ISBN 0816044872.

"Kansas City Massacre—Charles Arthur "Pretty Boy" Floyd".
Federal Bureau of Investigation, United States Government.
Burrough, Bryan (2009). Public Enemies: America's Greatest
Crime Wave and the Birth of the FBI, 1933-34. Penguin Books.
p. 469. ISBN 0143115863.
"Letters, Nov. 19, 1979". TIME. Time Inc. November 19, 1979.
Ingram, Dale (October 18, 2009). "Family plot: Pretty Boy Floyd
relative
recalls his infamous uncle". Tulsa World Archives .
Guthrie, Woody (1947). "Pretty Boy Floyd". Lyrics on line.
Wallis, Michael. "Floyd, Charles Arthur (1904–
1934)". Encyclopedia of Oklahoma History and Culture.
Oklahoma Historical Society.
Newton, Michael. Encyclopedia of Robbers, Heists, and Capers.
New York: Facts On File Inc., 2002.

Chapter 4

Newton, Michael. The Encyclopedia of Robberies, Heists, and
Capers. New York: Facts On File Inc., 2002. (pg. 261-263) ISBN
0-8160-4488-0
King, Jeffery S. (1999). The Life and Death of Pretty Boy Floyd.
Kent State University Press. p. 272. ISBN 978-0-87338-650-0.
Wallis, Michael (1994). Pretty Boy: The Life and Times of
Charles Arthur Floyd. Macmillan. p. 396. ISBN 978-0-312-
11046-8..
Burrough, Bryan (2009). Public Enemies: America's Greatest
Crime Wave and the Birth of the FBI, 1933-34. Penguin Group.
p. 624. ISBN 978-0-14-311586-1.
King, Jeffrey, "The Life and Death of Pretty Boy Floyd" Atlas
Books, 1998; ISBN 0-87338-582-9
Library of Congress, "End of the trail for desperado
Floyd", Library of Congress, 22 October 1934
Fisher, Jeffery S. (1998). The Life and Death of Pretty Boy
Floyd. Kent, OH: Kent State University Press.
Wallis, Michael. "Floyd, Charles Arthur (1904–
1934)". Encyclopedia of Oklahoma History and Culture.

FBI (2010). Kansas City Massacre – Charles Arthur "Pretty Boy" Floyd. Retrieved on 09 March 2016 from https://www.fbi.gov/about-us/history/famous-cases/kansas-city-massacre-pretty-boy-floyd

Newton, Michael (2002). The Encyclopedia of Kidnappings. New York: Chekmark Books. p. 158. ISBN 0816044872.

"Kansas City Massacre—Charles Arthur "Pretty Boy" Floyd". Federal Bureau of Investigation, United States Government. Retrieved 26 February 2011.

Burrough, Bryan (2009). Public Enemies: America's Greatest Crime Wave and the Birth of the FBI, 1933-34. Penguin Books. p. 469. ISBN 0143115863.

"Letters, Nov. 19, 1979". TIME. Time Inc. November 19, 1979.

Ingram, Dale (October 18, 2009). "Family plot: Pretty Boy Floyd relative recalls his infamous uncle". Tulsa World. Archived from the original on October 27, 2010

Guthrie, Woody (1947). "Pretty Boy Floyd". American Folksong. p. 27.

Wallis, Michael. "Floyd, Charles Arthur (1904–1934)". Encyclopedia of Oklahoma History and Culture. Oklahoma Historical Society.

Chapter 5

Downey, Patrick (2008), Bad Seeds in the Big Apple: Bandits, Killers and Chaos in New York City, 1920-40, Cumberland House, ISBN 978-1-58182-646-3

Jeffers, H. Paul (1993), Gentleman Gerald: The Crimes and Times of Gerald Chapman, America's First "Public Enemy No.1", St. Martin's Press, ISBN 978-0-312-13500-3

"Executions in Connecticut Since 1894". Connecticut State Library. Archived from the original on 20 September 2010.

"U.S. MAIL HELD UP IN BROADWAY; LOOT MAY BE $1,000,000" (PDF). The New York Times. 25 October 1921. Retrieved 19 January 2010.

"2,400,000 Hold-up of Mails Described; One of 13 arrested for Truck Robbery Tells all Details in U.S. Court. (PDF). New

York Times. 17 August 1922.

"Fought for His Life Chained to Burglar; Detective, with His Own Revolver Pressed Against Him, Dared Thief to Shoot." New York Times. 29 October 1911.

"CHAPMAN IS HANGED AT 12:04 A.M. AFTER HIS LAST PLEA FAILS". The New York Times. 6 April 1926. "The First "Public Enemy Number One"". Smithsonian Postal Museum.

"The Real Truth about Chapman—America's 'Super-Bandit', Part One". True Detective Mysteries: 40ff. November 1929.

"The Real Truth about Chapman—America's 'Super-Bandit', Part Two". True Detective Mysteries: p. 55. December 1929.

Gerald Chapman: http://www.crimemagazine.com/gerald-chapman

Downey, Patrick (2008), Bad Seeds in the Big Apple: Bandits, Killers and Chaos in New York City, 1920-40, Cumberland House, ISBN 978-1-58182-646-3

Jeffers, H. Paul (1993), Gentleman Gerald: The Crimes and Times of Gerald Chapman, America's First "Public Enemy No.1", St. Martin's Press, ISBN 978-0-312-13500-3

Walsh, Robert (2013). Gerald Chapman – America's First "Public Enemy No. 1"

Chapter 6

Tuohy, John William (December 2001). "The Owl". AmericanMafia.com. Archives.

Newton, Michael. The Encyclopedia of Robberies, Heists, and Capers. New York: Facts On File Inc., 2002. (pg. 12–13) ISBN 0-8160-4488-0

Ford, Miriam Allen, The Real Ma Barker: Mastermind of a Whole Family of Killers, 1970 Ace, New York. [b]

Mahoney, Tim, Secret Partners, p.15.

Claire Bond Potter, War on Crime: Bandits, G-Men, and the Politics of Mass Culture, Rutgers University Press, New Brunswick, 1998, p.175

Mahoney, Timothy, Secret Partners: Big Tom Brown and the Barker Gang, Minnesota Historical Society Press, 2013, passim.

Mahoney, Tim (2013). Secret Partners. Minnesota Historical Society Press. p. 244.

https://www.fbi.gov/news/stories/2003/september/hamm090803

Mahoney, Tim (2013) Secret Partners Minnesota Historical Society Press, St. Paul, Minnesota.

McIver, Stewart. Touched by the Sun, Pineapple Press, 2008, pp.71-77.

Burrough, Bryan (2004). Public Enemies: America's Greatest Crime Wave and the Birth of the FBI, 1933-1934. Penguin Press, New York, p.508-509;

Powell, Jack. Haunting Sunshine, Pineapple Press Inc, 2001, p.54.

Jones, Ken (1957) The FBI in Action Signet, New York;

Gentry, Curt (1991) J. Edgar Hoover: The Man and the Secrets W. W. Norton, New York, ISBN 0-393-02404-0

Karpis, Alvin with Trent, Bill (1971) The Alvin Karpis Story Coward, McCann & Geoghegan, New York.

Hardy, Philip (ed), The BFI Companion to Crime, British Film Institute, 1997, p.42.

Woodiwiss, Michael, Organized Crime and American Power: A History, University of Toronto Press, 2001, p.238.

Hardy, Phil. The BFI Companion to Crime, University of California Press, 1997, p.42.

Livesey, Robert (1980). On the Rock: Twenty-Five Years in Alcatraz : the Prison Story of Alvin Karpis as told to Robert Livesey. Canada: Beaufort Books, Inc., New York. p. 14. ISBN 0-8253-0019-3.

John Dillinger slept here: a crooks' tour of crime and corruption in St. Paul, 1920-1936; 1995; p.362.

Burrough, Bryan. (2004). Public Enemies. New York.

Gentry, Curt (1991). J. Edgar Hoover: The Man and the Secrets. New York: W. W. Norton. ISBN 0-393-02404-0.

Jones, Ken (1957). The FBI in Action – New York: Signet.

Karpis, Alvin with Trent, Bill (1971). The Alvin Karpis Story. New York: Coward, McCann & Geoghegan.

Ibid Burrough: p. 536, p. 540

St. Paul Daily News, 14 July 1936, p. 1 col. 7.

Albert Lea (Minn.) Evening Tribune, 29 July 1936, p. 1 col. what4.

"Alcatraz: The "Worst of the Worst"—Doing Hard Time on the Rock". Parksconservancy.org. Retrieved 2012-05-01.

Karpis, Alvin; Livesey, Robert (November 1980). On the Rock: Twenty-Five Years in Alcatraz (1st ed.). Beaufort Books, Inc. Newton, M. (2002). The Encyclopedia of Robberies, Heists and Capers. Checkmark Books, an imprint of Facts on File, Inc. ISBN 0-8160-4489-9.

Karpis, Alvin (1 January 1971). Public Enemy Number 1: The Alvin Karpis Story. McClelland and Stewart. ASIN B0007B4FK8.

"Alvin Karpis: Pursuit of the Last Public Enemy — Aftermath — Crime Library". Trutv.com. Retrieved 2012-05-01

"Vincent "Mad Dog" Coll - MAFIA GANGSTER - Great Donegal People". Greatirishpeople.com. 1932-02-08.

"Young thugs put on swagger in line-up". New York Times. October 6, 1931.

"Schultz product of dry law era". New York Times. January 22, 1933.

"Coll seized with his gang". New York Times. October 5, 1931.

"Dry era 'big shot' dies safely in bed". New York Times. September 20, 1939.

"Child slain, 4 shot as gangsters fire on beer war rival". New York Times. "Coll and 4 indicted for baby's murder". New York Times. October 6, 1931. "Coll to offer alibi in killing of child". New York Times. December 17, 1931. "Sole Coll accuser admits lie on stand". New York Times. December 25, 1931, pp.3-4.

"Police aim to drive Coll from the city". New York Times. January 13, 1932. "Coll Is Acquitted". The Daily Republican. Monongahela, Pennsylvania. 30 Dec 1931. p. 8 – via newspapers.com.

"Mrs. Coll pleads guilty in killing". New York Times. February 27, 1934. Perlmutter, Emanuel (October 3, 1963). "Informer tells more". New York Times.

Coll is Shot Dead in A phone Booth by Rival Gunman.

New York Times. 8 February 1932.

"Dutch Schultz dies of wounds without naming slayers". New York Times. October 25, 1935.

"Gangster's Widow Marked for Death". The Border Cities Star. 21 November 1932. p. 10.

"Owney Madden, 73, Ex-Gangster, Dead; Owney Madden, Ex-Racketeer, Dead in Hot Springs at 73" (PDF). New York Times. 24 April 1965. p. 1.

Chapter 7

Toland, John (1963). The Dillinger Days, Random House.

Kokomo Bandit In Prison Break article, Kokomo Tribune, Kokomo, Indiana, December 29, 1930, p.1

Many See Man Shot By Bandit article, Indianapolis Sunday Star, Indianapolis, Indiana, January 8, 1922, p. 1

Clemency Pleas From State Wards Granted By M'Cray article, Indianapolis Star, Indianapolis, Indiana, May 2, 1923, p. 12

Toland 1963, p. 18.

King 2005, p.k 19.

King 2005, p. 20.

Robbery Suspects Arrested article, Wabash Plain-Dealer, Wabash, Indiana, April 2, 1925, p. 1.

Alleged Bank Bandit Leader Held article, Marion Leader-Tribune, Marion, Indiana, April 3, 1925, p.1.

Bandit Trio Leave Today For Prison article, Marion Leader-Tribune, Marion, Indiana, January 4, 1925, p. 2.

Police Keep On Trail Of The Bandits article, Marion Leader-Tribune, Marion, Indiana, November 27, 1924, p. 1.

No New Clue Of Value On The Robbery article, Marion Leader-Tribune, Marion, Indiana, November 28, 1924, p. 1

Attempt Made To Rob Noblesville Bank Frustrated article, Marion Leader-Tribune, Marion, Indiana, December 17, 1924, p. 1

Bandits Fail In Attempt To Rob Noblesville Bank article, Indianapolis Star, Indianapolis, Indiana, December 17, 1924, p. 1

Auto Used By Bank Bandits Is Found article, Marion Leader-

Tribune, Marion, Indiana, December 28, 1924, p. 1
Upland State Bank Robbed of $2500 article, Marion Leader-
Tribune, Marion, Indiana, December 24, 1924, p. 1
Bank Bandits Confess to Sheriff Article, Marion Leader-Tribune,
Marion, Indiana, December 30, 1924, p. 1
Third Bandit Is Caught In The Trap article, Marion Leader-
Tribune, Marion, Indiana, December 31, 1924, p. 1.
Hold Woman As Bandit Accomplice article, Marion Leader-
Tribune, Marion, Indiana, January 1, 1925, p. 1
Two More Bandits Fall In The Trap article, Marion Leader-
Tribune, Marion, Indiana, January 3, 1925, p. 1.
Bandit Trio Now Serving Prison Term article, Marion Leader-
Tribune, Marion, Indiana, January 6, 1925, p. 1.
Father Surrenders His Bandit Son article, Marion Leader-
Tribune, Marion, Indiana, January 11, 1925, p. 1.
Posey Bank Bandits article, Evansville Courier, Evansville,
Posey Bank Bandits article, Evansville Courier, Evansville,
Indiana, March 11, 1925, p. 1.
Evansville, Indiana, March 11, 1925, p. 1.
Saws Are Found In Cells Of Alleged Bandits At Kokomo article,
Marion Leader-Tribune, Marion, Indiana, April 7, 1925, p. 1.
Identify Three Men As Kokomo Bank Bandits article, Kokomo
Daily Tribune, Kokomo, Indiana, April 3, 1925, p.1 New Suspect
In Bank Case Under Arrest article, Kokomo Daily Tribune,
Kokomo, Indiana, April 28, 1925, p. 1.
Bold Bandits Rob Bank At Kokomo Today article, Logansport
Pharos-Tribune, Logansport, Indiana, March 27, 1925, p.1.
Make Away With Loot From S. Kokomo Bank article, Kokomo
Dispatch, Kokomo, Indiana, March 28, 1925, p.1.
Police Lose Trail of Kokomo Bandit Gang, Blue Car Found
article, Marion Leader-Tribune, Marion, Indiana, March 28,
1925, p. 1.
Robbers Outwit Kokomo Police article, Elwood Call-Leader,
Elwood, Indiana, March 28, 1925, p.1
Laketon Bank Robbed Today article, Elwood Call-Leader,
Elwood, Indiana, March 31, 1925, p.1.
Laketon Robbers Traced To Warsaw article, Elwood Call-

Leader, Elwood, Indiana, April 1, 1925, p. 1.

Search For on for Bandits, Wabash Plain-Dealer, Wabash, Indiana, April 1, 1925, p. 1

Bandits Loot Laketon Bank article, Wabash Plain-Dealer, Wabash, Indiana, March 31, 1925, p.1

To Identify Bank Crooks article, Wabash Plain-Dealer, Wabash, Indiana, April 3, 1925, p.1.

Men Held In Detroit For Kokomo Theft article, Logansport Pharos-Tribune, Logansport, Indiana, April 2, 1925, p. 10.

Men Held In Detroit For Kokomo Theft article, Logansport Pharos-Tribune, Logansport, Indiana, April 2, 1925, p. 10

Local Bonds Are Found article, Marion Leader-Tribune, Marion, Indiana, April 4, 1925, p. 1.

Kokomo Robbers Held In Detroit article, Elwood Call-Leader, Elwood, Indiana, April 3, 1925, p.1

Prisoners To Stay In City Says Sheriff article, Kokomo Daily Tribune, Kokomo, Indiana, April 5, 1925, p. 1

Did Not See Bank Bandit article, Marion Leader-Tribune, Marion, Indiana, April 3, 1925, p. 7

Bandit Suspect's Plot For Escape Is Frustrated article, Logansport Pharos Tribune, Logansport, Indiana, April 7, 1925, p. 11.

Kokomo Bandit Suspect Released article, Logansport Pharos Tribune, Logansport, Indiana, May 2, 1925, p. 1

Fix Bonds At $10,000 article, Kokomo Daily Tribune, April 13, Harry Pierpont Turns State Evidence In His Trial For Bank Robbery article, Warsaw Daily Times, Warsaw, Indiana, May 6, p.1

Pierpont Asks Release From State Prison article, Kokomo Tribune, Kokomo, Indiana, August 25, 1933, p. 8

Kokomo Bank Bandit Is Believed Leader In Bold Escape Plot article,
Kokomo Tribune, Kokomo, Indiana, September 27, 1933, p. 10.

Girardin, George Russell (2009). Dillinger: The Untold Story, Indiana University Press.

King, Jeffery S. (2005). The Rise and Fall of the Dillinger Gang, Cumberland House Publishing.

JohnnieDillinger.com - The Dillinger Gang, information on
Dillinger and Company

Chapter 8

"Mail Bandit Is Captured". The Blair Press. Blair, Wisconsin.
June 2, 1921. p. 2.
MacCabe, Scott, "'Smiling Bandit' makes daring escape off
island", Crime History, The Washington Examiner, September 5,
2012, p. 6.
"Newspaper Claims Letter From Roy Gardner". Eugene Daily
Guard. Eugene, Oregon. September 26, 1921. pp. 1 - 6.
"To Operate On Skull Of Roy Gardner". Gettysburg Times.
Gettysburg, Pennsylvania. December 14, 1921. p. 3.
"Alcatraz: Search for the Truth: Famous Alcatraz
Inmates". History. 2015. Retrieved October 25, 2016.
Ward, David A.; Kassabaum, Gene G. (2009). "Alcatraz on
Trial". Alcatraz: The Gangster Years. University of California
Press. pp. 187–88. ISBN 9780520256071.

Chapter 9

"George 'Machine Gun' Kelly". Alcatraz History.com. 2015.
 Finger, Michael (September 7, 2005). "Public Enemy Number
One: The real story of Machine Gun Kelly, the Memphis boy
who grew up to become the most wanted man in
America". Memphis Flyer.
"FBI history. Famous cases. George "Machine Gun" Kelly". FBI.
O'Dell, Larry. "Urschel Kidnapping". Oklahoma Historical
Society. Encyclopedia of Oklahoma History and Culture.
Retrieved May 11, 2013. Family Tree Genealogy.
 The FBI: A Centennial History, 1908-2008. Washington, D. C.:
Government Printing Office. 2008. p. 24. ISBN 978-0-16-
080954-5.
Fee, Christopher R.; Webb, Jeffrey B. (31 August
2016). American Myths, Legends, and Tall Tales: An
Encyclopaedia of American Folklore (3 Volumes). ABC-CLIO.

p. 310. ISBN 978-1-61069-568-8.

"FBI 100. The legend of 'Machine Gun Kelly'". FBI. September 26, 2008. Retrieved May 6, 2009.

"George "Machine Gun" Kelly". Wise County Sheriff's Department. 2003. Archived from the original on September 27, 2006.

"Kathryn Kelly - Crime Museum".

Atkins, Ace (2010). Infamous. G.P. Putnam's Sons.

Hamilton, Stanley (2003). Machine Gun Kelly's Last Stand. University Press of Kansas. ISBN 978-0-7006-1247-5.

Kirkpatrick, E.E. (1934). Crimes' Paradise (1st ed.). San Antonio, Texas: The Naylor Company.

Urschel, Joe (2016). The Year of Fear:Machine Gun Kelly and the Manhunt That Changed the Nation. Minotaur Books. ISBN 978-1-250-10548-6.

Nickel, Steven; William J. Helmer (2002). Baby Face Nelson. Cumberland House. pp. 13–14. ISBN 1-58182-272-3.

Bourough, Bryan . (2004) Public Enemies. The Penguin Press, pg.98 ISBN 1-59420-021-1.

Baby Face Nelson on the web. www.babyface.com

Voorhees, Donal (May 3, 2001). The Indispensable Book of Useless Information: Just When You Thought It Couldn't Get Any More Useless--It Does. Penguin. p. 221. ISBN 0-399-53668-X.Stewart, Tony. Dillinger, the Hidden Truth Reloaded. p. 396.

Burrough, p. 99.

"Nelson Arrested as Thief When 13." New York Times. November 29, 1934.

"Baby Face" Nelson FBI Website

Burrough, p. 101.

Federal Reserve Bank of Minneapolis Community Development Project."Consumer Price Index (estimate) 1800–". Federal Reserve Bank of Minneapolis.

Burrough, pp. 101-2.

Burrough, pp. 102-3.

Burrough, pp. 104-5.

Burrough, pp. 105-6.

Burrough, pp. 175-78.

Burrough, pp. 243-4.

Nickel, Steven, and Helmer, William J. Baby Face Nelson. Cumberland House Publishing, pp. 150–167. ISBN 1-58182-272-3.

Burrough, Bryan. (2004) Public Enemies. The Penguin Press, pp. 234–247,ISBN 1-59420-021-1.

Nickel, Steven, and Helmer, William J. Baby Face Nelson. Cumberland House Publishing. p. 169. ISBN 1-58182-272-3.

Nickel, Steven, and Helmer, William J. Baby Face Nelson. Cumberland House Publishing, pp. 170–79. ISBN 1-58182-272-3.

Burrough, Bryan. (2004) Public Enemies. The Penguin Press, pp. 274–278,ISBN 1-59420-021-1.

Burrough, p. 259.

Cromie, Ronert; and Pinkston, Joseph. (1962) Dillinger: A Short And Violent Life. Chicago Historical Bookworks, pp. 207–230. ISBN 978-0-924772-06-1.

Nickel, Steven; William J. Helmer (2002). Baby Face Nelson: Portrait of a Public Enemy. Cumberland House Publishing, pp. 203–255. ISBN 1-58182-272-3.

Nickel, Steven, and Helmer, William J. Baby Face Nelson. Cumberland House Publishing, pp. 236–237, 250–251, 263–264. ISBN 1-58182-272-3.

Nickel, Steven, and Helmer, William J. Baby Face Nelson. Cumberland House Publishing, pp. 239–246. ISBN 1-58182-272-3.

Nickel, Steven, and Helmer, William J. Baby Face Nelson. Cumberland House Publishing. p. 240. ISBN 1-58182-272-3.

Cromie, Ronert; and Pinkston, Joseph. (1962) Dillinger: A Short And Violent Life. Chicago Historical Bookworks, pp. 207-230. ISBN 978-0-924772-06-1.

Nickel, Steven; William J. Helmer (2002). Baby Face Nelson: Portrait of a Public Enemy. Cumberland House Publishing. p. 222. ISBN 1-58182-272-3.

Nickel, Steven, and Helmer, William J. Baby Face Nelson. Cumberland

House Publishing. p. 256. ISBN 1-58182-272-3.

Nickel, Steven, and Helmer, William J. Baby Face Nelson. Cumberland House Publishing, pp. 272–273. ISBN 1-58182-272-3

Cromie, Ronert; and Pinkston, Joseph. (1962) Dillinger: A Short And Violent Life. Chicago Historical Bookworks, pp. 245–246. ISBN 978-0-924772-06-1.

Burrough, Bryan. (2004) Public Enemies. The Penguin Press. pp. 382-383 ISBN 1-59420-021-1.

Burrough, Bryan. (2004) Public Enemies. The Penguin Press. p. 383, ISBN 1-59420-021-1.

Nickel, Steven, and Helmer, William J. Baby Face Nelson. Cumberland House Publishing, pp. 289–302. ISBN 1-58182-272-3.

Burrough, Bryan. (2004) Public Enemies. The Penguin Press. pp. 384-387,ISBN 1-59420-021-1.

Nickel, Steven, and Helmer, William J. Baby Face Nelson. Cumberland House Publishing, pp. 305–306. ISBN 1-58182-272-3.

Nickel, Steven, and Helmer, William J. Baby Face Nelson. Cumberland House Publishing, pp. 308–309. ISBN 1-58182-272-3

Nickel, Steven, and Helmer, William J. Baby Face Nelson. Cumberland House Publishing, pp. 311–338. ISBN 1-58182-272-3.

Nickel, Steven, and Helmer, William J. Baby Face Nelson. Cumberland House Publishing, pp. 334–342. ISBN 1-58182-272-3.

Special Agent Herman E. Hollis. Officer Down Memorial Page.

Inspector Samuel P. Cowley. Officer Down Memorial Page.

article published by the New York Times. November 28, 1934.

"Blasting a G-Man Myth". Time Magazine. September 24, 1979.

http://www.babyfacenelsonjournal.com/nelson-death-2.html

Burrough, p. 482.

"Wife Lying in Ditch Saw Nelson Shot." New York Times. December 6, 1934. Retrieved June 12, 2008.

Nickel, Steven, and Helmer, William J., Baby Face Nelson,

Cumberland House, 2002, p. 364

"Kill Widow Of Baby Face!, U.S. Orders Gang Hunters". Chicago Herald-Examiner. November 30, 1934.

Nickel, Steven, and Helmer, William J. Baby Face Nelson. Cumberland House, 2002, pp. 343–363.

Alan Gevinson (1997). Within Our Gates: Ethnicity in American Feature Films, 1911-1960. University of California Press. p. 327. ISBN 978-0-520-20964-0.

Official website of the film: Public Enemies

FBI famous cases (public domain text)

Crime Library biography

Baby Face Nelson- FBI Archives

Chapter 10

Newton, Michael. The Encyclopedia of Robberies, Heists, and Capers. New York: Facts On File Inc., 2002. (pg. 303-304) ISBN 0-8160-4488-0

Morgan, R. D. The Tri-State Terror: The Life and Crimes of Wilbur Underhill. Stillwater, Oklahoma: New Forums Press, 2005. ISBN 1-58107-107-8

"Mad Dog" couldn't outrun police forever by Gene Curtis

Last of the Outlaws: Wilbur Underhill by R. D. Morgan

Wanted: Notorious Bank Robbers at CBSnews.com

Newton, M. (2002). The Encyclopedia of Robberies, Heists, and Capers. Checkmark Books, an imprint of Facts on File, Inc. ISBN 0-8160-4489-9. pp. 305–307.

Mason City Public Library. First National Bank Robbery Dillinger Gang, Crimelibrary.com

CourtTV.com. "People & Events: John Dillinger, 1903–1934". PBS.org.

Morton, James, The Mammoth Book of Gangs, Constable & Robinson Ltd., ISBN 9781780330884 (2012), p. 1931

George Russell Girardin et al, Dillinger, The Untold Story, Indiana University Press, 2004, p. 340

Homer Van Meter Walks Into Police Trap and Dies Shooting], Lawrence Journal-World, 24 August 1934

Dillinger Mob Man Shot Down, Prescott Evening Courier, 24 August 1934

Van Meter's Loot Sought From Girl, The New York Times, New York, August 25, 1934

Girardin, G. Russell, and Helmer, William J, Dillinger: The Untold Story, Bloomington, IN: Indiana University Press, ISBN 0253325560 (2005), p. 323

Vanmeter.com

The Real Homer Van Meter. Indianapolis Star, August 18, 1934.

Nickel, Steven, and Helmer, William J., Baby Face Nelson: Portrait Of A Public Enemy, Nashville, TN: Cumberland House Publishing, Inc., ISBN 1581822723 (2002), p. 316

Chapter 11

Elliott J. Gorn, Dillinger's Wild Ride: The Year That Made America's Public Enemy Number One (2009), p 101.

"A Byte Out of History - How The FBI Got Its Name". Federal Bureau of Investigation. March 24, 2006.

"Famous Cases & Criminals - John Dillinger". Fbi.gov.

Matera, Dary (2005). John Dillinger: The Life and Death of

"Primary Sources: 'What I Knew About John Dillinger' – By His Sweetheart", Public Enemy #1, American

Experience (represented by them as transcriptions of two installments in a series of articles by her, The Chicago Herald and Examiner, August 1934.

http://www.biography.com/people/billie-frechette-466520

"American Experience | Public Enemy #1 | Primary Sources". Pbs.org.

"American Experience | Public Enemy #1 | People & Events". Pbs.org.

America's First Celebrity Criminal. Carroll & Graf Publishers. ISBN 0-7867-1558-8.

Was John Dillinger German?, citing The Untold Story by G. Russell Giradin and William J. Helmer; and Dary Matera's John Dillinger.

"Famous Cases: John Dillinger". Federal Bureau of Investigation.

"Depression-era gangster John Dillinger's sister dies in Mooresville at 92.WTHR.com, January 15, 2015.

G. Russell Girardin, William J. Helmer, Rick Mattix, Dillinger: The Untold Story, pp. 11, 21.

"The Scoop Deck – Fireman 3rd Class John Dillinger". Militarytimes.com. 2009-07-06. Retrieved 2012-05-01.

"Certificate of Birth: Beryl Hovious." Morgan County Health Department, Martinsville, Indiana. Filed 9-1923.

Reading Eagle September 2, 1937 p.14

Daily News, June 21, 1933, pages 1 & 5.

Defining Documents in American History: The 1930s (1930-1939). Ipswich, Massachusetts: Salem Press. 2014. p. 269. ISBN 978-1-61925-4954.

Girardin/Helmer, Dillinger: The Untold Story

"YOUNGBLOOD IS SLAIN IN BATTLE". Lowell Tribune. Lowell, Indiana. 22 March 1934.

http://www.babyfacenelsonjournal.com/south-bend-2.html

"FBI History - Famous Cases, John Dillinger". FBI.

U.S. District Court, District of MN, USA vs. Evelyn Frechette, et al., p. 590-592

Girardin/Helmer, "Dillinger: The Untold Story," p. 274

Millett, Larry, AIA Guide to St. Paul's Summit Avenue & Hill District (2009), p. 68

USA vs. May/Frechette, et al., p.35

USA vs May/Frechette, Cutting's testimony, p. 75-80

USA vs May, Frechette, et al., testimony from Coffey and Nalls

Dillinger File 62-29777, Nalls report

USA vs. May/Frechette, et al. Nalls' testimony, p. 90

USA vs. May/Frechette, Coulter's testimony, p. 178-179

Dillinger File, 62-29777, Nalls report

USA vs. May/Frechette, Nalls' testimony, p.90

Girardin/Helmer, p. 134

USA vs. May/Frechette, et al., Cummings' testimony, p. 97-98

Cromie and Pinkston, "Dillinger: A Short and Violent Life, p. 189

USA vs. May/Frechette, Clayton May's testimony, p. 473-487, 501

FBI Dillinger File 62-29777

Cromie and Pinkston, p. 196

"Chicago Cubs History and News - Welcome to Just One Bad Century". Justonebadcentury.com. 1934-07-22. Retrieved 2012-05-01.

Piquett vs USA, Loeser's testimony, p. 154-155

Piquett vs USA, Loeser's testimony

Piquett vs USA, Loeser's testimony, p. 152-162

FBI Dillinger File 62-29777, Peggy Doyle statement

Helmer/Mattix, "The Complete Public Enemy Almanac"

Purvis, Alston W.; Alex Tresinowski (2005). The Vendetta. PublicAffairs. pp. 155–156.

Massad Ayoob (July–August 2008), "The death of John Dillinger",American Handgunner

FBI Dillinger File 62-29777, S.P. Cowley report, August 1, 1934.

Chicago Daily Tribune, 7-15-34 through 8-1-34 movie section

"On This Day (front page)". The New York Times. The New York Times Company. 1934-07-23. Retrieved 2015-06-28.

"FBI History - Famous Cases, John Dillinger". FBI. Retrieved 2009-07-18.

The Story of the FBI, E.P. Dutton and Co., Inc. New York, 1947, p. 195.

"Dillinger Slain in Chicago; Shot Dead by Federal Men in Front of Movie Theater." nytimes.com. Retrieved 2013-02-04.

May, Allan, and Marilyn Bardsley. "Biograph Encounter." John Dillinger: Bank Robber or Robin Hood? - Crime Library. trutv.com.

John Dillinger: The FBI Files. Filiquarian Publishing, LLC., 2007, 160 pages, ISBN 1599862468. ed. doc. refers to the document number)

F.B.I. comm.July 24, 1934

U.S. Government Accountability Office - Document : A-57405, OCTOBER 10, 1934, 14 COMP. GEN. 300 Eposito, Stefano; John Dillinger: "Hero for the angry masses" at the Wayback Machine (archived July 15, 2009), Chicago Sun-Times. June 28, 2009.

BAD MOON RISING: AMERICAN OUTLAWS
OF THE ROARING 1920'S AND 1930'S

"In Grave Condition - John H. Dillinger" at the Wayback
Machine (archived July 19, 2012), Lost Indiana.net.
Girardin, Helmer, p. 313
"Dillinger's grave attracting crowds due to Public Enemies
movie.". Wkowtv.com. 2009-06-29.
Girardin/Helmer, p. 280
Sennwald, Andre (June 8, 1935). "Movie Review: Public Hero
No. 1". The New York Times.
Costello, Mark (August 1, 2004). "Public Enemies Review". The
New York Times Book Review.
Gorn, Elliott. "The Real John Dillinger: Is Public Enemies
historically accurate?" Slate.com.